Identity, Inequity and Inequality in India and China

In the late 1990s, the post-reform India unveiled a global publicity campaign to create a different self image – from a third world nation to a major global player – just as China buoyed by its stunning economic growth sets out to become a superpower in science and technology. If these spectacular moments constitute the 'rise' of India and China in the early 21st century, they do so in entanglement with the everyday disquiet over inequity and inequality within these societies. From the Maoist struggle and contentious rural development schemes in India to the Chinese state's attempts to control and direct the rural migrant populations in the urban industrial zones, the two Asian powers are invested in a double edged project of governing difference – to create a distinct global identity for the outside gaze even as they struggle to contain growing unrest inside.

This book explores how *difference* is constructed, manifested, mobilized and obscured in socially uneven societies, particularly those fuelled by neoliberal economic growth in the recent years. The book approaches difference as a double edged concept that allows one to make sense of the tensions that are played out between 'cosmopolitan' convergence and 'multicultural' diversity, between expanding middle classes and increasingly disenfranchised poor groups, between the global and the local.

The chapters in this book examine how difference is articulated, desired, leveled, governed and even subverted in the socio-economically uneven landscapes of India and China. They consider how difference emerges out of daily practice, categorisation processes, dividing practices, nation building efforts and identity projects. Difference, here, is not just examined as celebration of diversity in multicultural settings, but also something deemed potentially disruptive and in need of containment by the state. The contributors explore how the states *construct* and *control* differences and how these interventions rearrange the social-political landscapes.

This book was published as a special issue of *Third World Quarterly*.

Ravinder Kaur is Associate Professor and Director of the Centre for Global South Asian Studies, Department of Cross-cultural and Regional Studies, University of Copenhagen. She is currently responsible for a research programme funded by the Danish Social Sciences Research Council on the ongoing social-political transformations in post-reform India.

Ayo Wahlberg is Postdoctoral Research Fellow with the Asian Dynamics Initiative, Department of Anthropology, University of Copenhagen. Ayo has published widely at the cross-sections of science and technology studies and medical anthropology/sociology. His current research project is in the field of reproductive technologies in south central China where he is carrying out an ethnographic study of sperm banking. Ayo holds a PhD in sociology from the London School of Economics and was recently awarded a Sapere Aude Young Researcher award from the Danish Council of Independent Research.

Thirdworlds
Edited by Shahid Qadir, University of London

THIRDWORLDS will focus on the political economy, development and cultures of those parts of the world that have experienced the most political, social, and economic upheaval, and which have faced the greatest challenges of the postcolonial world under globalisation: poverty, displacement and diaspora, environmental degradation, human and civil rights abuses, war, hunger, and disease. **THIRDWORLDS** serves as a signifier of oppositional emerging economies and cultures ranging from Africa, Asia, Latin America, Middle East, and even those 'Souths' within a larger perceived North, such as the U.S. South and Mediterranean Europe. The study of these otherwise disparate and discontinuous areas, known collectively as the Global South, demonstrates that as globalisation pervades the planet, the south, as a synonym for subalterity, also transcends geographical and ideological frontiers.

Terrorism and the Politics of Naming
Edited by Michael Bhatia

Reconstructing Post-Saddam Iraq
Edited by Sultan Barakat

From Nation-Building to State-Building
Edited by Mark T. Berger

Connecting Cultures
Edited by Emma Bainbridge

The Politics of Rights
Dilemmas for feminist praxis
*Edited by Andrea Cornwall and
    Maxine Molyneux*

**The Long War – Insurgency,
    Counterinsurgency and
    Collapsing States**
*Edited by Mark T. Berger and
    Douglas A. Borer*

Market-led Agrarian Reform
Edited by Saturnino M. Borras, Jr.

After the Third World?
Edited by Mark T. Berger

Developmental and Cultural Nationalisms
Edited by Radhika Desai

Globalisation and Migration
New issues, new politics
Edited by Ronaldo Munck

**Domestic and International Perspectives
    on Kyrgyzstan's 'Tulip Revolution'**
Motives, mobilizations and meanings
Edited by Sarah Cummings

War and Revolution in the Caucasus
Georgia Ablaze
Edited by Stephen F. Jones

War, Peace and Progress in the 21st Century
Development, Violence and Insecurities
Edited by Mark T. Berger and Heloise Weber

Renewing International Labour Studies
Edited by Marcus Taylor

Youth in the Former Soviet South
Everyday Lives between Experimentation and Regulation
Edited by Stefan B. Kirmse

Political Civility in the Middle East
Edited by Frédéric Volpi

The Transformation of Tajikistan
Sources of Statehood
Edited by John Heathershaw

Movement, Power and Place in Central Asia and Beyond
Contested Trajectories
Edited by Madeleine Reeves

People Power in an Era of Global Crisis
Rebellion, Resistance and Liberation
Edited by Barry K. Gills and Kevin Gray

EU Strategies on Governance Reform
Between Development and State-building
Edited by Wil Hout

Identity, Inequity and Inequality in India and China
Governing Difference
Edited by Ravinder Kaur and Ayo Wahlberg

The Personal and the Professional in Aid Work
Edited by Anne-Meike Fechter

Identity, Inequity and Inequality in India and China
Governing Difference

Edited by
Ravinder Kaur and Ayo Wahlberg

LONDON AND NEW YORK

First published 2014
by Routledge
2 Park Square, Milton Park, Abingdon, Oxfordshire OX14 4RN

Simultaneously published in the USA and Canada
by Routledge
711 Third Avenue, New York, NY 10017

First issued in paperback 2016

Routledge is an imprint of the Taylor & Francis Group, an informa business

© 2014 Southseries Inc.

This book is a reproduction of *Third World Quarterly*, vol. 33, issue 4. The Publisher requests to those authors who may be citing this book to state, also, the bibliographical details of the special issue on which the book was based.

All rights reserved. No part of this book may be reprinted or reproduced or utilised in any form or by any electronic, mechanical, or other means, now known or hereafter invented, including photocopying and recording, or in any information storage or retrieval system, without permission in writing from the publishers.

Trademark notice: Product or corporate names may be trademarks or registered trademarks, and are used only for identification and explanation without intent to infringe.

British Library Cataloguing in Publication Data
A catalogue record for this book is available from the British Library

ISBN 13: 978-1-138-20933-6 (pbk)
ISBN 13: 978-0-415-85969-1 (hbk)

Typeset in Times New Roman
by Taylor & Francis Books

Publisher's Note
The publisher would like to make readers aware that the chapters in this book may be referred to as articles as they are identical to the articles published in the special issue. The publisher accepts responsibility for any inconsistencies that may have arisen in the course of preparing this volume for print.

Contents

Citation Information	ix
Acknowledgement From the Publisher	xi

1. Governing Difference in India and China: an introduction
   Ravinder Kaur & Ayo Wahlberg — 1

2. Imperial Modernity: history and global inequity in rising Asia
   David Ludden — 9

3. Nation's Two Bodies: rethinking the idea of 'new' India and its other
   Ravinder Kaur — 31

4. China as an 'Emerging Biotech Power'
   Ayo Wahlberg — 51

5. Post-colonial Renaissance: 'Indianness', contemporary art and the market
   in the age of neoliberal capital
   Manuela Ciotti — 65

6. Making Gujarat Vibrant: *Hindutva*, development and the rise of
   subnationalism in India
   Tommaso Bobbio — 85

7. Between Egalitarianism and Domination: governing differences in a
   transitional society
   Swagato Sarkar — 101

8. Rule through Difference on China's Urban–Rural Boundary
   Jesper Zeuthen — 117

9. 'Winning Hearts and Minds': emotional wars and the construction
   of difference
   Nandini Sundar — 133

10. Religion, Secularism and National Development in India and China
    Peter van der Veer — 149

11. Between Party, Parents and Peers: the quandaries of two young Chinese
    Party members in Beijing
    Susanne Bregnbaek — 163

Index — 179

Citation Information

The chapters in this book were originally published in *Third World Quarterly*, volume 33, issue 4 (May 2012). When citing this material, please use the original page numbering for each article, as follows:

Chapter 1
Governing Difference in India and China: an introduction
Ravinder Kaur & Ayo Wahlberg
Third World Quarterly, volume 33, issue 4 (May 2012) pp. 573–580

Chapter 2
Imperial Modernity: history and global inequity in rising Asia
David Ludden
Third World Quarterly, volume 33, issue 4 (May 2012) pp. 581–602

Chapter 3
Nation's Two Bodies: rethinking the idea of 'new' India and its other
Ravinder Kaur
Third World Quarterly, volume 33, issue 4 (May 2012) pp. 603–622

Chapter 4
China as an 'Emerging Biotech Power'
Ayo Wahlberg
Third World Quarterly, volume 33, issue 4 (May 2012) pp. 623–636

Chapter 5
Post-colonial Renaissance: 'Indianness', contemporary art and the market in the age of neoliberal capital
Manuela Ciotti
Third World Quarterly, volume 33, issue 4 (May 2012) pp. 637–656

Chapter 6
Making Gujarat Vibrant: Hindutva, *development and the rise of subnationalism in India*
Tommaso Bobbio
Third World Quarterly, volume 33, issue 4 (May 2012) pp. 657–672

CITATION INFORMATION

Chapter 7

Between Egalitarianism and Domination: governing differences in a transitional society
Swagato Sarkar
Third World Quarterly, volume 33, issue 4 (May 2012) pp. 673–688

Chapter 8

Rule through Difference on China's Urban–Rural Boundary
Jesper Zeuthen
Third World Quarterly, volume 33, issue 4 (May 2012) pp. 689–704

Chapter 9

'Winning Hearts and Minds': emotional wars and the construction of difference
Nandini Sundar
Third World Quarterly, volume 33, issue 4 (May 2012) pp. 705–720

Chapter 10

Religion, Secularism and National Development in India and China
Peter van der Veer
Third World Quarterly, volume 33, issue 4 (May 2012) pp. 721–734

Chapter 11

Between Party, Parents and Peers: the quandaries of two young Chinese Party members in Beijing
Susanne Bregnbaek
Third World Quarterly, volume 33, issue 4 (May 2012) pp. 735–750

Please direct any queries you may have about the citations to
clsuk.permissions@cengage.com

Acknowledgement From the Publisher

The publisher would like to thank the India Brand Equity Foundation and the Saatchi Gallery for allowing Routledge to reproduce their artwork that had previously appeared in the special issue.

Introduction
Governing Difference in India and China: an introduction

RAVINDER KAUR & AYO WAHLBERG

Inequality and social difference are the primary themes that have come to define the current financial turmoil and political unrest in various parts of the world—from the market square in Sidi Bouzid, Tunisia to Zucotti Park in New York. As the financial crisis increasingly threatens the familiar global economic structures, the inequality such structures engender has been revealed in plain sight for everyone to see. Thus, it is hardly a coincidence that the resistance against a variety of inequalities and inequities appears precisely when the financial world is in a state of crisis of its own. These developments offer a fresh vantage point from where to rethink the questions of difference in the form of inequality and inequity together with that of national identity making in a globalised world. In this special issue, we approach these questions from two locations—India and China—that might be considered unusual given that both these nations have not only maintained high economic growth rates, and therefore are said to have circumvented the gloom of financial crisis, but are also seen as the 'rising' global powers that are expected to reshape the global institutional framework. Perhaps this is precisely what makes it interesting to rethink inequality, inequity and identity from these locations, which are said to be very different in their political frames of democracy and authoritarianism—to witness not only the concrete transformations taking place in these societies, but also how the very languages and hegemonic discourses that have long described the world for us are in a state of transformation. As we argue in this issue, not only are the patterns of global inequality between states and world regions in a state of flux, they are also being reproduced, sometimes violently so, within national boundaries of socially uneven neoliberal societies such as India and China as the various contributions to the special issue show. The contributions collectively also show how the popular conceptions of India and China based on their political framing—democratic and authoritarian

Ravinder Kaur is in the Department of Cross-Cultural and Regional Studies, University of Copenhagen, Denmark. Ayo Wahlberg is in the Department of Anthropology, University of Copenhagen, Denmark.

respectively—do not help us understand the transformations taking place in these societies. As the case studies show, the Indian state is capable of authoritarian actions against its own population while the Chinese state often engages in extensive negotiations at local levels. Clearly the simple classifications in currency do not allow us a clear understanding of the ongoing transitions that have positioned these nations as leading global players.

As we enter the second decade of the twenty-first century, the question of discourse—how to describe the contemporary world beyond the language of north /south, developing/developed and first/third—has understandably once again gained a particular urgency, especially within a narrative context of 'Asia Rising', this time with all focus firmly fixed on China and India.[1] The boundaries etched in the twentieth century seem unsettled and in fact plain ineffective in helping us understand the current geographies of difference. This is especially so as we confront the popular discourse of 'emerging powers' that seems to have destabilised the categories we have long been familiar with. The relentless 'rise' of India and China is now the subject of both hyperbolic and apprehensive speculations in international media reporting as well as academic deliberation spanning the fields of political science, economics, sociology, anthropology and humanities. This euphoric discourse is complicated by the fact that the impressive economic growth in these nations has not yet translated into lifting populations out of poverty or geopolitical rebalancing. The Indian and Chinese states struggle to govern tumultuous differences within—inequities and inequalities constitutive of the socio-economic and political terrain; rich/poor; urban/rural; cosmopolitan/ vernacular; ethnic majorities/minorities—accentuated by neoliberal market reforms, even as they seek to project a unified 'national difference' that can compete profitably with other nations on a global scale. Tensions are playing out between 'cosmopolitan' convergence and 'multicultural' diversity, between expanding middle classes and increasingly disenfranchised poor groups, between the global and the local. Difference, here, at once, appears as a desirable condition in relation to the concept of 'global nation' as well as a challenge that threatens to unravel the very weave of the nation.

In this special issue of *Third World Quarterly*, we address the problem of governing difference, or better yet of governing multiple forms of difference—objects of desire as well as fear—that are simultaneously courted and denounced. This multipronged approach to difference becomes particularly palpable in 'emerging' powers like India and China, witnessed in a snapshot of transformation—unsettled within and unsettling the current global order. While these nations actively seek to construct a distinctive global identity—nation branding—in order to demarcate themselves from other nations, they also seek to subordinate and eradicate difference within the nation. Difference in need of subordination is that which is seen as disharmonious, contrary and even threatening to the nation's externally projected image as a unified, prosperous and influential power. This unruly 'internal other' is witnessed under flexible and interchangeable signs: the poor, the rural migrants, the militants, the separatists, the dissidents and the religious minorities to name a few. When difference is permitted—sometimes even flaunted—under the signs of diversity and multiculturalism, it only comes into being within a prior consensual framework. The ungovernable difference, or the non-consensual, is what becomes subject to violence and coercion in one form or the other. It is in this broad sweep that we explore the taxonomies of difference and conflicts to govern those in contemporary India and China.

The notion of difference, of course, has a rich theoretical history. Since the closing decades of the twentieth century, it has in particular been fleshed out in the fields of multicultural, postcolonial, sexuality and disability studies.[2] One element that these strands have had in common is a theorising of difference as something that is staged, performed, maintained, fixed and/or contested as a matter of identity politics in contexts of domination/subjugation and power/knowledge. As argued by Stuart Hall: "'difference' is ambivalent. It can be both positive and negative. It is both necessary for the production of meaning, the formation of language and culture, for social identities and a subjective sense of the self as a sexed subject—and at the same time, it is threatening, a site of danger, of negative feelings, of splitting, hostility and aggression towards the "Other"'.[3] A second element that these strands of study have shared has been in glimpsing a kind of emancipatory potential within 'difference' as it hints at possible routes out of racist, chauvinist and Eurocentric hierarchies—one must 'pay attention to difference without creating a hierarchy of difference'.[4] Difference here emerges as a kind of platform for mobilisation, as suggested by Arturo Escobar whose Afro-Colombian informants 'engage in the defence of place from the perspective of the economic, ecological, and cultural difference that their landscapes, cultures, and economies embody in relation to those of more dominant sectors of society'.[5]

While sharing these scholars' preoccupation with matters of identity and inequality, we nevertheless propose to shift attention towards mundane questions of how *difference* is constructed, manifested, governed, mobilised and obscured. We are interested not so much in claims to difference as in the making of difference in socially uneven societies, particularly those fuelled by neoliberal economic growth, such as China and India.[6] In such contexts, as we have argued, dichotomies of developed/underdeveloped, north/south or emerging/backward as unifying national or regional categories are rendered entirely obsolete. At best they might be folded back into the nations as classificatory schemes to parcel out various demographic or political groups within the nations. What we argue in this collective intervention, however, is that such an analytic move will inevitably fall short. Instead we are compelled to seek another conceptual language, outside these binaries, that enables us to explore, describe and make sense of the ongoing transformations in these societies. We suggest a turn to the languages of difference as a frame within which to explore contemporary India and China as a contribution to ongoing conceptual development and innovation around which to rethink social unevenness and the making of global identities.

Central to this conceptual shift is the idea of difference that underpins projects of identification, classification and naming of objects, peoples, places and ideas. Difference is often seen as a readily discernible relation between two entities each with a prior identity. While such a relation is largely built upon contradiction and mutual negation of the two, Gilles Deleuze has argued for a positive approach towards difference.[7] This means moving beyond the identity of a given entity to look for the underlying processes that constitute the reasoning behind empirical distinctions. Instead of locating difference within a frame of dichotomies, we view it synoptically in its interwoven layers of multiplicity—linking seemingly disparate terrain, and revealing interconnections that make the inside and the outside of a nation. We approach difference as constitutive of a range of languages of difference revealing specific configurations and patterns that come together in various ways in disparate contexts. It is the effects of difference, rather than attempts to ascertain what differences there in fact are in India and China, that articles in this issue analyse.

Without claiming to be definitive, we isolate three languages of difference as especially relevant for understanding the problems posed in this special issue. These are difference spoken of as standardisation, commodification and alterity, produced upon a matrix of social unevenness and identity making. Each of these languages are seen in spectacular as well as ordinary, mundane processes that constitute everyday life. While none of these presuppose each other, they remain entangled even in their seemingly distinctive spaces where imperatives of governance, authority of state power and individual freedoms and desires compete, collide and cohere. These languages are not deployed by state powers alone to exercise authority and enhance legitimacy; state-like authorities as well as those in opposition also make use of difference as a ground for action.

First, the modernist discourse and practices of standardisation through which nations are arranged, classified and displayed in a global hierarchy—patches of difference woven in a universal frame. Over the past few decades, the nations have routinely been subjected to measurement and comparison with other nations on universal parameters. These parameters range from themes as diverse as poverty, human development, economic growth rate and per capita consumption to those of free speech, transparency, corruption and good governance, and even beauty.[8] The result is an array of standardised nation indexes through which distant societies become instantly familiar, knowable and comparable. This classification is predicated upon differences made palpable that distinguish one nation from the other within a comprehensible scheme—for instance, Indianness and Chineseness become legible only within such a universal frame. And, at the same time, it privileges one attribute—of comparison—over several others, thereby creating an internal play of elements that reveal a specific and limited gaze through which to know the nation. Shades of Derrida's notion of *differánce* here: reading difference together with its other meaning of deferment or absence allows one to witness the play of difference where one pattern of difference becomes prominent only to consign other patterns into the background.[9] The practice of standardising and indexing nations on various scales—upon which nations can aspire to 'rise' or risk a 'fall' if found lacking—now constitutes a global regime of knowledge that both informs and reconfigures the place of a nation within the world. To govern difference, therefore, is precisely to make it palpable, comparable and thereby calculable. Second, the related processes of commodification of thus created inalienable, essential cultural difference—identity—of nations, communities and regions that make tangible and intangible national or ethnic goods saleable in the global markets. In fact, the very idea of a viable nation has become interlinked with the ability of the nation to enhance and realise its exchange value in the global circulation of capital.

Third, the emotive claims and assertions of alterity deployed not only to identify the dangerous 'other', but also to justify one's disengagement—self alienation—from the society at large. The making of the other has long been noted as an imperial technology that enables the dominant power to define itself through marginalisation and exclusion of the other.[10] Difference is implicated in the processes of othering where fear and violence reinforce each other, and yet where the question of outrage largely remains in ambivalence. The power to outrage and be outraged allows one to arbitrate simultaneously on what is in excess and therefore in need of condemnation, and what actions are necessary to contain the outrage and are therefore praiseworthy. This privilege of arbitration is central to the drawing and redrawing of internal boundaries, and re/imagining the dangers that can be countered in new battlegrounds. The assertion of alterity can be witnessed in the double-edged exclusionary mechanisms—both in the processes of marginalisation where the other is pushed to the limit, and the processes of abandonment where the privileged retreat to their securitised exclusive zones beyond the reach of the other. The quest for alterity is similarly implicated in the processes of individual self-making in relation to—or sometimes in stark opposition to—the rapid transformations that seem to overtake the current way of life.

The articles that follow approach these issues at national, provincial and indeed individual levels, showing how national projects to firmly place India and China on to a global scene come into tension with the social unevenness found within their borders. David Ludden sets the stage, in his analysis of imperial modernity in Asia: 'Modern capitalist imperialism crowned Europeans with supreme status, and Asian nationalists fought European imperialists to make free nations, but a reproduction of old imperial forms of inequity also occurred inside transitions from empire to nation in Asia, which continues to shape patterns of global inequality today'. Structures of inequity, he argues, are part and parcel of Asia's rise, as patterns of global inequality—whereby the poorest 20 per cent of the world's population account for 1.4 per cent of global wealth and the richest 20 per cent account for 80 per cent—come to be reproduced in countries like India and China.

Within this context of inequity and social unevenness, a cluster of articles take on the challenge of analysing nation-building—or indeed nation-branding—processes in China and India, as these two countries take concrete steps to position themselves globally as modern nations with particular qualities and advantages. Ravinder Kaur's analysis of Brand India, shows us how images are mobilised in advertising campaigns to 'mediate the attractiveness of an investor friendly nation in aesthetically pleasing frames' in an emerging field of nation-branding. The article invokes image as the site where a desirable global identity for the nation is carved out in ways that sometimes bear little resemblance to the social life outside the image frames. Thus, the world of images is also where ruptures in the nation's body take place when the simulated model of the ideal nation is superimposed over the real territory to reveal the violent scars of market transition. Similarly, Ayo Wahlberg provides an analysis of ongoing global negotiations which have placed China on the global biotech map as an 'emerging power'. This negotiation has involved efforts, on the one hand, to specify those qualities and assets that make China attractive as a biotech nation, and on the other, to identify those ethical challenges related to the recruitment of volunteer research subjects that are specific to a 'Chinese context'. Such global negotiations contribute palpably to nation-building processes. And in yet another arena, namely an emerging global Indian art market, Manuela Ciotti argues that in circuits of the global art world, value is created through inscribing 'Indianness' to local objects. What these articles show in their different arenas is how India and China are jostling for place within global circuits of commodity exchange, knowledge production and nation-branding, and in the process articulations of what constitutes 'Indianness' or 'Chineseness' are set in motion. Both in terms of that which sets apart but also the contrasts and paradoxes they embody. At a subnational level, Tommaso Bobbio shows us how similar branding processes are going on within India, as he documents the emergence of a 'Vibrant Gujarat' campaign to lure global investors to the regional state. This campaign was the culmination of a wider set of articulations about the 'attractive' (from a business point of view) qualities of Gujaratis as a thrifty people who are 'more westernised and modernised than the rest of India'. In these cases, difference is mobilised as a value proposition, a way to make a case for the attractiveness of India or China as a destination for investors, corporations, biotech scientists or art dealers.

Yet, such 'success portrayals', of course, stand in glaring contrast to the inequity and unrest which permeate both countries and which are the focus of another cluster of articles in this special issue. For, as we have already noted, while concerted efforts are being directed towards building up and projecting 'unified wholes' in a global world, state authorities and officials are also struggling to contain differences within. Based on fieldwork among local government officials and villages in North and South 24 Parganas, Swagato Sarkar argues that the rise and fall of the Left Front government in West Bengal can be accounted for through its failed effort to guide industrial transition in West Bengal. He suggests that as the government embarked on acquiring land for industrialisation, marginalised groups remained dependent despite the introduction of a series of 'development' and 'self help' interventions. In China, Jesper Zeuthen has carried out fieldwork on the outskirts of Chengdu in Sichuan province, where he interviewed people who had been affected by urban–rural integration schemes. In his article, Zeuthen shows how urban–rural boundaries are rarely fixed as local peasants as well as local government officials frequently 'worked the system', mobilising categorisations as a way to get access to, for example, better compensation for a demolished house, funds earmarked for integration schemes or access to land. He argues that at the urban fringe in Chengdu, 'both rule and claims-making were powered by difference', as manifest in different categorisations. In an analysis of how the armed conflict between Maoist guerrillas and the government of India in Chattisgarh comes to be portrayed by government spokespersons and national media, Nandini Sundar argues that the conflict is as much an emotional war as it is an armed conflict. While outrage is directed at the death of 'worthy victims', the deaths of 'unworthy victims' are barely noticed in the media or in government statements. Emotions, she suggests, 'are brought in to justify and structure the course of war' through processes of emotional conscription aimed at 'winning hearts and minds'. In these cases, differences emerge out of interventions into the daily lives of villagers, suburban populations and soldiers. The formation of difference through administrative categorisations, media coverage of armed conflicts or industrialisation programmes has palpable effects on people, yet difference is also mobilised by these same people in their efforts to, for example, gain land, generate sympathy or make claims.

In a final cluster of articles, we are given insight into what Peter van der Veer calls 'secularism as a project' as opposed to secularisation as a process. He argues that in both India and China, secularism has been utilised as a strategy of national development: 'secularism is not simply anti-religious in these societies... it simultaneously attempts to transform religions into moral sources of citizenship and national belonging'. Such an approach, he shows, allows us to understand how different forms of secularism take hold in different places, rather than assuming that a uniform process of secularisation will take place the world over. In a secular China, the Communist Party has played an important role in the mobilisation of the masses, although, as Susanne Bregnbæk shows us in her article on the quandaries of young students aiming to become party members, the place and regard of the party has certainly undergone changes. Bregnbæk's very intimate account of the split subjectivities of two university students in Beijing who were aspiring party members, shows us how difference can be negotiated as a matter of self formation. As one of her informants, who had come to Beijing from another province, reflected: 'people from the rural areas... lack confidence because we live in a modern city but we are from less developed areas'.

Thus, by shifting our analytical focus to the ways in which difference is made and governed and away from the ways in which difference authorises certain claims or vantage points, we argue in this special issue that a new conceptual language is required if we are to come to grips with ongoing transformations and transitions in countries like India and China, and indeed globally. The empirical studies contained within demonstrate the traction that can be gained from such a shift, but this special issue remains a call to arms. If we indeed are to leave behind the kinds of dichotomies that have hitherto cemented global difference, then we must go to those locations in which difference is made, governed, mobilised and obscured.

Notes

1 The usefulness of the discourse of 'Third World' has already been a subject of intense debate. See for example, 'The Third World is Disappearing', in N Harris, *The End of the Third World. Newly Industrializing Countries and the Decline of an Ideology*, London, I.B. Tauris, 1986, p 300; '[T]he rise of East Asia, the demise of the "Second World" and the onset of a new era of global capitalism, throws the problems associated with the continued use of the term "Third World" into sharp relief', see M Berger, 'The end of the "Third World"?', *Third World Quarterly*, 15(2), 1994, p 257; '[There is a] need to move beyond the paradigm of modernity within which the Third World has functioned as a key element in the classificatory hierarchy of the modern/colonial world system', Arturo Escobar, 'Beyond the Third World: imperial globality, global coloniality and antiglobalisation, social movements', *Third World Quarterly*, 25(1), 2004, pp 224–225; and 'the age of the Third World has passed irrevocably into history', M T Berger, 'After the Third World? History, destiny and the fate of Third Worldism', *Third World Quarterly*, 25(1), 2004, p 30. See especially *Third World Quarterly* (25(1)) special issue 'After the Third World?' from 2004, guest edited by Mark Berger.
2 On multicultural, postcolonial, sexuality and disability studies respectively, see S Hall, 'The spectacle of the "other"', in S Hall (ed.), *Representations. Cultural Representations and Signifying Practices*, London, Sage and The Open University, 1999, pp 223–279; A Escobar, *Territories of Difference*, Durham, NC, Duke University Press, 2008; J Butler, *Bodies That Matter: On the Discursive Limits of 'Sex'*, London, Routledge, 1993; J Butler, *Gender Trouble: Feminism and the Subversion of Identity*, New York, Routledge, 1990; D Pothier & R Devlin, *Critical Disability Theory: Essays in Philosophy, Politics, Policy, and Law*, Vancouver, UBC Press, 2006.
3 Hall, 'The spectacle of the "other"', p 238.
4 Devlin & Pothier, *Critical Disability Theory*, p 12.
5 Escobar, *Territories of Difference*, p 6.
6 While we focus on India and China in this special issue of TWQ, one could easily include countries like Brazil, Russia or South Africa, among many others, in the analysis.
7 Deleuze makes a critique of the Hegelian approach and argues that difference should be an object of affirmation rather than negation. See G Deleuze, *Difference and Repetition*, London, Continuum, 2009.
8 Some examples would include the Human Development Index, Transparency International Index, Freedom Index and the annual Ms Universe competition.
9 J Derrida, *Writing and Difference*, London, Routledge, 2001.
10 H Bhabha, 'Of mimicry and man: the ambivalence of colonial discourse', *October*, 28, 1984, pp 125–133.

Notes on contributors

Ravinder Kaur is Associate Professor and Director of the Centre for Global South Asian Studies, Department of Cross-Cultural and Regional Studies, University of Copenhagen, Denmark. Her work includes *Since 1947: Partition Narratives among Punjabi Migrants of Delhi* (Oxford University Press, 2007); editor, *Religion, Violence and Political Mobilisation in Contemporary South Asia* (Sage Publications, 2005) and several articles and book chapters. She is currently responsible for a research programme funded by the Danish Social Sciences Research Council on the ongoing social-political transformations in post-reform India.

Ayo Wahlberg is Asian Dynamics Initiative Postdoctoral Research Fellow at the Department of Anthropology, University of Copenhagen. He is co-editor (with Laurence Monnais and C. Michele Thompson) of *Southern Medicine for Southern People – Vietnamese Medicine in the Making* (Cambridge Scholars Publishing, 2012) and (with Susanne Bauer) *Contested Categories – Life Sciences in Society* (Ashgate, 2009). His current project, for which he has received a Sapere Aude Young Researcher Award from the Danish Council of Independent Research, focuses on reproductive technologies in China.

Imperial Modernity: history and global inequity in rising Asia

DAVID LUDDEN

ABSTRACT *In the recently generalised historical coincidence of neoliberal free-market policy trends with accelerating global economic growth and inequality, India and China stand out as world regions with distinctive histories of imperial inequity. The rise of Asia shows that globalisation does not work the same way everywhere. In Asia historical dynamics of imperial territorialism generate inequities that fit global patterns through their absorption and mediation of capitalism. Economic reforms that brought Asia into global leadership ranks express imperial forms of power, authority, and inequity whose long histories need to be understood to make sense of Asia and global capitalism today. This article focuses particularly on India.*

In both India and China central state reforms in the 1980s facilitated national integration into a globalising market economy, increased economic growth, and aggravated inequality; all these trends accelerated in later decades.[1] In smaller Asian countries—Sri Lanka, Nepal, Bangladesh, and the Philippines—external financial pressure propelled neoliberal structural adjustment policies, but the two Asian giants have joined the trend of global marketisation on their own terms, at their own pace, for their own reasons. In both cases it was a top-down process that not only changed economic policy but also altered the substance of national sovereignty, increasing the influence of big business and of regions that gained political stature as privileged sites for economic growth, aggravating inequities that divide urban from rural areas, industry and services from agriculture, and rich from poor, and casting minorities into deepening marginality. Economic reforms that have brought Asia into the leadership ranks of global capitalism express imperial forms of power, authority and inequity, whose long histories need to be understood to make sense of Asia and of globalisation today.

Three features of global inequity frame recent trends in Asia. First, increasing spatial complexity emerges when we look at geographies of inequality inside and across national boundaries. In many countries national borders are battlefields where poor migrants face barbed wire and high walls, in deadly no man's land, as national territorialism also concentrates privilege

David Ludden is in the Department of History, New York University.

and deprivation. Affluent people increasingly tend to inhabit areas of concentrated affluence, both inside and among nations, reinforcing advantages such as access to first-rate services within safe, secure and resource-rich environments. The territorial expression of material and political interests among rich and poor people diverge increasingly with spatial concentration. Second, inequality trends tend to be invisible in mainstream public discourse, despite outbursts of protest in 2011. This invisibility is surely explained in good measure by mass media filters that support neoliberal cultural hegemony, not only in the USA, but in most of the so-called developing world, including India and China, where the rising rich, middle class, mass media and politicians have deeply invested in neoliberal globalisation. Third, authoritative knowledge production remains a privilege of the rich and powerful, most of all in rich countries, islands of knowledge production which are getting richer and smaller, encouraging scholars to expand their global reach, while budgets for education, research and libraries decline even faster than income moving down the scale of wealth, inside and across countries. The concentration of wealth reinforces the tendency for world knowledge to be formulated by and for people at the top of the heap, as well as the reciprocal tendency for knowledge produced in poor places to be inferior in quality and designed to serve the status quo.

All this indicates that historians need to think beyond statistics on economic inequality to understand how structures of inequity operate in culture, politics, social organisation and knowledge production, temporally and spatially. I argue here that history also becomes more useful politically when it escapes national territorialism to focus on inequality as an historical process, to isolate the specific newness of the present—what the United Nations Development Programme (UNDP) calls 'the inequality predicament'—inside historical dynamics operating over long periods of time, into the future. I want to further argue, indeed, that we can only explain trends and patterns of inequality today—and formulate appropriate politics—by adopting a long-term perspective on the reproduction of inequity in the present.

What is globalisation?

Locating history inside globalisation, rather than inside national boundaries, opens up historical analysis in three ways: temporal, spatial and analytical. Temporally we should think of globalisation as a distinctively contemporary moment in a very long history of globalising territorialism. It is a political project, operating amid increasing spatial interconnectedness, fed by technological change in communications and transportation, and producing new formations of national sovereignty, which facilitate more spatially flexible and rapid rearrangements of human affairs. Globalisation as a form of territorial politics moved ahead more rapidly and decisively when the world of nations came into being after 1945. The national state became the first truly global institution; the nation became the first global form of cultural identity. This gave rise to a global territory of culture and political economy, which has been rapidly restructured in the past several decades, by technological space–time compression, to make the world seem smaller every day, and by politically expansive, deepening marketisation, to make more and more human assets private property for sale.

Spatially globalisation is an aggregation of individual moments of mobility, transfer, relocation and flow in a world that is *also* composed spatially by forces of containment, that is, by territorial powers of confinement, enclosure and boundary-making; so that people, things, and ideas are always moving inside and among territories defined by official boundaries. Analytically globalisation provides a mobile perspective on history, covering more human space over time, moving the mind's eye across boundaries, among separate territories, where historians always find that most documentation implicitly articulates territorial attachments to enclosed spaces of human identity, fellow-feeling and social order, even as mobility is always at the same time cutting across and inflecting territorial sensibilities.[2]

Instead of focusing solely on national territories, therefore, historians need to analyse inequality inside interactions of mobility and territorialism. Ankie Hoogvelt provides a good point of departure by arguing that global capitalism operates in networks of mobility where markets move assets from place to place by privileging some places over others as sites of accumulation.[3] This 'networking capitalism' raises the crucial question of what forces guide the uneven flow of capital and its differential accumulation. Markets do move assets around and articulate capital accumulation, but markets never fully explain why wealth moves and accumulates the way it does. Studies of territoriality provide additional explanatory force by revealing how social power produces bounded territories that privilege some places and people as sites and as actors in markets. For instance, territorial systems of property ownership define legal entitlements to assets moving around in markets; rules of citizenship, inheritance, taxation and state patronage construct territorial authority, power and order by means that structure circuits of capital flow and accumulation, thereby organising inequality.

Nevertheless, national territories of globalisation do not conform to the flat world described by national maps. Global territory is also organised vertically by inequities of power and inequalities of wealth and influence, forming mountains of power and privilege and swamps of dependency and deprivation. Describing that world of inequity historically remains a major challenge. The word 'empire' serves a useful purpose by evoking a supranational and vertically elaborate institutional space of power relations which lock national territories into globalisation. Historically, moreover, all nations are entangled with empire in one way or another, although nationalism has constituted itself as the opposition to imperialism and postcolonial nations see themselves as the idealistic negation of empire. In the world of nations the narration of modernity prominently includes progress from empire to nation, forming a national teleology as progress from slavery to freedom forms an irreversible process of transition, negation and replacement. In that context empire and nation appear to be incompatible opposites, and the old archaic world of empire appears to have disappeared inside the new modern world of nations, as represented by the formal framework of international law.

I think Michael Hardt and Antonio Negri are right to theorise globalisation as a new territorial formation of power at a planetary scale, but wrong to detach it from the history of imperialism.[4] Territorial empires spawned nations that formed the bounded spatial domains of power and authority where globalisation operates today. Despite their structural differences and conflicts, imperial and national forms of territoriality interweave one another. Empires produced, sustained and enriched national territories. Imperial territories became national territories. As nations covered the world, national cultures consigned empire to the past and nations became definitive territories of human identity and progress, but the legal frame of national sovereignty that covered the world did not eliminate imperial forms of territoriality. The reproduction of imperial forms continued *de facto*, though not *de jure*, in the world of national states, comprising an unofficial but licit territorial basis for patterns of inequity which have accelerated inequality over the past four decades.[5]

Imperial modernity

Imperial territories that structure inequality under global capitalism are not only of the modern, Western kind, as theorists since Marx have believed, assuming that world capitalism spread out from Europe, carried by Western imperialism. Now it is apparent, however, largely because of the recent rise of Asia, that capitalism evolved from the beginning in transcontinental spaces, in networks of mobility transecting many imperial territories. In the 19th century capitalism evolved inside expansive European imperial spaces where intellectuals saw capitalism as being European by definition. Now we know, however, that inside very old Asian imperial territories, distinctively Asian imperial forms of power and authority also fed markets and structured circuits of capital accumulation, forming foundations for imperial modernity. Modern capitalist imperialism may have crowned Europeans with supreme status, and Asian nationalists may have fought European imperialists to make free nations, but a reproduction of old imperial forms of inequity also occurred inside transitions from empire to nation in Asia, something which continues to shape patterns of global inequality today.

Inequality in the world of globalisation is increasing in Asia at the intersections of two kinds of imperial history: one is global and emanates from the West, now most powerfully in US global circuits of power; the other operates inside Asia and reflects the articulation of Asian and Western imperial forms over three centuries.[6] It is certainly true, therefore, that today's increasing inequality results from a recent technology-assisted surge of globalisation inside a neoliberal policy regime devised and enforced by Western powers, but it is not true that the imperial dimensions of this process are formed only by Western supremacy. Technologies and policies of neoliberal globalisation have been developed by national elites in many countries, who form a new kind of multinational, imperial ruling class whose global dominion is emerging from long intersecting histories of imperial territoriality on all continents. In these histories we can better understand how social, political and spatial inequity produce increasing inequality at various levels of scale under globalisation.

Three features of imperial territory are most critical for this kind of history: ranking, mobility and unevenness. First, in contrast to the formal equivalence of people and places inside national territory, imperial space consists of explicitly visible cultural ranks of authority and privilege, supported implicitly by coercive power, in which, however horizontal and voluntary social transactions appear—notably market transactions—they always entail coercive potential in ranks above, and subordinate response and adaptation in ranks below, in vertically structured relationships among unequal actors whose transactions dramatise inequality and represent dynamics of power.[7] In imperial territory spatial and social relations are pervasively vertical: each place, person and group occupies a rank. National rankings on global scales of economic development are condensed symbols of imperial order. In this context geographical mobility, which appears horizontal on maps, also travels vertically up and down ranks of wealth, power, status and authority. Upward social mobility typically involves physically moving from lower to higher status locations; this is driving urbanisation, the concentration of affluence and cross-border immigration around the world, as poor people move in millions from poorer villages to richer cities, creating a planet of slums and borderlands of conflict over territorial rights.[8]

Second, imperial territory is inherently mobile. Imperial power and authority move constantly in networks of mobility to inscribe ranks in the realm, and resulting imperial boundaries are never firmly fixed: they form moving frontiers. In contrast to the static, fixed boundaries of a national state, imperial territories typically overlap as entangled boundaries move and mobile authorities struggle for space and supremacy. Imperial territory is dynamic, expansive, working to incorporate new regions, locations, forming ever more complexly layered domains, a many layered cake of ranked people and places. Elites rise above the rest as imperial authority incorporates more expansive domains, with more layers of subordination, to secure the accumulation of capital flowing up the ranks, in many forms. The mobility of power outward from the metropolitan centres, down the ranks of central places, into frontiers of imperial authority, secures the reciprocal flow of assets up the ranks into elite hands at every level.

Third, and also in contrast to the national state, where legal authority spreads comprehensively from boundary to boundary, in empire gaps and grey areas always appear inside territorial domains, at all levels, not only because rebellion and resistance counteract and negate top-down imperial power and authority, but also because imperial incorporation produces layered domains of legal authority,[9] while some places simply do not warrant the effort to integrate fully into an imperial order. Imperial territory is unevenly controlled by people of higher status ranks: it always contains dynamic struggles in its many layered cake that shift power up and down the ranks, producing various outcomes in space and time; and it typically includes people and places so lowly and marginal as to be left out of the status ranks entirely. Strategic places and people in networks of imperial mobility secure the flow of power and assets that feeds and expresses imperial authority: imperial territory is defined not so much by boundaries on maps as by connections among critical urban sites in networks of imperial mobility, with each urban site in turn ranked above descending ranks in its domain.

Its ranks, mobility and unevenness—and thus spatially adaptive qualities[10]—make imperial territory impossible to map accurately on the static horizontal plane of modern cartography. Firmly fixed boundaries of the national sort do not exist in imperial space, where places and regions are not equivalent, but rather ranked as superior and inferior, central and peripheral. Some people and places represent imperial order more than others. People live on various cultural planes, higher and lower, the higher being more advanced, more civilised, authorised to lead, in charge of the future for people lower down the ranks, who must follow, adapt, learn the rules and adjust, but who often resist, fight back and contest power held at higher ranks by exerting force to alter vertical transactions, to produce more wealth, power and authority in lower ranks, while some people and places elude or escape inclusion entirely. Unlike the nation, empire is a dynamic, shifting and ever-changing territorial form, deeply invested in its own capacities for mobility.

The articulation of mobile market space with mobile imperial territorialism is indeed a central dynamic force in globalisation. In this context it is important to note that temporal boundaries of empire are as elusive as spatial boundaries. Imperial expansion, integration and ranking operate in changing patterns over time. Imperial forms of power and authority assume various guises, sometimes appearing as massively coercive and domineering, sometimes being composed primarily of rituals and symbols. All elements of imperial order can be combined, separated, dispersed and recombined variously over time, creating kaleidoscopic possibilities, impossible to chart with chronological or geographical precision.

Historians nevertheless typically treat empire as a unitary political form whose shifting geographies and fluid temporalities can be crammed into flat maps and rigid timelines that describe the 'rise and fall' of each empire as a separate institutional entity.[11] This kind of enclosed regime history provides an orderly chronology of imperial succession and creates a logical endpoint for imperial history in the mid-twentieth century, but obscures the fact that imperial forms of power and authority have structured human space for millennia. Setting aside this scholarly tradition of imperial historiography, we can shift our focus to histories of imperial territoriality and their structuration of modern culture and political economy. In this kind of history, we see that imperial forms of power and authority reproduce themselves repeatedly in new guises and across regime transitions, including the global transition to national state hegemony in the mid-twentieth century. Instead of framing histories of empire with chronicles of rising and falling regimes, we can look across times and spaces occupied by empires and nations to find histories of imperial territoriality forming dynamic cycles of

Imperial inequity

Asian history is a composite of many imperial cycles, and modern cycles have occurred in the embrace of imperial territories built on a global scale.[12] In eighteenth century South Asia, regional authorities, enriched by European trade, broke the Mughal Empire into constituent domains that shifted imperial power down territorial ranks into regions where elites became more independent and Mughal authority became increasingly symbolic. Then, in one region after the other, East India Company imperialists altered Mughal imperial forms, added the force of emerging industrial capitalism, and built a new imperial order. British India expanded Indian imperial territory into new frontiers across the nineteenth century. Early in the twentieth century the British built a new capital for imperial India around the old Mughal capital in Delhi, as Indian nationalists mobilised middling ranks of imperial authority against the British. At the same time upward mobility in the wider world of empire generated conflict, as upstarts—including the USA and Japan—rose to challenge imperial Europe, and nationalists fought to bring more power over the flow of assets into the lower imperial ranks. Nationalists undermined British authority in India at the same time as war among globe-trotting imperialists produced two world wars that weakened all imperial nations, except the USA, which moved up the ranks. After 1945, British imperial territory fractured into national state territories; a world covered by independent, sovereign national states came into being. And in this world, and well as in South Asia, imperial forms of power and authority acquired new life. The organisation of the United Nations expressed international ranks of power and authority that formed the so-called developed and developing world, ranked as the First, Second, Third, and later even Fourth worlds. Recent globalisation has occurred inside this new formation of imperial inequity, which has produced what the UN calls the 'inequality predicament'.

This predicament—described in the 2005 UN *Report on the World Social Situation*—results from a persistent tendency of empire to channel wealth up the ranks and to concentrate wealth in upper echelons. This upward mobility of wealth provides capital for elites to spend and invest, which can spur economic growth, but also reduces the proportion of new wealth available to people in lower echelons. The resulting tendency for inequality to increase aggravates a range of endemic imperial problems. The UN emphasises one in particular: the increasing difficulty that people in the lowest echelons have in moving out of poverty and up the ranks, thereby to benefit from—and acquire good reasons for loyalty to—imperial order.[13]

Martin Ravallion succinctly states the relevant economic axiom: 'At any positive rate of growth, the higher the initial inequality, the lower the rate at which income-poverty falls'.[14] This means that increasing inequality reduces the rate at which people move out of poverty as it channels more wealth into richer hands, disadvantaging the poor,[15] even though this same trend might also stimulate growth, at least for a time, and thus benefit a majority, each person according to their rank, in a capitalist economy where markets reward investors in proportion to investments.[16] Thus, imperial inequity operates under capitalism to generate productive power and distribute profits inside a system of ranks that resulting inequality trends express and alter in various ways. In standard economic jargon we can say that imperial inequity in capitalism has a poverty effect and a growth effect and, as Robert Wade has argued, we can expect elites to prefer state policies that stimulate growth by channelling wealth up the ranks, even though this aggravates the poverty effect, which is concentrated in lower echelons and on peripheries, among groups on the outskirts of elite priorities.[17]

Such an imperial framing helps to make sense of the UN's contemporary 'inequality predicament', which is this: in recent decades, total wealth has been increasing globally under free-market-oriented economic policies and a surge of globalisation, but asset inequality has also been increasing in and among countries. More wealth is available for reducing poverty globally, but smaller proportions of new wealth are serving that purpose. This upward mobility of wealth is in general producing a trend of relative impoverishment among people in lower echelons, and overall rates of poverty reduction are bound to be declining. Statistics to reveal this picture became available in the 1990s,[18] when the landmark 1996 *Human Development Report* showed that 'The poorest 20% of the world's people saw their share of global wealth decline from 2.3% to 1.4% in the [preceding] 30 years ... [as] the share of the richest 20% rose from 70% to 80%'.[19] This trend is also visible inside the imperial nation most influential in setting global economic policy, the USA, where, during two decades following 'the Reagan revolution', in 1980, the richest 20 per cent increased their share of national income from 44 per cent to 50 per cent, and the richest 1 per cent increased theirs proportionately six times more, from 7 per cent to 13 per cent.[20] Twenty per cent of the US population now owns 84 per cent of private assets, and today the USA is more unequal—and the rich and poor are separated by a wealth gap more expansive—than at any time since the start of the Great Depression.[21]

Amid these trends, absolute poverty is decreasing in some parts of the world, stagnating in others and increasing in others,[22] while overall poverty reduction must be slowing down, making future poverty more intractable. In the 1990s the world poverty problem began to be of concern at the World Bank, where increasing inequality began to appear as a hindrance to sustainable growth, but alarm bells became louder in 2005, when the UNDP *Report on the World Social Situation* warned that current inequality trends not only threaten economic growth by depressing demand, reducing labour productivity and degrading human and natural environments, but also foster social and political conflicts that undermine governance and encourage nations to seek stability by drawing back from globalisation.

We can usefully locate this present-day scene in a long historic cycle, stretching back to the nineteenth century, during which imperial forms of power and authority have been reproduced at various levels of scale. At the global level, in the aftermath of World War Two, old imperial elites sat on the UN Security Council, met at Bretton Woods, in NATO, at Davos and elsewhere, to refashion their imperial position in a new world of nations, where the Cold War expressed a new kind of inter-imperial struggle. In the 1970s a new phase of globalisation began, when a long postwar economic boom ended, and a new global development regime took shape—led by the richest countries, the World Bank and the IMF—which gained increasing influence, mostly by financial means, over economic policies in most poor countries. This global development regime supported competitive capitalist strategies in the post-boom decades by enforcing structural adjustment policies, which composed an unprecedented global uniformity of free-market-oriented state policy regimes, inducing poor country exports, promoting imports and opening up states to global investors.[23] After 1980 rapid technological change also lowered transport and communication costs, most rapidly after 1989, when the end of the USSR inspired the American regime to proclaim the USA 'the world's only superpower'.

Echoes of imperial history reverberate across the nineteenth and twentieth centuries. The aggressive hubris of imperial America echoes imperial Britain, to which the USA is now frequently compared.[24] And long-term trends in international wealth inequality also suggest a century-long imperial cycle, which connects the present to the late nineteenth century. Lant Pritchett has famously shown that between 1870 and 1985 ratios of per capita income between rich and poor countries increased over six-fold, as income levels dispersed over an ever-widening range, with rich and poor countries clustering more and more on opposite ends of a widening spectrum.[25] In that global context development efforts in poor post-colonial countries after 1950 were an uphill struggle against the tide of modern history, for new wealth produced by economic development around the world has tended since the late nineteenth century to augment the wealth of already richer countries disproportionately.

And yet, in neoliberal public culture, the imperial implications of such trends have been rendered largely invisible by analysts who agree with *New York Times* columnist David Brookes that 'today's rich don't exploit the poor; they just out-compete them'.[26] In this view the UN's inequality predicament is simply that more competitive, productive people earn more by merit, and inequality increases because markets do not provide uncompetitive, unproductive people with what they need to compete successfully. This logic has induced all major development agencies to promote what they call 'pro-poor growth' policies, which rely on governments, NGOs and business to provide loans, education, health, housing, jobs and other things poor people need to compete more successfully.[27] Despite pro-poor initiatives, however, inequality is increasing in the world and in most countries; faster, it seems, with each passing year.

Imperial Asia

It is tempting to see Asia as a collection of poor post-colonial countries where recent economic policy trends are having the same kinds of growth and poverty effects that we see in many countries and in the world as a whole. But that appearance is deceptive. It is true that Asia's recent surge in economic growth under neoliberal policy influence has spawned increasing inequality, but globalisation in Asia also has temporal, spatial and social patterns that derive from imperial histories in Asia. Focusing on India, Tirthankar Roy evokes one such history by saying insightfully that the Indian government has returned to the free-market policy framework that prevailed in Queen Victoria's day.[28] We can see this recent 'return', however, as a moment in a long, dynamic process of imperial transformation, which can be outlined briefly as follows.

In the nineteenth century, the British regime refashioned India's old imperial ranks into a modern entitlement system that channelled wealth upwards through state institutions and markets. Imperial capitalism was deeply embedded in India during a great surge of globalisation before World War One, when the proportion of world GDP travelling around the world grew faster than during any decade thereafter until the 1990s. In 1914 the US Consul at Bombay described British India as 'one of the few large countries of the world where there is an "open door" for the trade of all countries'.[29] In 1914 most goods arriving at South Asian ports were for export. British India was then the world's fourth largest industrial cotton textile producer, and manufactured goods comprised 20 per cent of exports, a figure never since surpassed. In the next two decades industrial output grew faster in India than in the UK and Germany,[30] as trade with the UK at India's five major ports fell to less than one-third,[31] and Indian labour also went global. By 1921 Indian emigration exceeded immigration and what we now call diaspora began moving people to Ceylon, Malaya, East and South Africa, Fiji and West Indies, all in the embrace of the British Empire.[32]

Following typically imperial trajectories, capitalism in British India channelled wealth upwards to benefit people of superior status in all layers of the empire's many layered cake, from top to bottom, benefiting most of all the British 0.0001 per cent in topmost ranks, but also Indian professional, business and landowning elites in lower ranks, all the way down to the village. Wealth moving upwards enriched the Empire more than either India or Britain.[33] Imperial priorities dampened profit incentives for productive investment, so rates of growth were low and rates of poverty high. Extremes of inequality in India appeared during famines that killed many millions, the last several million in Bengal during World War Two, where imperial priorities focused on feeding Calcutta and left lowly villagers on the outskirts of empire to starve.[34]

By 1880 the upward mobility of wealth in the Empire had become apparent to Indian nationalists, led by Dadabhai Naoroji. Staunching the flow of wealth out of India to increase wealth inside national territory became a central goal for nationalists. The results were stunning, especially when we compare trends in India to the world trend of steadily increasing inequality between rich and poor countries, measured by Lant Pritchett, across the whole of the 20th century. By contrast, data compiled by Gregory Clark show that Indian per capita GDP relative to the UK and USA declined sharply and steadily after 1870, but only until 1947, when India's long trend of increasing impoverishment compared to the two great imperial nations stopped abruptly.[35] The reason is simple. British India's development regime channelled wealth up the ranks and out of India, but after Independence, in 1947, national regimes in India (and then Pakistan and Bangladesh) kept and created more wealth inside national territory.[36] National independence accomplished a radical shift of wealth and power downwards in the world's imperial ranks by increasing the power of people to control economic resources inside their national territory. India remained comparatively poor, with per capita GDP hovering since 1947 around 10 per cent of the US–UK average (Figure 1)—and India is still the poorest of the world five largest national economies[37]—but India's relative impoverishment trend stopped dead at independence (Figure 2).

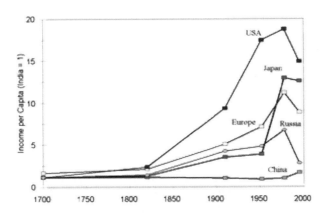

FIGURE 1. Per capita incomes per capita relative to India.

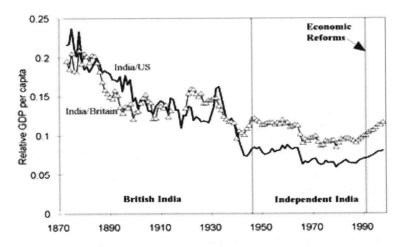

FIGURE 2. Indian GDP per capita relative to the UK and USA, 1873–1998.

Today most analysts point to 1991 as the year of great economic change in India, but 1947 was a much bigger watershed, when the end of the Empire shifted India's comparative national wealth trend from negative to positive for the first time in modern history. The same trend holds for China, though details differ, and the weight of the combined populations of India and China would have brought global inequality down significantly in the early decades after 1950, when François Bourguignon and Christian Morrison have shown the overall rate of increase in world inequality slowed down considerably.[38]

After 1980 India's comparative wealth trend accelerated and then, after 1991, sped up again (Figure 3).[39] And, again, the same trend holds for China, so if we weight national wealth by population, rapid growth in India and China today is reducing the rate of increase of international inequality.[40] But inequality has also been increasing and poverty reduction slowing down in India and China, as freeing up markets has aggravated the imperial tendency for wealth to move up the ranks. A decline in intra-country inequality during the three decades after 1950 has reversed itself, with inequality increasing after 1980 in two-thirds of the 73 countries analysed by Giovanni Andrea Cornia and Sampsa Kiiski, representing over half the world's population.[41]

India's imperial dynamics help to explain why it is getting richer faster today, for in India, as well as in China, a substantial part of the explanation lies in a downward territorial shift in political power over economic resources into regions. In India an analogous downward shift or devolution of economic power underlay an upsurge in growth in coastal regions in the late eighteenth century, when independence from the Mughal Empire coincided with increasing overseas trade. Likewise, after 1947, nationalists in India built a new state that held dividends from public and private investment inside India. Inside independent India the reorganisation of states after 1956 repeatedly delivered growth benefits to regions that thereby gained state power over economic resources. The process called 'nation building' in Asia can be interpreted in India as a new round of imperial incorporation, in

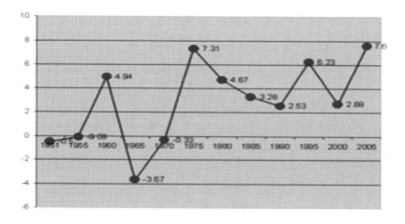

FIGURE 3. Growth of India's real GDP per capita (constant prices: chain series), 1950–2006.

which regions and peoples on the margins of British Indian territorialism, in mountains, jungles and so-called 'native states' were aggressively subordinated to the centralising Indian state.

Liberalisation in India after 1991, and in China after 1979, has been accomplished by political processes that typify dynamic cycles of imperial territorialism, as devolutions of power down vertical ranks have composed what Yongnian Zheng calls a 'state transformation'.[42] As a result, national political systems have changed drastically, and in India, where the Congress Party once ruled without rivals, coalitions of regional parties came to control the central government.[43] Currently high growth rates in India and China derive significantly from economic and political devolution; in that context domestic and international businesses seek new opportunities in both countries,[44] as they also did during analogous periods of imperial change in earlier times.[45]

Imperial inequality in India

India's imperial dynamics also help to explain internal patterns and trends in inequality. At independence nationalists produced a new India by extracting territorial layers from the many layered cake of British Empire, welding them into a much more tightly integrated national territory. Freed from global empire, India instituted a state regime that forcefully integrated old frontiers and erstwhile Native States,[46] invested heavily in infrastructure, increased growth, eliminated famine, kept Gini coefficients of income inequality stable for 50 years, and lowered inequality through land reforms, food and public goods provisioning, and subsidies for productive inputs like water, electricity, fertiliser and high yielding varieties of wheat and rice.[47] From the 1930s onwards, nationalism in India stood for an equalisation of all Indian citizens, a politically sustained commitment which reduced inequality inside India for three decades after independence.

These national efforts did not, however, eliminate India's imperial ranks. In agrarian regions where Mughal and British empires had privileged landlord property owners, levels of private and public investment in agriculture and human development (health and education) remained comparatively low.[48] India's national development regime actually accentuated wealth accumulation by people and in places already privileged at various levels in 1947. National development policy—to quote its critics— 'bet on the rich' to secure economic growth. In the 1980s the upwardly mobile social strata—people who had benefited most from their status in British imperial ranks and in India's imperial regime of national development—propelled the government's return to a free-market regime, which was by then no longer identified with empire, but rather with being progressively, proudly Indian, most notably during the political transition of the 1980s.[49]

In 1991, after a decade of national debt-driven growth, India joined a global trend by returning to the same kind of free-market, import-export-oriented economic policies that prevailed in 1914. By then inequality among Indian states had been increasing along inherited lines since the 1960s,[50] and today, spatial inequality is seen to be 'a serious problem' in India, having remained entrenched 'in spite of planning' and increasing notably after 1991.[51] After India's devolution of political power and its return to free-market policies, higher growth rates ensued but spatial inequality began to increase visibly, as richer regions got steadily richer compared with poorer regions.[52] After 1991 faster growth increased inequality quickly and more broadly. Relevant data are complex and contentious, but convincing. Gini coefficients of income inequality have risen since 1999. In 2004 National Sample Survey data indicated that, after 1991, new wealth went mostly to wealthier classes with privileged access to government and new market opportunities. The urban rich benefited most: the top quintile of income groups in cities increased its per capita consumption by 40 per cent, but in rural areas by 20 per cent. The rural rich got much richer although poorer compared with urban rich, a comparison that politicians took seriously and which helps to explain the change in Indian governments in 2004, when the new prime minister had to face the fact that 600 million Indians, in the bottom 80 per cent of rural income groups, had suffered a steady decline in per capita consumption under reforms he introduced as finance minister, in 1991, and which he vowed to accelerate after 2004. Manmohan Singh could, however, feel good that 300 million Indian citizens did get richer under liberalisation after 1991, and that the richest among them became media stars for his aggressive ad campaign promoting India as 'the world's fastest growing free-market democracy'.[53]

Patterns of inequality and its increase in India today are not haphazard. Neither are they new. They can be understood as products of a unitary world capitalist system,[54] or as symptoms of India's unique political economy, with its distinctive culture of inequality.[55] Viewing them instead as features of a dynamic, changing imperial order helps to explain them better, because these patterns arise over and again in various geographical frames and historical contexts, which are not unique to India, as they are also not the same in all countries across the capitalist world. They represent what we can usefully call generic patterns of imperial inequity, reproduced across centuries and across modes of production, and structuring inequality in India today during a general increase in inequality worldwide.

Four prominent generic forms of imperial inequity operate in India, as in China and elsewhere, according to ranks defined by location, gender, ethnicity and class, all tightly entangled in ranks of state power and authority. Imperial landscapes define spatial inequality in core locations that form privileged sites for capital accumulation, and in both China and India urban–rural and regional disparities institutionalised long before 1980 have become rapidly worse since 1990.[56] For India Angus Dean and Jean Dreze have showed that recent growth favours states in the south and west, distressing states in the north and northeast, which had been previously disadvantaged by public and private investment decisions.[57] The poverty of regions in the eastern Gangetic basin compared to the West and the Punjab goes back to the nineteenth century, when the east–west divergence in North India became a feature of imperial politics that moved the capital to New

Delhi. That same spatial divergence continued after Independence, with disproportionate state and private investments in the west.[58] Regions more dependent upon agriculture had declining economic returns in the 1990s, as annual growth in agriculture and allied services dipped to less than half (3.2 per cent) the rate of growth in India's aggregate per capita GDP (6.7 per cent), and the ratio of rural-to-urban poverty rapidly increased.[59] Regions of Asia that are most out of the loop of capital accumulation generally lie on the far peripheries of old empires—of the Mughals, the British, Dutch, French and Chinese—in mountain regions spanning Nepal, northeast India, the Chittagong Hill Tracts, and highland Burma, Thailand, Vietnam and southern China. All these are homelands of tribal minority groups on the peripheries of national control.[60] In cities slums can be viewed as internal peripheries, like distant, remote villages from which people come to live in cities to find employment and services they rarely fully secure. Slums are effectively out of the loop of capital accumulation and, like the poorest remote villages and highland fringe areas, they are homelands for criminal gangs that often provide basic public services, making them more dangerous, unruly and marginal.

Gender inequality in patriarchal ranks pervades imperial forms at each level, from the global to the local.[61] In 2003, a national study of gender disparities in India concluded in line with earlier research that the poorest Indian states (with about half the total population, mostly in the eastern Gangetic Plain) had not improved the condition of women, while the worst gender disparities continued to prevail in richer and faster growing states, above all, Punjab and Haryana. Women's wages and working conditions, and the social and environmental conditions of their domestic and communal labour, all seem to be worsening under free-market globalisation, along lines that indicate a reproduction of old imperial forms of patriarchy, particularly in agrarian contexts, but also in new urban sites of female industrial work in garment, electronics and global sweatshops.[62]

Ethnic inequality hits minority cultural and religious populations. Recent studies have found that India's Muslim population has become poorer, relatively in most states and absolutely in some, including the fast growing, highly urbanised state of Gujarat.[63] Ethnic minority and tribal populations in poor Indian northeastern states and in the Chittagong Hill Tracts have lost ground, reflecting their location on national peripheries and imperial frontiers.[64]

Class inequality divides people with and without proprietary entitlements that people translate into education, business and employment opportunities. M. Atchi Reddy and others have shown that upward trajectories of social mobility into urban elite ranks typically began in rich market towns and in irrigated, rice-growing villages, where up-and-comers owned property whose value increased much more than poor dry farmland. Even today people who own dry land are much less likely to benefit *in situ* from connections to urban sites of globalisation,[65] and impoverished farmers in dry regions on the outskirts of booming cities like Bangalore and Hyderabad, always on the verge of famine, now routinely commit suicide under the humiliation of crushing debt.[66] Landless workers in villages and cities dominate the lowest income groups, who have seen their real income decline in recent times. Jan Breman and others have shown how deindustrialisation and casualisation of labour under free-market flexible production regimes render urban and rural workers more vulnerable to distress and poverty, while the 2005 UNDP report emphasises the poverty effects of being cast into the world's growing informal economy.[67] Exchange entitlements for poor wage workers have been further distressed by inflation and reduced subsidies for basic commodities.[68] Proportionate wage increases favour more educated workers in settings where education is unavailable to improve the position of poorer workers.

It is important to note that these four generic forms of imperial inequality in power over resources overlap and generate dynamics of increasing inequality. Health inequalities arise from and compound all others, and conflict zones wracked by violence arise at their intersections, as the UN report indicates. Today, there is a 'Maoist rebel crescent' that runs across poor mountain regions from Nepal and northeast India through Bihar, Orissa and Andhra Pradesh. In northeast India and Gujarat relative and absolute impoverishment for poor groups has fed violent upheavals in state politics. Caste violence in Tamil Nadu and religious violence in Bangladesh (pitting Muslims against Muslims and against minority Hindus) are also incited by struggles sparked by growing disparities in control over critical resources.

History as the present

In conclusion I would say that we can enrich Ankie Hoogvelt's idea that world capitalism operates in urban-based networks of mobility by emphasising that these networks take shape in spaces of imperial power and authority. Markets are embedded not only in societies, as Karl Polanyi theorised, but also in expansive spaces of social power that generate inequitable market outcomes.[69] Neoclassical economics arose in the heyday of European imperialism to theorise the market as a free-standing system of value making, at a time when major capitalists began to see empire as a constraint to their expansion. A century later neoliberal economic policies became a means to free markets from external constraints imposed by national efforts to restrict the upward mobility of wealth. Imperial inequity in the world of nations then spread neoliberal policies that once again accelerated the upward mobility of wealth—most notably in financial forms—to foster disproportionate accumulations in the higher echelons. It is critical to remember, however, that demographic expansion in wealthier middling ranks—that is, the rise of a global middle class, fired by neoliberal cultural ideals—made this renewed upward shift in the imperial power structure possible. Stepping back to look at this critically important imperial middle class in long-term perspective, we can say that economic growth in Asia has long been driven by the productive deployment of dividends accruing to people according to status inside explicit, well-understood, changing ranks of imperial entitlement. Thus when people deploy their legitimate entitlements in market transactions, they typically secure dividends in systematically recurring patterns of inequity. The neoliberalism of the global middle class thus emerges inside middling imperial ranks, which benefit accordingly, thus becoming politically invested in imperial inequity, whose worst effects are heaped on lower echelons, most often out of sight.

Imperial forms of power and authority thus have a changing cumulative impact, which we can trace over centuries. Decolonisation produced a dramatic downward shift in imperial power during the decades after 1945, and for several decades virtually every national state regime strove to reduce inequality. This policy trend produced a serious reduction of world inequality, which was temporary, because, in the same decades, a reproduction and transformation of imperial forms of power and authority also occurred, globally and inside old imperial spaces like India and China. New imperial formations emerged that now engage one another in the globalisation of territorial structures devoted to the marketisation of all human resources. Government and big business formed an imperial partnership to enforce structural adjustment policies and a devolution of political authority that shifted power down the ranks, into regions of urban expansion linked to one another by competitive liberalisation. This increased economic growth and also inequality by allocating more wealth through markets and producing more wealth by channelling more of it, more productively, into privileged sites inside increasingly unequal big city-centred regions, networked with one another globally.

History indicates therefore that inequality and the influence of the top 1 per cent will not be seriously reduced without dismantling the infrastructure of imperial inequity, because, made free to do as they will, in the world as it is, markets can be relied upon to strengthen imperial forms of entitlement and thus to aggravate inequality. Focusing history in this way on present-day problems, I now find to my great surprise that old European imperialists do not seem the bad guys they once seemed to be, when national independence seemed to pave the way to social justice. For, as Tirthankar Roy says, it did not matter so much that the imperialist were foreigners: what mattered was how they ruled. And now we can see that any ruler who imagines that national independence eliminates imperial power and authority may be likewise engaged in moving more wealth up the food chain. Solving the inequality predicament requires sustained and transnational downward shifts in power over all forms of wealth, which calls for many more and much deeper studies of imperial regimes to inform anti-imperial struggles in every nook and cranny of globalisation.[70]

Acknowledgements

I want to thank Ravinder Kaur for her encouragement and patience during the revision of this paper, which was composed for the 2010 'Governing Difference' workshop, supported by the Asian Dynamics Initiative, University of Copenhagen. Some of these ideas appeared initially in the 2006 Wertheim Lecture for the International Institute for Asian Studies at the University of Amsterdam (http://www.iias.nl/asia/wertheim/lectures/WL_Ludden.pdf).

IDENTITY, INEQUITY AND INEQUALITY IN INDIA AND CHINA

Notes

1 A Kohli, *Poverty amid Plenty in the New India*, New York: Cambridge University Press, 2012.

2 See K Satchidanandan, 'That third space: interrogating the diaspora paradigm', in M Paranjape (ed), *In Diaspora: Theories, Histories, Texts*, Delhi: Indologue Publishers, 2001, pp 15–24. Thanks to Rosemary George for this reference. See also D Ludden, 'Maps in the mind and the mobility of Asia', *Journal of Asian Studies*, 62 (3), pp 1057–1078; and Ludden, 'Nameless Asia and territorial angst', *HIMAL South Asian*, June 2003, at http://www.sas.upenn.edu/~dludden/LuddenHIMALmaps1.htm.

3 A Hoogvelt, *Globalization and the Postcolonial World: The New Political Economy of Development*, Baltimore, MD: Johns Hopkins University Press, 1991.

4 M Hardt & A Negri, *Empire*, Cambridge, MA: Harvard University Press, 2001.

5 On 'licit' realities, see W van Schendel, 'Introduction: the making of illicitness', in W van Schendel & I Abraham (eds), *Illicit Flows and Criminal Things: States, Borders, and the Other Side of Globalization*, Bloomington, IN: Indiana University Press, 2005, pp 1–37.

6 For a compelling account of this intersection as it appears to a perceptive activist author in India, see A Roy, *An Ordinary Person's Guide to Empire*, Boston, MA: South End Press, 2004.

7 Focusing on these dynamics in India was the great initial contribution of Subaltern Studies, which, interestingly, began its career at the onset of contemporary trends in globalisation and inequality, and then diverted attention from those trends with its 'cultural turn' in the mid-1980s. See D Ludden, *Reading Subaltern Studies: Critical Histories, Contested Meanings, and the Globalisation of South Asia*, New Delhi/London: Permanent Black/Anthem Press, 2002.

8 M Davis, *Planet of Slums*, London: Verso, 2006; W van Schendel, *The Bengal Borderland: Beyond State and Nation in South Asia*, London: Anthem, 2005.

9 L Benton, *A Search for Sovereignty: Law and Geography in European Empires, 1400–1900*, Cambridge: Cambridge University Press, 2010.

10 See A Miller & AJ Rieber (eds), *Imperial Rule*, Budapest: Central European University Press, 2004.

11 J Burbank & F Cooper, *Empires in World History: Power and the Politics of Difference*, Princeton, NJ: Princeton University Press, 2010.

12 See Ludden, 'Maps in the mind and the mobility of Asia'.

13 For the implications, see AO Hirschman, *Exit, Voice, and Loyalty: Responses to Decline in Firms, Organizations, and States*, Cambridge, MA: Harvard University Press, 1970.

14 M Ravallion, 'Can high-inequality developing countries escape absolute poverty?', *Economic Letters*, 56, 1997, pp 51–57.

15 A good account is SL Engerman & Kenneth L Sokoloff, *Factor Endowments, Inequality, and Paths of Development among New World Economies*, NBER Working Paper 9259, at http://www.nber.org/papers/w9259, which demonstrates: 'systematic patterns by which societies in the Americas that began with more extreme inequality or heterogeneity in the population were more likely to develop institutional structures that greatly advantaged members of elite classes (and disadvantaged the bulk of the population) by providing them with more political influence and access to economic opportunities'.

16 This is a basic characteristic of capitalism, which the *American Heritage Dictionary* defines nicely as 'an economic system in which the means of production and distribution are privately or corporately owned and development is proportionate to the accumulation and reinvestment of profits gained in a free market'.

17 R Wade, 'Income inequality: should we worry about global trends?', *European Journal of Development Research*, 23, 2011, pp 513–520.

18 United Nations Development Programme (UNDP), *Human Development Report*, Baltimore, MD: Johns Hopkins University Press, 1992; UNDP, *Human Development Report*, Baltimore, MD: Johns Hopkins University Press, 1999; and United Nations, *The Inequality Predicament*, New York: United Nations, 2005, p 18.

19 http://hdr.undp.org/reports/global/1996/en/pdf/hdr_1996_overview.pdf. See also Gavin Kitching, *Seeking Social Justice Through Globalisation*, University Park: Pennsylvania State University Press, 2001, p 175.

20 Congressional Budget Office data, analysed by Center on Budget and Policy Priorities, reported in the *New York Times*, 5 September 1999.

21 Dollars & Sense and United for a Fair Economy (eds), *The Wealth Inequality Reader*, New York: Economic Affairs Bureau, p 1.

22 The worst absolute poverty trend is in sub-Saharan Africa, where the average household consumed 20 per cent less in 1998 than 25 years earlier. UNDP, *1998 Human Development Report*, New York: Oxford University Press, 1998. However, the most dramatic relative poverty trend is in Latin America, where the number of poor fell in the 1970s, then nearly doubled in the 1980s, and was 33 per cent of the total population in 1997, and not falling despite renewed economic growth. N Birdsall & JL Londono,

IDENTITY, INEQUITY AND INEQUALITY IN INDIA AND CHINA

'Asset inequality matters: an assessment of the World Bank's approach to poverty reduction', *American Economic Review*, 87(2), 1997, pp 32–37.

23 Structural Adjustment Participatory Review International Network (SAPRIN), *Structural Adjustment: The SAPRIN Report—The Policy Roots of Economic Crisis, Poverty, and Inequality*, London: Zed Books, 2004.

24 N Ferguson, *Empire: The Rise and Demise of the British World Order and the Lessons for Global Power*, New York: Basic Books, 2002; D Lal, *In Defense of Empire*, Washington DC: American Enterprise Institute Press, 2004.

25 L Pritchett, 'Divergence, big time', Washington, DC: World Bank, 1995 at http://ideas.repec.org/e/ppr27.html.

26 See the OpEd section of the *New York Times*, 9 March 2006, p A23 on Annette Lareau, *Unequal Childhoods: Class, Race, and Family Life*, Berkeley, CA: California University Press, 2003, which analyses child-rearing practices in rich and poor American families.

27 World Bank, *World Development Report 2000/1*, Washington, DC: World Bank; and UNDP, *Choices for the Poor: Lessons from National Poverty Strategies*, March 2001, at http://www.undp.org/dpa/publications/choicesforpoor/ENGLISH/.

28 T Roy, 'Economic history and modern India: redefining the link', *Journal of Economic Perspectives*, 16(3), 2002, pp 109–130.

29 US Department of Commerce, *British India, with Notes on Ceylon, Afghanistan, and Tibet*, Special Consular Reports, No 72, Washington: Government Printing Office, 1915, p 9.

30 MD Morris, 'The growth of large-scale industry to 1947', in D Kumar (ed), *The Cambridge Economic History of India, Volume II, c 1757–c1970*, Cambridge: Cambridge University Press, 1983, pp 569, 576, 609.

31 *Annual Statement of the Sea-Borne Trade of British India with the British Empire and Foreign Countries for the Fiscal Year ending 31st March, 1926*, Calcutta: Government of India, 1926, Table 10.

32 JE Schwartzberg (ed), *A Historical Atlas of South Asia*, Chicago, IL: University of Chicago Press, 1978, p 115.

33 See G Balachandran (ed), *India and the World Economy, 1850–1950*, Delhi: Oxford University Press, 2003; DM Peers, *Between Mars and Mammon: Colonial Armies and the Garrison State in India, 1819–1836*, London: IB Tauris, 1995; D Washbrook, 'Agriculture and industrialization in India', in P Mathias & A Davis (eds), *Agriculture and Industrialization: From the Eighteenth Century to the Present Day*, Oxford: Basil Blackwell, 1996; Washbrook, 'Changing perspectives on the economic history of India', unpublished keynote presented to the Economic History Workshop, University of Pennsylvania, 23 April 2006; and D Wasbrook, 'The Indian economy and the British Empire', in N Gooptu & DM Peers (eds), *Oxford History of the British Empire: India*, Oxford: Clarendon Press (forthcoming).

34 A Sen, *Poverty and Famines: An Essay on Entitlement and Deprivation*, Oxford: Oxford University Press, 1981. For a recent account of the famine's imperial dimensions, see M Mukerjee, *Churchill's Secret War: The British Empire and the Ravaging of India During World War II*, New York: Basic Books, 2010.

35 G Clark, 'The great divergence—world economic growth since 1800', at http://www.econ.ucdavis.edu/faculty/gclark/GlobalHistory/Global%20History-12.pdf; and Clark, 'One polity, many countries: economic growth in India, 1873–2000', at http://www.econ.ucdavis.edu/faculty/gclark/210a/readings/One%20Polity.pdf.

36 D Ludden, 'India's development regime', in N Dirks (ed), *Colonialism and Culture*, Ann Arbor, MI: University of Michigan Press, 1992, pp 247–287; Ludden, 'Development regimes in South Asia: history and the development conundrum', *Economic and Political Weekly*, 10 September 2005, pp 4042–4051; and Ludden, 'A useable past for a post-national present: governance and development in South Asia', *Journal of the Asiatic Society of Bangladesh*, 50(1–2), 2006, pp 259–292.

37 B Milanovic, *Half a World: Regional Inequality in Five Great Federations*, World Bank Policy Research Working Paper, September 2005, at http://www.worldbank.org/research/inequality/pdf/5countries1.pdf.

38 F Bourguignon & C Morrisson, 'Inequality among world citizens, 1820–1992', *American Economic Review*, September 2002, pp 727–744.

39 Clark, 'The great divergence', p 28, Figure 2.

40 'More or less equal?', special report on global economic inequality, *The Economist*, 11 March 2004, at http://www.economist.com/displaystory.cfm?story_id=2498851.

41 GA Cornia with S Kiiski, 'Trends in income distribution in the post-World War II period', UNU/WIDER Discussion Paper No 2001/89, September 2001.

42 Y Zheng, *Globalization and State Transformation in China*, Cambridge: Cambridge University Press, 2004.

IDENTITY, INEQUITY AND INEQUALITY IN INDIA AND CHINA

43 D Ludden (ed), *Making India Hindu: Community, Conflict, and the Politics of Democracy*, New Delhi: Oxford University Press, 2005.

44 For a recent example, see *The Men Who Would Conquer China*, a First Run Icarus film about how a US–Hong Kong business partnership bought state-owned Chinese companies.

45 See Ludden, 'Development regimes in South Asia'; and Ludden, 'A useable past for a post-national present'.

46 For Pakistan, see M Sokefeld, 'From colonialism to postcolonialism: changing modes of domination in the northern areas of Pakistan', *Journal of Asian Studies*, 64(4), 2005 pp 939–974.

47 T Besley & R Burgess, 'Land reform, poverty reduction, and growth: evidence from India', *Quarterly Journal of Economics*, 115(2), 2002, pp 389–430. For a descriptive account of policy trends, see FR Frankel, *India's Political Economy, 1947–2004: The Gradual Revolution*, Delhi: Oxford University Press, 2005.

48 A Banerjee & L Iyer, 'History, institutions and economic performance: the legacy of colonial land tenure systems in India', October 2004, at http://econ-www.mit.edu/faculty/download_pdf.php?id=517. I thank Yuthika Sharma for this reference.

49 See Kohli, *Poverty amid Plenty in the New India*. For concurrent trends in cultural politics, see Ludden, *Making India Hindu*.

50 A Kishore, 'Towards an Indian approach', in D Gruen & T O'Brien, *Globalisation, Living Standards, and Inequality: Recent Progress and Continuing Challenges*, Sydney, Australia: Reserve Bank of Australia, 2002, p 126, at http://www.rba.gov.au/publications/conf/2002/kishore.pdf, accessed 10 December 2009.

51 BB Bhattacharya & S Sakthivel, 'Regional growth and disparity in India: comparison of pre- and post-reform decades', *Economic and Political Weekly*, 6 March 2004, pp 1071–1077. See also NJ Kurian, 'Widening regional disparities in India: some indicators', *Economic and Political Weekly*, 12–18 February 2000, pp 538–550.

52 Milanovic, *Half a World*; and Milanovic, 'Social justice and stalled development: caste empowerment and the breakdown of governance in Bihar', Philadelphia, PA: Center for the Advanced Study of India, University of Pennsylvania, 2006.

53 See A Deaton & J Dreze, *Poverty and Inequality in India: A Reexamination*, Working Paper No 107, Centre for Development Economics, New Delhi, 2002; J Ghosh, 'Income inequality in India', at http://pd.cpim.org/2004/0215/02152004_eco.htm; and A Deaton & V Kozel (eds), *The Great Indian Poverty Debate*, Delhi: Macmillan, 2005.

54 G Datt & M Ravallion, 'Is India's economic growth leaving the poor behind?', *Journal of Economic Perspectives*, 16(3), 2002, pp 103–106 state that cross-country regressions support the idea that several factors explain why growth reduces poverty in some places, for some people, more than others: 'credit market imperfections and greater initial inequality of assets (particularly of land)', 'low educational attainment', urban–rural sector divisions in 'dualistic' labour markets, They reiterate their earlier conclusion, from M Ravallion & G Datt, 'Why has economic growth been more pro-poor in some states of India than others?', *World Bank Economic Review*, 8(1), 2002, pp 1–25, that some conditions in Indian states in 1960—eg average farm yield, ratio of urban to rural average consumption, proportion of the state's landless population, literacy rate, and mortality rate—'are significant predictors of the elasticity of poverty with respect to growth'. They find that poor initial conditions in rural development 'inhibited the prospects of the poor participating in growth of the nonagricultural sector' (p 104). They particularly emphasise 'the role played by initial literacy', noting 'India's relatively poor performance in expanding literacy' and the fact that Kerala's high literacy rate largely explains its success in poverty reduction.

55 J Assayag, *The Making of Democratic Inequality: Caste, Class, Lobbies and Politics in Contemporary India, 1880–1995*, Pondichery: Institut Français de Pondichery, 1995.

56 For China, a large proportion of inter-regional inequality can be explained by urban–rural disparities. AS Bhalla, S Yao & Z Zhang, 'Causes of inequalities in China', *Journal of International Development*, 15, 2003, pp 133–152; and R Kanbur & X Zhang, 'Fifty years of regional inequality in China: a journey through central planning, reform, and openness', cited in Milanovic, *Half a World*.

57 Deaton & Dreze, *Poverty and Inequality in India*. Datt & Ravallion, 'Is India's economic growth leaving the poor behind?', note that the two richest states in the 1980s (Punjab and Haryana) hit a low-growth trend in the 1990s but that, leaving these two states out, 'there is a strong positive relationship between level of GDP in the mid-1980s and growth rate in the 1990s; that is, there is divergence between per capita GDP among all but the richest states in India' (p 97).

58 D Ludden (ed), *Agricultural Production and South Asian History*, Delhi: Oxford University Press, 2005.

59 Datt & Ravallion, 'Is India's growth leaving the poor behind?', pp 97–98.

60 Being out of the globalisation loop may not be so bad, as incorporation is exceptionally destructive for livelihoods and environments on these far peripheries and frontiers of imperial nations based in the

lowlands. For a wider view of economies on the margins, see van Schendel & Abraham, *Illicit Flows and Criminal Things*.

61 MG de la Rocha & A Grinspun, 'Private adjustments: households, crisis, and work', in UNDP, *Choices for the Poor*, ch 3.

62 'Disparities in inequality', at http://www.indiatogether.org/2003/mar/wom-states.htm; and DM Siddiqi, 'Miracle worker or woman-machine? Tracking (trans)national realities in Bangladeshi factories', *Economic and Political Weekly*, 27 May 2000, pp L11–L17.

63 I Ali & Y Sikand, 'Survey of socio-economic conditions of Muslims in India', at http://www.counter currents.org/comm-sikand090206.htm; *The Sachar Committee Report*, Government of India, Ministry for Minority Affairs, Delhi, 2006. On Muslim women, see Z Hasan & R Menon, *Unequal Citizens: Muslim Women in India*, New Delhi: Oxford University Press, 2004.

64 S Adnan, *Migration, Land Alienation, and Ethnic Conflict: Causes of Poverty in the Chittagong Hill Tracts of Bangladesh*, Dhaka: Research and Advisory Services, 2004.

65 MA Reddy, *Lands and Tenants in South India: A Study of Nellore District 1850–1990*, New Delhi: Oxford University Press, 1996; and D Ludden, *Peasant History in South India*, Delhi: Oxford University Press, 1989.

66 For a broad view, see D Ludden, *An Agrarian History of South Asia*, Cambridge: Cambridge University Press, 1999.

67 J Breman, *Footloose Labour: Working in India's Informal Economy*, Cambridge: Cambridge University Press, 1996. For the USA, see L Uchitelle, *The Disposable American: Layoffs and their Consequences*, New York: Knopf, 2006.

68 Datt & Ravallion, 'Is India's economic growth leaving the poor behind?', p 100.

69 For updated readings of Polanyi, see A Bugra & K Agartan (eds), *Reading Karl Polanyi for the Twenty-First Century: Market Economy as a Political Project*, Basingstoke: Palgrave, 2007.

70 The effectiveness in reducing poverty of egalitarian state policies that shift power over resources down the class ranks is well demonstrated by the Indian state of Kerala, where the poverty rate was as high as that of India's poorest state, Bihar, in 1960, but less than half by 1990. Datt & Ravallion, 'Is India's economic growth leaving the poor behind?', p 98. Thus for promoting poverty reduction, Datt and Ravallion conclude that, in addition to economic growth, 'The sectoral and geographic composition of growth is also important, as is the need to redress existing inequalities in human resource development and between urban and rural areas' (p 106).

Notes on contributor

David Ludden is Professor of Political Economy and Globalization in the Department of History, New York University. His four edited volumes, three monographs, and many articles and chapters explore various aspects of inequity in South Asia. A recent essay is 'Spatial inequity in national territory: remapping 1905 in Bengal and Assam', *Modern Asian Studies*, 20, 2011, pp 1–43.

Nation's Two Bodies: rethinking the idea of 'new' India and its other

RAVINDER KAUR

ABSTRACT *The idea of a post-1990s re-formed India is shaped by an imaginary of a fractured body of the nation—a 'new' nation in tune with the neoliberal desires of a structurally adjusted world and the 'old' nation constitutive of superfluous matter in excess of that seductive world. This imaginary is not only etched in popular discourses but also in the policy-making apparatus engaged in the task of creating a global identity for India. Taking the Brand India initiative—promoted by the Indian state to produce positive images of the nation for global publicity—as a case study, this article argues that in this shift from nation building to nation branding, the very idea of prosperity and equity has now become first and foremost a matter of image. In this world of images, one can also witness how a competitive strategy to seek more corporate investments through concerted brand campaigns has redefined the relationship between the nation and corporations. While earlier it was the corporations which sought the endorsement and patronage of the sovereign, now it is sovereign nations which are seeking to become the most 'favoured investment destinations' that purvey global capital.*

India. Right place, Right time.[1]

There are two Indias in this country.
One India lives in the optimism of our hearts.
The other India lurks in the skepticism of our minds.[2]

When Tata Group's ambitious Nano car project was withdrawn amid violent protests in Singur in 2008, Suhel Seth, a Delhi-based managing partner of a strategic branding firm described it as 'a slap on the face of Brand India'.[3] This rather visible depiction of violent affront and vexation caused to India's new global face was spiked with a further warning: 'Which foreign company will want to come in when India's most respected group cannot set up industry in a state?'. The question was laden, at once, with a sense of palpable anxiety, provocation, and even foreboding that had become emblematic of

Ravinder Kaur is in the Department of Cross-cultural and Regional Studies, University of Copenhagen, Denmark.

the current debates about the perceived obstructions to India's brand image in the world.

The violent protests could not have been more ill-timed as far as the Indian state and the corporations were concerned. The neoliberal economic reforms set in motion in the late 1980s were finally said to be bearing results—India was increasingly described as an assertive nation taking long economic strides to create a vast, prosperous middle class, attract unprecedented levels of foreign direct investment, and even boast of four Indians in the top 10 of the *Forbes* billionaire list.[4] The state led efforts began in the mid-1990s to establish a viable and globally competitive corporate brand for the Indian nation. Brand India had a decade later gained world-wide recognition among multinational corporations as well as the rich industrialised nations as an attractive destination for investments. The global displays of a *re-formed* nation at the annual meetings of the World Economic Forum at Davos and the enticing images of 'Incredible India' campaigns had by now successfully iterated and circulated the idea of a market-friendly India. The sixtieth anniversary of India's independence had similarly served as an opportune moment to take stock of the past decades, through which the nation had arguably transformed from a Third World country mired in a Nehruvian vision of 'mixed economy' to a 'structurally adjusted' Asian economic giant which, together with China, was about to change the course of global history. 'India Rising' was now a popular subject adorning coveted magazine covers, newspaper features, documentaries, short films, vision papers and *re*aligned foreign policy strategies all over the world. This new global discourse on India served an additional purpose of creating a stark contrast to its neighbour, Pakistan, with which it shared its genealogy as well as a protracted history of unresolved conflicts. It seemed that India's moment of celebration had finally arrived: a moment that just a generation ago was difficult to imagine outside the limits of desire.

At precisely this moment of alliance between the nation and corporation the violent unrest in Singur erupted to draw out in plain sight the unruly to reveal the two bodies of the nation: the nation of seductive brand images and its undesired shadows that stubbornly refuse to disappear from the global gaze. The notion of shadow, here, suggests the undesirable matter—the poor, the unbeautiful and the unruly—seemingly in excess of the neoliberal dreams of the Indian middle class. The question this article addresses is: how do images and their shadows produce the imaginary of 'new' India in the world of strategic brand making? And how is the carefully assembled world of images realised, circulated, subverted and even emptied out? Through a close reading of Brand India campaigns, I examine the visual production of new India through a range of advertising campaigns that seek to corporatise and commodify the imagined essence of the nation. Rather than read the nation's brand-making campaigns under the sign of state propaganda, I approach them not only as sites of visual communication, where seductive images invite and address the global public, but also as sites of interrogation, when the public gaze is turned back critically on the content, form and social space these images occupy. To this end, the article examines the modes of address visible in the recent Brand India campaigns and the visual and discursive ruptures that shape the historical imagination of new India.

Shadow of images

Two related theoretical concerns frame my argument. First, how the new relationship between the nation and corporation is shaped in an increasingly hyper-competitive environment where nations compete to gain the most favoured 'investment destination' status. The favoured mode of address is to 'dress up' the nation to make it more 'attractive' for potential investors through nation-branding campaigns that showcase the effects of structural adjustments, open access to markets, and less government regulation. In the past decades, we have witnessed how the traditional relationship between the nation and corporation has altered as the nation is transformed in the image of the corporation, and its legitimacy is contingent upon its ability to draw corporate patronage.[5] What I show in this article is the intensification of this role reversal between the nation and corporation. Whereas it was once the corporation that sought patronage and endorsement as purveyor to the sovereign, now it is the nation that is revealed as *purveyor to the global capital* – as provider of raw material, cheap skilled labour and an unfettered access to open markets. This particular relationship is most visible in the world of advertising and nation branding, where national and corporate interests seem to be in full convergence.

Second, how does the social life framed within the visual surface of nation-branding campaigns interact with the life outside them? Or, put another way, what kind of relations bind the semiotics of the nation brand to the messy world of its materialisations? These questions have gained urgency in the past few years as glossy images contained within the frames of Brand India campaigns are routinely juxtaposed with the undesirable images—impromptu showcasing of extreme poverty, deprivation, farmer suicides, corruption, inefficiency, unruly mass protests, and violent state repression against demands for autonomy—of the nation. What meanings does this counter-imagery render to the nation-branding campaigns? And how do brand consultants and policy makers eager to build a positive image of the nation deal with this shadowy flow of unregulated images in a liberal democratic setting? As we will see, these questions and dilemmas are inextricably linked to the discourse of 'two nations' that frequently appears in the public debate. But before we get ahead of ourselves, a brief account of the idea of image makeover of the nation-form is in order.

A defining aspect of neoliberal economic restructuring over the past few decades has been the remaking of the nation-form in the image of the corporation—Nationality, Inc—complete with its own trademark and a brand image. The shift marks the move from the ideas and practices of nation building to those of nation branding, which is often suggested as the attainment of a higher and more complete form of nationhood appropriate to the era of globalisation. While this unabashed public alliance of the nation-state and corporation is not entirely a new phenomenon, the relationship has become more transparent as the state increasingly becomes a manager of capital.[6] The nation and its image, in this species of relationship, become a rich resource that can be commodified to generate and attract capital through tourism and investment. Not surprisingly, a number of nations, especially those decolonised in the mid-twentieth century and sometimes labelled 'emerging powers', have invested in image makeovers to alter the world's perceptions.[7] While the discourse of development lay at the core of the nation-building attempts of the post-Independence years, the nation-branding exercise is inextricably connected to the magical world of seductive images.[8] One can frequently witness, for example, the national essence of Malaysia, Qatar, South Africa, Croatia, Brazil and India in 'an avalanche of images' circulated on international media that evokes cultural difference within an aesthetic frame informed by Western sensibilities.[9]

The most characteristic sign of identification of 'new' India is its recently made-up face—Brand India—which has been specifically designed for display in the outside world.[10] Its distinctive feature, separating it from other similar initiatives such as India Shining, is its almost invisible visibility: Brand India barely figures in the Indian public imagination, even while it successfully creates spectacular displays of India globally. In a way Brand India has emerged as a discreet image machine—limited to the world of policy makers and advertising professionals—that produces, translates and propels the Indian nation into the global orbit of big businesses, international financial institutions and leaders of rich nations without revealing itself in the process.

The India Brand Equity Foundation (IBEF) was created under the aegis of the Ministry of Commerce in 1996 as part of liberal reforms to promote 'Made in India' brands around the world.[11] This lagging project was revived in late 2002 by the BJP-led government, although with a redefined task—not only to showcase Indian brands abroad but to transform India itself into a corporate brand. The official brief was to 'celebrate India' as the 'destination of ideas and opportunities' in order to bring in foreign direct investment (FDI) as well as to invigorate tourism.[12] By 2004 Brand India was set to 'build positive economic perceptions of India globally'. In 2011 the purpose was further developed 'to portray the distinctive qualities of all things Indian and...the dynamism to build an enduring reputation [of India] in the competitive global arena'. A Delhi-based advertising agency specialising in place branding was recruited to create a distinctive logo, a slogan and a 'business kit' to be presented through glossy campaigns in international print and electronic media. The new initiative not only formalised the corporate approach to governing the nation, it also confirmed the alias by which the nation is known in the corporate world—India Inc—an entity consequently governed by a CEO rather than a political representative.[13]

Brand India offers a synoptic vision into this new historical imagination of India—a young nation seeking to find its place in the global scheme of things. It is conceptualised, in branding terms, both as a generic mother brand that brings together various initiatives on tourism and businesses, as well as the public face of a government agency, IBEF. While Incredible India has by now become a well recognised brand that sells India to tourists around the world, corporate branding is done through a more strategically targeted series of campaigns, such as 'India Everywhere', 'India Now', 'Resilient India' and 'India Marches Ahead', assembled under the theme of 'India—fastest growing free market democracy'. Both the initiatives are aimed at the outside to attract global attention; although the former is a mass campaign visible in international media and global publics, the latter is directed more discreetly at leaders of states and corporations seeking profitable alliances.

In the world of strategic image makers, creating brand images for a young nation is seen as a necessary tool to close gaps between the perception and reality of the nation.[14] According to a nation branding consultant, 'the running of countries is no different from the running of a large company' and 'a nation that does not engage in proactive branding runs the risk of being positioned anyway by its competitor to the competitor's advantage'.[15] While the project of constructing a national imaginary is nothing new and is considered integral to the developmental project of nation building, this reasoning about nation branding signifies a momentous shift.[16] The old imperative to build national identity to secure internal cohesion and unity within the 'imagined community' is now supplemented by the logic of external competition within the 'family of nations'. In fact, nation branding is a globally recognised practice which Simon Anholt, a nation-branding expert, describes as 'national identity in the service of enhanced competitiveness'.[17] This advice to brand nations is considered particularly applicable to 'young nations' which 'are in a unique position to brand themselves because they are in an early stage of development'.[18]

Two significant assumptions underpin this belief. First, the nations thought to be in particular need of a globally recognisable brand image are presumed to be 'young', that is, inexperienced, immature, unpredictable, and often without a sufficiently 'proper' history. This description of youthful nations is not only reserved for the postcolonies in Asia, Africa and Latin America, but also applied to post-socialist nations that crossed over to a liberal market economy in late capitalism. Compared with mature nations across the North Atlantic, the nations in the global South are imagined as beginners who have merely tiptoed out of the 'waiting room of history'. In other words, their history proper is only seen as beginning with market reforms. Second, the trope of 'reality'—the transcendent and radiant domain produced by the 'gains' of free market forces—seeks to surface the subterranean transformations within neoliberal societies. In this new landscape of reality the nation's complex histories are erased only to be revealed as an archive of 'facts' and 'events' that can be teleologically rearranged to construct a proper history. The images of familiar objects, ideas, people and places appear in this new narrative, yet they are connected in a wholly new sequence that might bear little resemblance to the original.

The challenge, then, is how to *engage* with these nation-brand images beyond the registers of 'reality' and 'fiction'. While nation-branding these days is increasingly offered as a quick-fix solution to enhance, repair and restore a nation's image in the eyes of the world, it is frequently dismissed as an empty gesture, an imaginary nation that is nothing other than an image. However, as Ranciere reminds us, if there is nothing other than the image, 'the very notion of the image becomes devoid of content'.[19] This means taking the image seriously to engage with its paradoxical being and not succumbing to the temptation of looking for meanings confined within the visual frame.[20] Instead we may turn our attention to the 'work of imagination' that produces the visual frame itself, its modes of address, paths of circulation and the wider social setting within which the surfaces of display are produced.[21] To this end, the specific modes of address deployed by Brand India campaigns offer an insight into the imagination of 'new' India within a global publicity where familiar meanings are displaced and signs reverted in order to create a new nation. This article foregrounds the social life inside and outside brand images and the ways in which they are shaped under a critical global gaze.

The image machine

While Brand India was initiated in the mid-1990s, it was not until roughly a decade later that it became an image machine for the nation—manufacturing and circulating worldwide alluring images of India and the discourse of 'global Indian-ness'. The biggest challenge has been to sort out what to publicise and which messy realities to deflect attention away from. One might ask, then, what secreted logics of the new nation are articulated in the global publicity, and how? The function of these forms in singularity and collectivity is to seek out, empty and remould the essence of the Indian nation in harmony with global free markets. It is not a coincidence that one of the first major spectacles organised to unveil the Brand India campaign was in 2006 at the annual meeting of the World Economic Forum in Davos. The choice of location itself is instructive. The annual meeting has been bringing together more than 1000 top-earning businesses in the world, heads of states and influential policy makers for the past 40 years.[22] According to the Forum's own description, it is a critical platform that has introduced 'emerging economies such as China and India to the international community'.[23] It is by now a well known global venue where businesses network and gain easy access to policy-makers in various nations. Similarly nations in search of investments are likely to find businesses eager to expand into new markets in this setting. Thus, for 'emerging powers', Davos is said to be an obvious location where the nation must be displayed before an elite audience popularly described as 'world leaders' in business, government, academia and civil society.

The advertising professionals entrusted with the Brand India project in the mid-2000s were given a seemingly simple brief: to create a new look for India that would reflect its post-economic reform achievements and consolidate it as a prime investment destination.[24] The task was more complex than it initially seemed, as it meant severing ties with the 'old' India, as I was told frequently, without letting go of the essence of its unique cultural brand-value

FIGURE 1. India: Best country to be an investor in.
Source: Courtesy of India Brand Equity Foundation.

built over centuries. The 'new' India seemingly was to be based on a combination of bits of 'old' India surgically removed from its larger body, so that it could fit the growing global narrative of a re-formed nation. In other words, the task was to create the look of an ancient civilisation turned global power ready to conduct business with the world. I describe three key stages in this process of visual rearrangement of the nation's body—disrupting the familiar, the 'new' familiar, and finally corporate endorsements of the new nation—which seek to visually transform the nation into an attractive partner for global businesses.

The first set of images—what I call disrupting the familiar—produced to attract the world's attention at Davos was a short film called *India Now*. The film was part of a digital package distributed to more than 2000 delegates in information CDs and Ipods, and was screened at major public venues too. The idea was to invoke objects, places, people that are instantly associated with India and then visually break that connection in order to form new associations. The 1½-minute-long film begins with a stream of white, green and saffron shades that come together to form a digital inscription—India: fastest growing free market democracy. The subsequent visuals are composed of a series of facts and figures about India's liberalised economy and democratic foundations in order to support the main theme. The visuals are layered with moving images tracing familiar ideas, objects, people and places across different temporalities associated with the popular imagination of India, and are superimposed with simple statements of facts that testify to the claims of a robust economy and democratic state. At first, the choice of images signifying India seems eclectic and even random: Taj Mahal, the national flag, Jawaharlal Nehru making a historic speech, *bindis*, bangles, elephants interwoven with images of shiny computers, mobile phones, wires, headsets, smooth highways, high-rise buildings, cars and hi-tech machinery. These objects and places are the background against which men and women in white coats, headsets and microphones are seen deliberating or posing to display the rational scientific temperament. A visual scheme slowly begins to emerge from what initially seemed the random order and selection of images.

The array contains some iconic images of the essential cultural and historical symbols, interwoven with new images depicting universally identifiable symbols of techno modernity. The colour scheme sets off one set of images against another—black and white to suggest the foundational aspects of a 'young' India and vibrant colours to indicate the global translation of the nation. The images appear in rapid succession one after another, so much so that the viewer is eventually unable to distinguish one from another after a while—the familiar and the unfamiliar; faded black and white shots from colourful visuals. In one sequence, a well recognised object such as the national flag traces associations with another familiar object, the Taj Mahal, and then disappears instantly to make way for new objects—a glossy high-rise building and shiny car on a highway. The technique is to seamlessly weave seemingly different objects and themes together, and precisely in doing so to disconnect the old from the new in such a way that a wholly new narrative is produced. The familiar is invoked only to have the sign reverted and displaced with new associations in order to articulate new meanings. The rapid chain of quickly shifting images brings the iconic images to the surface and places them in a new frame together with hitherto unrelated objects. Thus the Taj Mahal is no longer isolated from IT professionals in Bangalore; likewise the India associated with natural, animal themes—elephants and tigers—is now framed together with visions of industrial development. In this way the cultural and historical images are displaced and reclaimed from the older contexts of colonial subjugation and Third World underdevelopment. This chain of new associations forms the rough outline within which the narrative of a reformed nation can be witnessed.

The second set of images constitutes the 'new familiar'—an identity of the nation that grows out of a gradual erasure of the old sign system. In a 2007 campaign called 'India: Right place, Right time', a series of elongated, vertical digital posters appear in bright fluorescent colours that carry an image and new facts about India. As the title suggests, the campaign was to invite investors to come and partake in the vast market that is India. The late 2000s were seen as the ripe moment for investment when Western markets had just begun talking of a property bubble and investors had started looking for alternative markets in which to invest. The re-formed India represented the right place and right time for investment. The posters, each carrying a depiction of a globalised Indian market scene, were displayed in Davos and other major cities of the world and were available for digital download as well.

One of the posters contains a visual of a shoe shop, probably located in a shopping mall. The counter is lit by halogen lights fitted in a lowered semicircular false ceiling which reflect brightly upon the marble floor. A customer dressed in *salwar kameez* is seen gazing at a shoe, while other customers and shop attendants participate in the labour of consumption. The lower part of the poster is a rich magenta shade with two words inscribed in bold—Super Market. A text in smaller print follows to reiterate India's status as a large emerging consumer market. The posters, rather than relying upon recognisable symbols within the image, are framed as panels of colourful saris, with borders decorated with a *phool-butti* design. The coloured background is also composed of the same flowered motif that runs across all the posters. The images in this series of digital posters suggest modernity symbolised by objects representing high technology, computers, walls of blinking computer screens, aeroplanes, metro, bridges, cars and mobile phones. Yet they are framed discreetly within the edges of sari borders—suggesting Indian-ness as the broader frame—within which a new sign system is revealed to facilitate the public encounter with the new relationship between hi-tech objects and India. Unlike in the earlier images, which are characterised by bold use of well known signs of Indian-ness, the latter images are distinguished by a more discreet use of objects and patterns signifying India. In fact, practices and objects termed as modern appear under the sign of India as suggested by the sari borders which frame the activity of consumption.

FIGURE 2. Branding India as a hub of scientific knowledge.
Source: Courtesy of India Brand Equity Foundation.

FIGURE 3. Supermarket.
Source: Courtesy of India Brand Equity Foundation.

The most important set of images, however, is the third one, which reveals a new orbit of connections that bring objects and people not directly connected together under the sign of India. This form of nation branding based on corporate endorsement not only visually discloses what is already well known—the collapsed boundaries between the domain of politics and the domain of economy—in addition, it tells us the extent of role reversal between the sovereign and the corporation. The official website of IBEF is designed so as to show the attractiveness of the nation to investors through testimonies and endorsements from big businesses already in India or about to be there.

The following is an example of glossily designed corporate frames of the nation. A slideshow of snapshots begins with an image of diamond jewellery displayed on rich, red velvet cloth, suggesting old wealth and luxury. The image disappears to make way for a text which simply states, 'India is a growing market for luxury'. This text is an endorsement offered by Julius Kruta, the 'head of Tradition' at Bugatti Automobiles, the car manufacturer for the wealthiest in the world. The brand Bugatti is associated with the worlds' fastest and the most expensive car, with a base price tag of €1.1 million that can speed up to 407 kmph on smooth roads. Since 2010 Bugatti has been available in India, which the company sees as an emerging market for luxury goods. In this brief slideshow, images and voices from outside the nation are drawn to create a new grammar of the image. Instead of direct links, various, unrelated elements such as diamonds, red velvet background are sequenced together with a factual statement about India's growing luxury market articulated by a luxury car maker. The embedded meanings of the objects in the image and the text are transferred to India as they are enclosed within the same image frame. This transference is made as an undisputed matter of fact, suggesting that different objects do share meaning. Within this image frame, the relationship between the objects becomes apparent as one complements the other and even turns into a substitute for the other.

While this is a routine advertising strategy to draw alliances and con-nections where none may exist, we are witnessing something novel in this sequence of images: a commodity (desirable foreign car) manufacturer endorsing the nation. This is the reversal of the previous relationship between the nation-state and the corporation. One usual practice which bound the two was the grant of a royal warrant to the manufacturer or merchant of commodities consumed by the sovereign. The favoured company was then allowed to use the logo and symbol inscribed in the coat of arms on its product—bestowing the prestige value enjoyed by the sovereign on the corporation. Such a favoured corporation joined the ranks of the 'purveyors to the royal court' and could advertise their products as such. The company and the commodities thus patronised came to be seen as quality products fit for the sovereign, and thus signified a higher exchange value than did similar products. In the case of Brand India it is the corporations which are aggressively sought by the nation in order to seek patronage and the use of their logos. The success of the nation is predicated upon its ability to attract big corporations so as to guarantee its enhanced value in the global market. Thus, in a role reversal, the nation is now revealed as the purveyor to global capital.

This mode of address is designed for global publicity where corporations are enclosed together with the sign of India within the same visual frame. As corporations add their logos and voices to make a pitch for the nation, this new alliance inaugurates India into expansive markets, along with other similarly re-formed nations. Here, cultural–historical facts about India become useful props that help the nation differentiate itself from other nations seeking the corporation's attention. Thus, a new imaginary of the nation—composed of carefully assembled images—that is at once global as well as characteristic of its vernacular particularities is made palpable.

India vs India

The convergence of the corporate interest with that of the nation visible in the brand initiatives is only part of the story. The other part is the contestation and subversion from within the nation which disrupts the smooth imagery. While the Indian state is heavily invested in the creation of the country's global identity on the one hand, it is also beset by a variety of scandals said to be corroding the inviting visage of Brand India on the other. The anxiety over the negative publicity has also set in motion a form of public and collective introspection. The question at the heart of these sometimes intimate and candid reflections is: why does India keep on failing to realise its full potential and destiny as a great power? This question in different modes and forms has been the subject of innumerable newspaper articles, television discussions, internet blogs and policy debates in recent years. These concerns are becoming especially palpable when framed in the context of China's stupendous economic growth in relation to which India lags far behind. A common discourse shaping various debates is that of a ruptured nation constantly at war with itself. While a number of dichotomies are usually employed to describe the bodily rupture—rural/urban; rich/poor; cosmopolitan/vernacular—it is the contrast between the 'old' and 'new' India that has come to define the current post-reform schism. This theme became particularly popular during the Commonwealth Games debacle, when India's image as a global player was said to be in the course of unravelling.

A note on the corrosive scandals contaminating the image of new India would be in order here. When the city of Delhi became host to the 2010 Commonwealth Games (CWG), it was expected to follow the Chinese precedent of hosting flawless Olympics Games in Beijing two years earlier. That spectacular cultural extravaganza was not merely a mega-gathering of sportspeople, rather its carefully choreographed show was read worldwide as a memorable debut of China as a great power on the global stage. The CWG, though less prominent in scale, nevertheless offered an international backdrop against which India could showcase its post-reform achievements and build its global brand of world-class road infrastructure, airports, public transport facilities, fresh modes of governance based on public–private partnerships, and well behaved citizens who had been especially asked to politely observe the rules during the Games period. In short, Delhi was to emerge as a world-class city on par with other mega-cities in the rich industrialised world. However, these ambitions were dented a few months before the Games were to begin as the Commonwealth Federation expressed its doubts about the readiness of the sports infrastructure. In the following weeks the images that began circulating within global media were in deep contrast to the image world of Brand India.[25] Not only were the sporting and housing facilities for the athletes found to be in a semi-finished state, they were declared 'unfit for human habitation' as images of filth and animal excreta in the apartments were circulated widely around the world.[26] While the games officials tried to explain this criticism as 'differences in standards of our hygiene from theirs',[27] the strategic brand image-makers interpreted this visible depiction of shame to India's new global face as 'essentially as saying that we are not world class yet, we are still a third world country...we are not your level yet'.[28] In short, Brand India was said to be in jeopardy and at the risk of unravelling precisely at the moment when the global gaze was upon India.

If the hope of the Games officials and the Delhi state government was that the moment of shame would disappear once the actual Games had been successfully concluded, then that was clearly undone in the avalanche of bad publicity that followed. On the one hand, the social activists were drawing attention to the exploitation of labour and poor conditions under which the CWG construction workers lived and worked, on the other hand Games officials had come under scrutiny for taking bribes and for corrupt practices in handing out building contracts. The poor quality of construction work was clearly revealed when an overhead bridge collapsed days before the Games inauguration, while part of the ceiling in a newly built stadium fell down on the spectators. In the subsequent weeks allegations of corruption had compounded to an extent that the CWG scandal, estimated at £2.5 billion, came to be regarded as one of the largest ever financial scams in India. The image of a corrupt India governed by inefficient bureaucrats was further entrenched in 2011 when corruption became a rallying ground for mass mobilisation following revelations of financial embezzlement worth scores of billions. The domain of the political was now defined by spectacular scandals and the failure of an unworthy political class to govern the nation efficiently.

It is against this background that the idea of a split nation gained currency within the public domain. The most explicit description of this idea was articulated by a well-known weekly newspaper columnist, Vir Sanghvi, as the negative news coverage of the Games began gathering ground. In a widely circulated article called 'Old India vs new India', the author voiced public anger and frustration at the national shame that had to be endured because of corrupt, incompetent Games officials. The crux of the analysis was pegged around the essential and unbridgeable distinctions between the old and the new. The 'old' was described as 'corrupt, slothful, incompetent, chaotic, unconcerned with the pursuit of excellence, and unwilling to benchmark global standards', whereas the 'new' was the emerging superpower 'that can do things to global standards, whose competences and intelligence are highly regarded all over the world, an India where people work hard, where there are high levels of accountability and where commitments are treated as sacred'. Clearly the old/new distinction, here, does not pertain to time and space differences. Rather it reveals two distinct nations under the sign of India as fetishised embodiment of opposing personal attributes and a web of associations. In fact, the two figurative imaginaries of India seem to have become autonomous subjects in their own right, displaying affective relationships with other subjects (state, investors and citizens) directly. The personalisation of the nation easily translates to a larger public the current antagonistic discourse of a split body where each part appears as a sovereign subject capable of independent action and designs for the future. It is hardly surprising, then, that the failure of the Games organisers to create an enviable spectacle like China's was explained as 'old India having failed the new India' which had made the nation 'in eyes of the world...a laughing stock'.[29] In short, the limits to progress, development and transformation of the nation into a great power commanding awe and respect were seen as marked from within. And unless this internal saboteur was controlled, India's ambitions and potential would never be fully realised.

The spectre of a ruptured nation circulates a well rehearsed logic of internal conflict and the underlying threat of subversion. In a 2007 television campaign, 'India Poised', created to mark India's sixtieth Independence anniversary, the idea of a ruptured nation's body was rendered poetically within the popular domain. The short, black and white video called *India vs India* featured the Bollywood superstar Amitabh Bachan articulating the idea of two nations. The video—a mixture of optimism, hope and anxiety—begins with the assumption that India is poised at a 'rarely ever moment' when 'history is turning its page...and a pulsating, dynamic new India is emerging'. Yet the historic moment is seen as fragile, and its precariousness accentuated by a fractured body of the nation where 'one India is straining at the leash, eager to spring forth and live up to all the adjectives the world has been recently showering upon us; the other India is the leash'.[30] The contrast is clearly laid out to demarcate the *new* nation imagined and realised in conjunction with the world from its isolated *other* that keeps on holding it back. The idea of a schismatic India that is out of synch with itself as well as the world, and therefore unable to mobilise its full resources to reach its natural destiny of world leader is a worrisome theme frequently voiced in the media. The fear of alienating investors, tourists and influential global opinion makers from Brand India is what informs the discourse of a split nation.

This sense of urgency can be witnessed in the domain of politics too, as was visible in the recent anti-corruption mobilisation. While ordinary citizens were mobilised around the 'plight' of the common man by a social activist turned protest leader, Anna Hazare, a different kind of rationale had spurred corporate actors into activism to eradicate corruption and 'governance deficit' in public life. At the heart of this corporate activism was the fear that

Brand India was being damaged beyond repair. Consider the following: at the height of the CWG scandal the Federation of Indian Chambers of Commerce and Industry (FICCI) issued a statement calling for probity in governance in order 'to preserve India's robust image and keep the growth story intact'.[31] This was followed by an open letter by 14 prominent individuals—corporate leaders, reform-minded economists and bureaucrats assembled together under the sign of 'citizen'—who identified corruption as the 'biggest issue corroding the fabric of our nation'. The recommendation of the group was to address the 'governance deficit' that had permeated every level of state institutions, and to restore the self-confidence of Indians in themselves and in the Indian state.[32] The biggest support to fight corruption came from the corporate sector too. Corporate leaders expressed their support publicly, proclaiming that 'We completely support Hazare in his fight against corruption which has been denting India'.[33] The fear of losing India's place as an attractive investment destination has been at the heart of this corporate mobilisation on the one hand, and of the government's acquiescence to the broad demands for an anti-corruption legislation on the other. This anxiety of alienating corporations was visible in a recent controversy over a court case involving the largest financial scandal in India yet. The Minister of Law, Salman Khurshid, berated the Supreme Court for not granting bail to businessmen accused in the 2G spectrum scam. His matter of fact question 'If you lock up top businessmen, will investment come?' voiced concerns over threats to the pace of economic growth and investment in the nation.[34] The logic of corporate patronage and investment in the nation has clearly become a matter of common sense to the extent that even the domain of law is deemed open for rearrangement so as to create exceptional spaces within the legal framework.

Intimate alterity

The idea of India conceived by the makers of postcolonial India was essentially a modernist project built on the embers of a fading empire and faced with the task of levelling geographies of unevenness within. The emphasis was on the 'idea of concrete' as Sunil Khilnani has memorably described it—initiating massive construction projects of dams, industries, cities and public works—on the one hand and, on the other, creating the institutional framework of democracy that has by now become one of the most defining characteristics of India.[35] Through a variety of developmental interventions the state had hoped to address the questions of poverty, illiteracy, social inequity and overpopulation at different points in history in order to 'uplift' the masses lagging behind. This unfinished project has reappeared in post-reform India in new formations particularly visible in the world of images. The most characteristic feature of this new form is that the modernist project of development itself has become first and foremost a matter of image. The strategy of the Indian state is clearly no longer limited to the 'concrete', but has moved to the plane of image making, where the production and projection of images of a prosperous nation becomes as imperative a task as the creation of a prosperous nation itself. This shift is a reminder of what Baudrillard described as the hyperreal—the making of the real without origin or reality—that has become the hallmark of contemporary postmodernist sensibilities.[36] In fact, in initiatives such as Brand India, we witness the relationship between the image and the real in reverse. It is not the real that precedes the image, rather it is the image that precedes the real. The tensions in such a project are inevitable, as we have seen the past few years.

The abstract world of images created in campaigns such as Brand India is probably more akin to what WJT Mitchell describes as the drawing of desires—perhaps even a model of the ideal—conjured to attract investors and wealthy tourists to engage with India.[37] Once such an abstract model of an investor-friendly nation populated with a multitude of prosperous consumers and cheap skillful labour is created, the project becomes something else altogether—to make the real coincide with the model. This is where we witness the ruptures and tensions as policy makers attempt to superimpose the social life inside the frame on the social life outside of the image. Since the economic restructuring the major push has been to introduce an ever greater degree of reforms that will enable access to markets as well as resources. The recent political mobilisation against FDI in the retail sector and conflict over special economic zones in West Bengal are examples of incongruity between the image and the real. While the state is committed to the creation of cheerful consumers—as seen in the images of Brand India—on the one hand, and the creation of an investor-friendly environment on the other, political society mobilises itself to create a world that is at odds, sometimes violently so, with the image conjured by the neoliberal state. The trope of two nations, often invoked as a lamentation, thus captures precisely this tension between a nation that is in harmony with the markets, and its other, which continues to resist the same. It also invokes the most intimate form of otherness, a part of oneself that nevertheless remains inaccessible and resistant. It is here that the magical sign system of the hyperreal also breaks down, revealing not only the rupture in the image, but also the ruins and shreds left behind in the violent shift to free markets.

Acknowledgements

I remain deeply thankful to Aniket Alam, Ananya Jahanara Kabir and Srirupa Roy for providing critical readings of this article. The article has benefitted from discussions at the 2010 Asian Dynamics Initiative workshop 'Governing Difference', University of Copenhagen as well as South Asia History Seminars 2011 at SOAS, London. I wish I knew how to include more of the good ideas generated in these conversations.

Notes

1 Brand India campaign, 'Right Place, Right time', 2007, India Brand Equity Foundation, at www. ibef.org

IDENTITY, INEQUITY AND INEQUALITY IN INDIA AND CHINA

2 India vs India, 'India Poised' campaign 2007, Times of India Group, at http://www.youtube.com/watch?v=wP-TwHwLc98, accessed 15 December 2011.

3 'Protests force Tata to stop building car plant', *New York Times*, 2 September 2008; and 'Singur is a slap on the face of Brand India', *Indian Express*, 3 September 2008.

4 'India dominates Billionaires' List', *Wall Street Journal*, 6 March 2008, at www.blogs.wsj.com/wealth/2008/03/06/india-dominates-billionaires-list/, accessed 15 December 2011.

5 John Comaroff & Jean Comaroff, *Ethnicity, Inc*, Chicago, IL: Chicago University Press, 2009.

6 For a detailed account of corporate activity under colonial rule, see R Birla, *Stages of Capital: Law, Culture and Market Governance in Late Colonial India*, Durham, NC: Duke University Press, 2009.

7 The idea of emerging powers is explored in C Jaffrelot (ed), *The Emerging States: The Well Spring of a New World Order*, New York: Columbia University Press, 2009.

8 See P Chatterjee, *Nationalist Thought and the Colonial World: A Derivative Discourse*, London: Zed Books, 1986; and D Ludden, 'India's development regime', in N Dirks (ed), *Colonialism and Culture*, Ann Arbor, MI: Michigan University Press, 1992, pp 247–288.

9 D Gaonkar, 'An avalanche of images', *Public Culture*, 22(2), 2010, pp 217–222.

10 William Mazarella describes brands as conceptual extensions of trademark that assert legal ownership of identity through logos and advertising images. However, Brand India does not make any legal claim towards ownership of India; rather it appears mainly as a marketing discourse. W Mazarella, *Shoveling Smoke: Advertising and Globalization in Contemporary India*, Durham, NC: Duke University Press, 2003, pp 185–187.

11 For an account of the shift towards brand making in newly re-formed India, see A Rajagopal, 'Thinking through emerging markets: brand logics and the cultural forms of political society in India', *Social Text*, 17(3), 1999, pp 131–149.

12 'Towards creating Brand India', *Financial Express*, 15 February 2003.

13 Manmohan Singh is popularly and complimentarily called the CEO of India Inc, a shift that is meant to mark the market friendliness of the nation. See, for example, the recently published portrait of the prime minister by A Ahuja (ed), *Manmohan Singh: CEO, India Inc*, Delhi: Pentagon Press, 2009.

14 Y Johnston, 'Developing Brand South Africa', in K Dinnie (ed), *Nation Branding: Concepts, Issues, Practices*, Oxford: Butterworth-Heinemann, 2008, p 5.

15 F Gilmore, 'A country—can it be repositioned? Spain—the success story of country branding', *Journal of Brand Management*, 9(4–5), 2002, p 283.

16 See S Roy, *Beyond Belief: India and the Politics of Postcolonial Nationalism*, Delhi: Permanent Black, 2007.

17 'Problem with your country's image? Mr Anholt can help', *Guardian*, 11 November 2006.

18 Gilmore, 'A country—can it be repositioned?', p 283.

19 J Ranciere, *The Future of the Image*, London: Verso, 2009, p 1.

20 WJT Mitchell, *What do Pictures Want? The Lives and Loves of Images*, Chicago, IL: Chicago University Press, 2005, pp 28–56.

21 A Appadurai, *Modernity at Large: Cultural Dimensions of Globalisation*, Minneapolis, MN: Minnesota University Press, 1999.

22 The annual meeting is an exclusive by 'invitation only' assembly of big businesses eager to network and influence policy makers. The paid membership is open to companies with an average turnover of $5 billion. See www.weforum.org/members, accessed 15 December 2011.

23 'A partner in shaping history: the first forty years 1971–2010', Web Economic Forum, Geneva, 2009.

24 Interview with Amit Shahi, Creative Director of Ideaswork, a Delhi-based advertising agency specialising in place branding, 15 October 2010.

25 CNBC-TV18 'CWG mess and Brand India', at http://www.youtube.com/watch?v=3XE2WPzM-sA&feature=related, accessed 5 December 2011.

26 'Commonwealth Games village is "unfit for human habitation"', *Guardian*, 21 September 2010, at http://www.guardian.co.uk/sport/2010/sep/21/commonwealth-games-unfit-human-habitation, accessed 5 December 2011.

27 L Bhanot, Secretary, Commonwealth Games Organising Committee, comments in 'Games village world class', 21 September 2010, NDTV news reportage, at http://www.ndtv.com/video/player/news/games-village-world-class-lalit-bhanot/164966, accessed 15 December 2011.

28 S Desai, CEO, Future Brands, 'Can India be found among the rubble?', CNBC-TV18 reportage and discussion, 18 October 2010.

29 V Singhvi, 'Old India has failed new India again', *Hindustan Times*, 25 September 2010. A longer version of the article is 'Old India vs new India', available at www.virsanghvi.com/CounterPoint-ArticleDetail.aspx?ID=552, accessed 15 December 2011.

30 India Poised campaign.

31 'FICCI fears corruption will damage Brand India', *The Hindu*, 14 December 2010.

32 'An open letter to our leaders', *Hindustan Times*, 17 January 2011.
33 'Corporate India says it backs Anna Hazare', *Deccan Herald*, 8 April 2011.
34 '2G scam: Supreme Court upset with Khurshid's remarks, asks "Are we wasting our time?"', 12 October 2011, at www.ndtv.com/article/india/2g-scam-supreme-court-upset-withkhurshid-s-remarks-asks-are-we-wasting-our-time-140599, accessed 15 December 2011.
35 S Khilnani, *The Idea of India*, New Delhi: Penguin, 1999; and R Guha, *India after Gandhi: The History of the World's Largest Democracy*, Basingstoke: Pan Macmillan, 2007.
36 J Baudrillard, 'Simulacra and simulations', in M Poster (ed), *Jean Baudrillard: Selected Writings*, Stanford, CA: Stanford University Press, 1988, pp 166–184.
37 Mitchell, *What do Pictures Want?*, p 56.

Notes on contributor

Ravinder Kaur is Associate Professor and Director of the Centre for Global South Asian Studies, Department of Cross-cultural and Regional Studies, University of Copenhagen, Denmark. Her work includes *Since 1947: Partition Narratives among Punjabi Migrants of Delhi* (Oxford University Press, 2007); editor, *Religion, Violence and Political Mobilisation in Contemporary South Asia* (Sage Publications, 2005), as well as a number of articles and book chapters. She is currently responsible for a research programme funded by the Danish Social Sciences Research Council on the ongoing social-political transformations in post-reform India.

China as an 'Emerging Biotech Power'

AYO WAHLBERG

ABSTRACT   *Asia's dramatic entry on to the global biotech scene has not gone unnoticed by commentators and social scientists. Countries like China, India, South Korea and Singapore have been identified as 'emerging biotech powers'. Consequently scholars have begun examining the particularities of how biotechnologies (eg stem cell science, genetic testing and reproductive medicine) have come to be taken up and grounded in a variety of cultural, legal and socioeconomic contexts. They have also examined how governments, scientists, clinicians and others have been engaged in efforts to build up endogenous biotech sectors as a part of nation-building strategies. In this article, rather than attempting to answer questions of what makes biotechnology particularly Asian, I will instead investigate how demarcations and boundaries are mooted in global negotiations of what constitutes 'good' biotechnology. The analysis is based on a collaborative project between Chinese and European scientists and experts on the ethical governance of biomedical and biological research. I show how an underlying condition for the negotiations that took place within this collaboration was the proposition that difference matters when it comes to developing, organising, carrying out and overseeing biotechnological research in a particular country.*

At a workshop on ethical challenges surrounding stem cell research held in Shanghai in 2007, one of the presenters projected an introductory slide on to the screen behind him with the words 'Open in 2009' in bold. The backdrop of the slide was an architect's portrayal of a spectacular new biomedical research complex under construction in the south of China. The presenter had recently returned to China from the USA to head up a team of embryonic stem cell researchers at this new research centre. Other presenters had similar slides and, during discussions, the mood of the workshop was captured in the reflections of one workshop participant: 'One of the characteristics of Chinese policies on stem cell research is the ambition to be a power in bioscience and biotechnology. A huge amount of resources is invested in it.' A year later, during a site visit to a biotechnology research institution at another workshop in Shenzhen, participants were introduced to an impressive wall display featuring several *Nature* cover stories resulting

Ayo Wahlberg is in the Department of Anthropology, University of Copenhagen, Denmark.

from their research. Following a guided tour of the institute filled with numerous multimillion-dollar DNA sequencing and digital data storage machines, we each received a postcard featuring a cartoon of a staff member answering an awed group of international visitors (like ours)—'Wow so many machines!'—with a deadpan 'It's still not enough'.

In recent years a string of publications has analysed Asia's dramatic entry on to the global biotech scene.[1] State-led investment programmes, turning brain-drain into brain-gain by luring back young researchers from Europe and the USA, political mobilisation around biotechnology as a potential engine of economic growth, nationalist aspirations in a global race 'to be the first', as well as anxieties surrounding biosecurity risks have all been highlighted as catalysts of 'Asia's Rising Science and Technology Strength'.[2] With titles and subtitles like 'Biopolitics in Asia', 'Biopolitics in China', 'Asian Biotech' and 'Imagining Biotech India', one of the common tasks of this literature has been to examine whether there is something particular to biotechnology in Asia, or indeed whether there is something which might qualify as Asian biotechnology.

In a special issue of *New Genetics and Society* on the theme of 'Biopolitics in Asia', Herbert Gottweis suggests that 'despite all general trends towards globalization a distinctive picture of biopolitics in Asia is in the process of emerging... Asia today is neither a "Wild East" nor simply, one big, research and experimental population in the service of the global bioeconomy'.[3] Instead, contributors to the special issue show how governments, scientists and others are engaged in 'binational' efforts to build up endogenous biotech sectors. In a similar vein Bharadwaj has argued that, in the context of the rise of neo-India in a global biotechnology sector, 'the twentieth-century development discourse which privileged the unidirectional flow of knowledge from the "global" North/developed to the "local" South/developing is now both an untenable orthodoxy and an unsustainable project'.[4] The point being that we need to approach these developments in India and other Asian countries as 'biotechnological autoproduction' rather than 'mere' technology transfer. Ong and Chen, on the other hand, shift the focus from what is happening in Asia to the question of what it is that makes biotechnology Asian. 'Asian biotech', they suggest, denotes a 'historical moment when biotechnologies articulate powerful nationalist aspirations in newly affluent Asia', as contributors to their volume show how biotechnology harnesses and aligns with ongoing nation-building efforts, thereby palpably contributing to the negotiation and production of 'Asianness'.[5] For example, in a chapter on 'Chinese DNA' Wen-Ching Sung shows how the 'introduction of genomics since the 1990s... adds another spin to the discourses and practices on China's ethnic categorization',[6] while Charis Thompson analyses the 'Koreanness' of fallen stem cell scientist Hwang Woo Suk, who had suggested that dexterous Korean chopstick users had sharpened the cell work done in his laboratory.[7]

In this article I will show how difference is actively mobilised on a global scale in the realm of biotechnology. Rather than attempting to answer the question of what makes or when is biotechnology particularly Asian, I will instead investigate how demarcations and boundaries are mooted in global negotiations of what constitutes 'good' biotechnology. Through his studies of mobilisation practices among indigenous activists of the Colombian Pacific, Arturo Escobar has argued that an important way in which a politics of difference plays out is in struggles against the terms of globality. 'People mobilize against the destructive aspects of globalization from the perspective of what they have been and what they are at present … in the defense of place from the perspective of the economic, ecological, and cultural difference that their landscapes, cultures, and economies embody in relation to those of more dominant sectors of society'.[8] Indeed, as noted in the introduction to this special issue, 'difference' has analytically often been used in contexts of resistance, as a way to circumvent hegemonies and hierarchies and to stake claims 'from below'. My analysis will show how difference can also be mobilised by 'dominant sectors of society', in my case the biotech sector, in the making of the figure of an 'emerging biotech power'. That is to say, the mobilisation of difference is not something restricted to emancipatory struggles against dominance, but can also be found in concrete contexts of nation building led by scientists, government officials, lawyers and other experts.

The context within which I will examine this field of problematisation is that of an international collaborative project between Chinese and European social and natural scientists that took place over a three-year period (2006–09) called Bionet.[9] Over the course of these years I participated in and helped to organise a series of six workshops and conferences, five of which took place in China (Beijing, Shanghai, Changsha, Xian and Shenzhen). These events focused on ethical challenges surrounding the governance of biomedical research involving volunteer human subjects in the fields of stem cell research, clinical trials and genomics, and were attended by more than 300 leading life scientists, ethicists, lawyers, social scientists as well as government representatives from China and Europe. Simultaneous translation was provided for European and Chinese participants at each of these events and presentations and discussions were recorded and summarised in workshop reports. The objective of these events was to map out practices of ethical governance of biomedical and biological research in China and Europe. The following analysis is based on my attendance and participation in these events (including my field notes), informal discussions with participants during lunches and dinners, as well as on the reports that were prepared during the course of the project. I have read through my field notes, copies of presentation slides and the workshop reports to identify common themes and issues. As such what follows is an analysis of *one particular forum* of global negotiation of difference.

I begin the article by asking what kind of biotechnology it is we are talking about that apparently can be characterised in terms of particular national or regional traits—namely a global biotechnology. I then move on to analyse how difference was explicitly mobilised during the course of the workshop and conference presentations and discussions, which all addressed in some way the question of what makes biotechnological research 'ethical'. I focus in particular on two kinds of difference that were consistently brought up during the project over the three years. First, a kind of carving out of a competitive advantage niche and, second, debates around whether bioethics are universal and if so whether that allows space for an 'Asian bioethics' or indeed 'Chinese bioethics'. I conclude by reflecting on how difference helps us to think about global biotechnology.

Global biotechnology

There is nothing particularly 'new' about life sciences research, not even about some of the much-hyped twenty-first century fields of genomics or regenerative medicine. Both have long histories dating back decades. Yet new developments are of course happening within these fields, many of which are linked to ongoing technological developments, on one hand, and globalisation processes on the other. A 'molecular gaze' has emerged out of the life sciences, propelled by high-powered microscopy and imaging technologies, as well as by the development of DNA sequencing techniques and associated bioinformatics computing software.[10] At the same time life science has become mobile as scientists, biological samples, digital information databases, technologies and biomedical treatments travel across national and continental borders. A biological sample procured in one place can be couriered across the world to be sequenced and chemically analysed and the information derived can be electronically transmitted to relevant parties around the world. A biomedical treatment developed in Switzerland can be transported to China for clinical testing on Chinese volunteers before being approved for use on American citizens. Immortalised stem cell lines can be ordered online from various stem cell banks and shipped globally.

Yet this globalisation of biotechnological research has raised numerous questions about the ethics of such endeavours. According to which standards should such research be judged? Whose ethical guidelines and regulations are applicable in situations where Chinese and European scientists collaborate? Which safeguards should be put in place to avoid exploitation of vulnerable patients and populations? These are not logistical questions concerning how best to organise scientific collaboration projects most efficiently; rather they are questions which concern what it is that makes particular forms of research 'ethical'.

It is with these kinds of questions that the Sino-European project which I took part in engaged. As such, the presentations and discussions that I observed were characterised by exchanges between Chinese and European scientists and experts regarding how to go about ensuring that biotechnological research was ethical when multiple languages, cultural backgrounds, socioeconomic contexts, regulatory traditions and the like were at stake. The common point of departure was that, for biotechnological research requiring volunteer human subjects (such as stem cell research, genomic research and clinical trials) to be 'good', not only did it have to be scientifically rigorous and efficiently organised, it also had to be 'ethically sound'. Yet, despite the existence of such global reference documents as the Helsinki Declaration on Ethical Principles for Medical Research Involving Human Subjects or the Universal Declaration on Bioethics and Human Rights, there was plenty of room for interpretation and negotiation as to how such universal principles might apply in particular contexts. It is on the basis of my observations of such negotiations between workshop participants that I present the following analysis of difference in global biotechnology.[11] What I will show is how an underlying condition for such negotiations to take place was the proposition that *difference matters* when it comes to developing, organising, carrying out and overseeing biotechnological research in a particular country.

Many different Chinas

Let us begin with the question of how biotechnological research can be organised, carried out and overseen in China. As noted in the opening of this article, there can be no question about the stated ambition of political leaders, government officials and scientists that China become a so-called 'global player' in biotechnology. This ambition has been backed up by state investment programmes, new laboratory facilities and regulatory reforms. And one can already discern the results of this strategy in the form of one of the world's largest genome sequencing centres, an increasing number of published articles in renowned life science journals stemming from research units in China, as well as a sharp increase in the number of international research collaborations involving Chinese partners.[12]

Just as Sunder Rajan has shown how numerous actors are currently 'building clinical research infrastructure in India [while] also promoting India as a clinical trial destination globally',[13] the same can be said of China. Indeed, in 2007, a report by the *Financial Times* suggested that 274 of those clinical trials registered on the US government's clinicaltrials.gov website were being carried out in China, while 260 were being carried out in India.[14] At a workshop held in Xian, a senior medical college representative proclaimed that 'we welcome more clinical trials in China, we are ready'. In the workshop discussions the 'attractive' characteristics of China as a clinical trials destination were debated. Clinicians and other experts pointed out that the country had a large population and relatively easy patient recruitment, it had good quality medical and research infrastructure at substantially lower costs and—perhaps most importantly—a growing domestic pharmaceuticals market. Yet not only have government officials, scientists, companies and other actors been engaged in building up a physical clinical research infrastructure, over the past decade or so they have also been engaged in the building up of what Reubi has referred to as the 'soft infrastructure' of biomedical research ethics.[15] As pointed out by a lawyer in our Shanghai workshop, 'almost every bioethical aspect regarding biomedical manipulations has been addressed to protect the rights of human subjects and public morality'. He was referring to a flurry of ethical guidelines, regulations and norms that have been promulgated by both the Ministry of Health and the Ministry of Science and Technology in recent years regarding extraction and export of genetic resources (1998), stem cell research (2003), Good Clinical Practice (2003), scientific integrity and misconduct (2007), ethical review of biomedical research involving human subjects (2007) and more. Such an infrastructure of biomedical ethics was deemed necessary by some participants, not least as a way to counter misguided assumptions that 'the development of biomedical research and biotechnology without constraint or unbounded freedom will allow China to more rapidly catch up with efforts in developed nations'. The scandal surrounding and reputational damage caused by Korean stem cell scientist Hwang Woo Suk was raised in many presentations and discussions as a kind of warning: 'Chinese science and technology could lose its essential integrity and public support both at home and abroad. The scandals over Hwang Woo Suk in [South] Korea and Chen Jin[16] in China convincingly illustrate this point'.

Yet the China that was being assembled in these accounts was very much one of elite centres of excellence which had the resources and capacity to carry out large-scale scientific research projects in accordance with international and national ethical guidelines. Other workshop participants were quick to point out a marked lack of capacity in many of the clinics and laboratories found in smaller cities, with some suggesting that one should indeed differentiate between high-capacity centres of excellence and those lagging behind. Evoking anthropologist Adriana Petryna's notion of 'ethical variability',[17] one participant commented: 'China is a big country. Implementation of ethical regulations varies drastically among regions and institutes. This situation may not be easily changed in a short time.' There were, in other words, many different Chinas within China, with access to vastly different amounts of resources, and, when the case was made for China as an 'attractive' biotechnological research destination, this attraction was very specific to certain centres. An important point raised by numerous speakers concerned the gaps that remained between regulations and guidelines, on the one hand, and the situation on the ground in many clinics and laboratories, on the other.

Biomedical research infrastructure was not the only attraction that was flagged by participants at our many workshops. One of China's perhaps most internationally notorious features is its large population of some 1.2 billion people. This was an advantage, it was suggested, not only in terms of recruitment of volunteers into biomedical research. It also represented a kind of 'treasure trove' of both genetic diversity and wide-ranging disease profile (from infectious to lifestyle diseases), both of which were 'available', waiting to be researched. In a workshop on biobanking, a senior scientist explained how 'there are 56 ethnic groups in China, each of them having independent inhabitation areas and some of them are genetically isolated as populations. In terms of genetic phenotypes, each ethnic group has its unique characteristics. There are significant differences in categories, enzyme systems, HLA antigens and incidences of some genetic diseases.' One could therefore take biomedical advantage from the 'homogeneous' marrying habits of particular cultural groups within China, but the task was urgent he pointed out since 'at present, more and more youths are marrying across different nationalities, and as a result the genomes of some nationalities face the danger of extinction'.

Yet, as already pointed out, it was not only the genetic diversity of China's 56 ethnic groups that was described as a valuable and 'attractive' research resource. The fact that China was in the midst of massive socioeconomic transformation meant that its population was host to a diversity of diseases which made it especially conducive to medical genomic research. For example, when introducing a large-scale prospective cohort study aiming to determine environmental risk factors, life-course causes and genetic risk factors underlying common chronic diseases, one of the project's scientists explained the reasoning behind choosing the city of Taizhou as the study site: 'Why Taizhou? Well, it is located in the area connecting north and south China with an admixture of northern and southern populations. The population is right at the start of economic transformation and it is a well established site for epidemiology studies with strong local government support.'

While there are clear similarities between, for example, China and India, what I am suggesting here is that an important component of the casting of China as an 'emerging biotech power' has been the carving out of a competitive advantage niche that sets it apart, in particular, from the 'West'. Difference here sets China apart in terms of the relatively low cost of its otherwise high-quality biomedical research infrastructure but also in terms of its biological 'assets', which in turn parcel out different groups and areas *within* China in terms of genetic diversity and a diverse disease profile. So China's attractiveness as a biotech research site is not only related to its difference from the West, but also to differences (or diversity) within China.[18]

Overseeing biomedical research in China

What bound the various forms of biotech research covered in our workshops together was their reliance on volunteer human subjects, either as donors of biological samples (eg blood samples for genomic research or 'leftover embryos' from fertility treatment for stem cell research) and associated biographical data (eg about lifestyle, family medical history, socioeconomic background) or as recipients of experimental therapies (eg new pharmaceuticals or stem cell therapies). As such these were forms of research which required not just scientific oversight in the form of peer review but also ethical oversight in the form of ethical review. The point being, as noted earlier, that, for scientific research requiring volunteer human subjects to be 'good', not only did it have to be scientifically rigorous it also had to be ethically sound.

There is a growing critical literature on the shortcomings of what are sometimes referred to as 'global' bioethics, understood as a universalised and instrumentalised set of principles and practices aimed at safeguarding and protecting those individuals who voluntarily participate in biomedical research.[19] For the purposes of this article I will not engage with this literature; I will instead show how during often lively debates about the ways in which ethical oversight of biomedical research should be organised, cultural and socioeconomic differences were mobilised. There are two particular debates that I will recount in this section: the first is between European and Chinese scientists about the moral status of an embryo in the context of human embryonic stem cell research; the second concerns which different forms of interaction between researchers and volunteer human subjects should or should not be allowed.

Chinese values

One of the most vocally contested areas of stem cell research worldwide has been that of human embryonic stem cell (HESC) research. Such research requires access to human embryos, which has raised questions about whether or not a human embryo constitutes a human life and thereby requires appropriate protection and safeguards, and, if research on embryos is allowed, then under which circumstances they can be procured. For example, should women and men be allowed to donate gametes for research purposes, should it be permissible to create embryos purely for research purposes, should HESC research only be carried out on so-called 'leftover embryos' from infertility treatment? One of the liveliest discussions in the course of our project took place in Shanghai, when participants at our stem cell workshop discussed the moral status of a human embryo. Throughout the world, different countries have different legal positions on whether or not it should be permissible to carry out research on human embryos—some countries prohibit it while others allow it under specific conditions.

The discussion quickly centred on the question of when a human life begins—is it at the moment of fertilisation (when egg and sperm mix), nidation (when an early embryo implants into the uterus), perception of 'primitive streak' (a structure in the embryo that becomes visible under the microscope around 14 days after fertilisation) or birth? While the discussion was very technical concerning the biology of reproductive processes, it was clear that the answer to whether or not, or at which point, a human embryo constitutes a human life would not come from biology: 'Ethical standards stem from cultural and religious background and they are highly diversified among different regions and countries'. Some presenters suggested that in China a traditional Confucian view still prevailed and that the 'governance of biotechnology and biomedical research should be exclusively based on unique Chinese culture, eg Confucian values and principles'. According to Confucian principles, it was argued, 'a person begins with birth and ends with death...and is an entity which has the capacity for social relationships', although 'a human embryo is a human biological life, a precursor of person, not merely "stuff" like placenta...so it deserves due respect: if there is no sufficient reason, it should not be permitted to manipulate or destroy it'. Another participant pointed out that this view was very much in line with the UK's Warnock

Committee, which has suggested that there should be a 'gradation in the respect accorded to a foetus as it develops from zygote to early embryo to its birth'. However, in Germany full moral status was accorded by the Embryo Protection Act to 'any fertilised human oocyte after that point in time at which the pronuclei have fused, any later stage of its development and to any totipotent parts which could, under the proper circumstances, be able to develop into an individual being'.

What this exchange between workshop participants gave insight into was precisely a negotiation of difference, however caricatured. What was it that counted as a Chinese, German or UK 'position' or view on the moral status of the embryo and how might such a view be 'established'? In the discussions that followed various processes for establishing a national position were discussed, including public opinion polls, existing laws or law proposals and national Ethics Commissions. There was no clear answer to this latter question, rather various options were identified, although workshop participants did arrive at a conclusion: 'each culture must find the right mix of biology, theology and metaphysics to satisfy it—to fit with its cultural narrative. "Drawing the line" it seems paradoxically, [i]s both arbitrary and essential'.

These kinds of discussion concerned ethical oversight of biomedical and biological research from a national point of view—a kind of national stewardship of biotech science. The questions of what forms of manipulation and disposal of early human life should or should not be allowed could not be answered within the confines of a laboratory, but rather required the involvement of other experts, members of the public, government officials, etc. Yet it was up to each country to organise the ways in which their respective inputs would be fed into the crystallising of some kind of a national position or 'consensus'. Notwithstanding the fact that multiple positions on the moral status of a human embryo might be found within a nation's borders, the conclusion among workshop participants seemed to be that this fell within a national remit. It should be pointed out that Chinese regulations do allow, as do UK regulations, research on human embryos up to 14 days after fertilisation and both countries are therefore described as having 'permissible' stem cell regulation, which adds to their 'attraction' as global sites of stem cell research.

'Cultural sensitivity' in the recruitment of volunteers

Once a biomedical research project proposal has been ethically and peer reviewed and thereby funded, the everyday work of the principal investigators and/or clinicians begins. Research staff have to be hired and trained, informed consent protocols have to be designed and modified to fit target patients, recruitment efforts have to be put in motion and follow-up procedures have to be agreed upon. It is precisely this moment—when researchers and clinicians must interact with potential participants in biomedical research—that is considered ethically precarious. It is at this moment that possibilities for coercion, exploitation, inducement and undue influence emerge, which could be driven by commercial motives, personal career advancement considerations, lack of healthcare services in resource-poor settings, etc.

What I found was that, regardless of the type of biomedical research that was under scrutiny (stem cell research, biobanking or clinical trials), there seemed to be an ongoing negotiation around the precise form that interaction between researchers and potential research subjects should take place, depending on the particular context 'on the ground'. One element of this context was the particular 'culture' in which the research was to take place. I will show how by discussing the way in which the question of informed consent in the context of clinical trials and biobanking was debated by participants from China and Europe.

Ever since the Nuremberg code from 1949 insisted that, when it comes to recruiting participants for medical research, 'the voluntary consent of the human subject is absolutely essential',[20] one of the most prominent tools to have been developed for ensuring that interaction between researchers and potential participants is ethical and appropriate has been the informed consent procedure/form. The conversation between researcher and potential participant, the form which explains the research, and the signature of the potential participant on that form are meant to ensure voluntariness as well as symbolise respect for a person. As already noted, there is a vast literature on the shortcomings of such a formalised approach to bioethics. What I will discuss here instead is how workshop participants argued for an adjustment of this process so as to fit a particular cultural and socioeconomic context. So what kind of 'Chinese context' could be discerned from the debates at our workshops?

I would point to two particular areas related to: 1) who has the authority to consent; and 2) how to recruit in a climate of commercialisation. One of the assumptions behind the idea of genuine voluntary informed consent is autonomy—individuals are the ones who should be deciding whether they would like to participate in biomedical research as symbolised in the signature. The spectre of 'many Chinas' once again emerged in discussions about whether such an individualised approach to consent is at all relevant or realistic in certain contexts. Some speakers argued that, since any kind of interaction with hospitals (whether for treatment or participation in medical research) in China had some kind of financial implication, then any decisions would always be taken in the context of families, with heads of households often having a final say. Moreover, in the context of large-scale biobanking projects requiring thousands of volunteers, for example from a particular ethnic community, consent would never be merely individual, as village leaders and other community heads would often have to sanction any kind of large-scale medical research in their communities.[21] So there were certain circuits of authority that needed to be followed if medical research was to be made ethical in a particular context. And although such distinctions tend to produce caricatured generalisations, many speakers pointed to a collectivist China vs an individualist Europe as an important difference that it was crucial to take into account when adapting recruitment and informed consent procedures into Chinese contexts. Indeed, Bionet's Expert Group[22] ended up recommending that 'before any research collaborations [between Chinese and European researchers] are approved or begin, participating researchers must receive training on how potential research participants are to be engaged with, as well as on how informed consent is to be obtained, while focusing on the particularities of the kind of research at stake...as well as the socioeconomic and cultural context'.[23]

Secondly, as anyone with a minimal interest in health care issues within China will know, over the past two decades medical care has come to be commercialised, as collective insurance systems have been overtaken by individualised healthcare plans and out-of-pocket medical service fees. At many of our workshops, clinicians would highlight the problems that this had brought in its wake, in particular regarding a worsening of doctor–patient relations thanks to increasing corruption as the only means of ensuring access to good quality care; decreasing trust between doctors and patients; increasing litigation against doctors and hospitals; and an epidemic of violence directed at doctors and nurses, among other things. Recruiting potential research participants in such a climate raises particular challenges, which many workshop participants from China argued need to be taken into account in the planning and carrying out of medical research. For example, one speaker suggested that 'patients, physicians/investigators and health care administrators regularly confuse clinical trials with medical care' and that 'some physicians/investigators seem deliberately to treat clinical trials as medical care'. The fact was that participating in medical research could 'save patients and their families from heavy economic burdens'. In such a climate of commercialisation, another participant argued that 'instead of empowering, informed consent can be disempowering if donors do not have the ability to nurture, sustain and develop themselves'. And so the particularities of China's health care system in the twenty-first century raised challenges for the ethical governance of biomedical research which had to be addressed.

The kinds of discussions I have briefly summarised here concerned oversight of interaction between researchers and potential research subjects as a way of minimising risks of exploitation, undue influence and coercion. While not all were agreed on exactly how, there was some kind of agreement among many workshop and conference participants that the ways in which such interaction should be structured, organised, carried out and monitored needed to be adapted to a 'Chinese' context which was circumscribed in terms of culture as well as socioeconomic stratification. It was through such differentiation—which required establishing the particularities of that which makes up Chinese contexts—that the ethical governance of biomedical research could be ensured. So in this sense differentiating was what would allow the adaptation of the universal to the particular. In the words of one workshop participant: 'Basic values, such as respect, non-maleficence/beneficence and justice are shared by Western and Eastern cultures alike...though as Confucius said, "By nature men are similar; by practice men are wide apart"'.

Conclusion

In this article I have demonstrated how difference organises global negotiations about how to ensure that biotechnological research in a time of increasing global mobility is 'ethical'. On the one hand, difference is mobilised in such negotiations as a way to carve out certain competitive advantages that make a particular nation, such as China or the UK, an 'attractive' place to carry out biomedical research. On the other hand, difference is invoked to insist that institutionalised, 'universal' bioethical tools, such as national ethics committees, declarations, ethical review boards or informed consent procedures, be adapted to particular cultural, socio-economic contexts. That is to say, *difference matters* in global biotechnology.

Much has been made of the emancipatory potential of difference in the mobilisation strategies of marginalised groups against dominant narratives, groups or sets of actors as a way of 'dissolving some of the strong structures of Euro-modernity at the level of theory by favouring flat alternatives; positing the fact that epistemic differences can be—indeed are—grounds for the construction of alternative worlds'.[24] What I have shown here is that difference can also be actively mobilised in these 'dominant' settings, as particular strategies of nation building. By focusing on a specific forum of global negotiation—a three-year collaborative project between European and Chinese experts on the ethical governance of biomedical and biological research—I have shown how difference organised the terms of debate among participants. In this sense difference can be a leveller in that, rather than invoking a universal global bioethics system, it authorises multiplicity, thereby invoking the particular. Hence, by shifting analytical focus to the governing of difference, we are able to see the multiple ways in which this can be mobilised in various contexts—whether among marginalised groups or dominant sectors of society.

In the foregoing I have not attempted to explain or account for differences between, say, China and the UK; rather, I have honed in on those occasions where difference was actively made through global negotiations between European and Chinese scientists, clinicians, experts and others. Such mobilisations of difference played their part in the kinds of nation-building strategies that seek to establish a certain country as a global 'biotech power'.

Acknowledgements

From 2007 to 2009 I was Research Fellow for the Bionet project, based at the BIOS Centre, London School of Economics. I gratefully acknowledge all Bionet partners as well as the funders of Bionet which included the European Commission Sixth Framework Programme (FP6), the United Kingdom's Medical Research Council (MRC) and the Wellcome Trust.

Notes

1 See A Bharadwaj & P Glasner, *Local Cells, Global Science: The Rise of Embryonic Stem Cell Research in India*, London: Routledge, 2009; H Gottweis (ed), 'Biopolitics in Asia', special issue of *New Genetics*

IDENTITY, INEQUITY AND INEQUALITY IN INDIA AND CHINA

and Society, 28(3), 2009; D Reubi, 'The will to modernize: a genealogy of biomedical research ethics in Singapore', *International Political Sociology*, 4, 2010, pp 142–158; A Ong & N Chen (eds), *Asian Biotech: Ethics and Communities of Fate*, Durham, NC: Duke University Press, 2010; K Sunder Rajan, *Biocapital: The Constitution of Post-Genomic Life*, Durham, NC: Duke University Press, 2006; and B Salter & C Waldby (eds), 'Biopolitics in China', special issue of *East Asian Science, Technology and Society*, 5(3), 2011.

2 National Science Foundation, *Asia's Rising Science and Technology Strength*, Arlington, VA: Division of Science Resources Statistics, National Science Foundation, 2007.

3 Gottweis, 'Biopolitics in Asia', pp 203–204.

4 Bharadwaj & Glasner, *Local Cells, Global Science*, p 20.

5 Ong & Chen, *Asian Biotech*, p 5.

6 W-C Sung, 'Chinese DNA: genomics and bionation', in Ong & Chen, *Asian Biotech*, pp 263–292.

7 C Thompson, 'Asian regeneration? Nationalism and internationalism in stem cell research in South Korea and Singapore', in Ong & Chen, *Asian Biotech*, pp 95–117.

8 A Escobar, *Territories of Difference: Place, Movements, Life, Redes*, Durham, NC: Duke University Press, 2008.

9 See the following reports for summaries of Bionet's work: Bionet, *Informed Consent in Reproductive Genetics and Stem Cell Technology and the Role of Ethical Review Boards*, first workshop report, Peking University Health Science Centre, Beijing, 1–5 April 2007; Bionet, *Ethical Governance of Reproductive and Stem Cell Research and Stem Cell Banks*, second workshop report, CAS-MPG Partner Institute for Computational Biology in cooperation with the Shanghai Medical Ethics Association, Shanghai, 9–11 October 2007; Bionet, *Ethical Governance of Reproductive Technologies, Therapeutic Stem Cells and Stem Cell Banks*, conference report, Institute of Reproduction and Stem Cell Engineering, Central South University & Reproductive and Genetic Hospital, CITIC-Xiangya, Changsha, 1–3 April 2008; Bionet, *Clinical Research and Clinical Research Organisations in EU–CN Research—Ethics and Governance Issues*, third workshop report, Research Center for Bioethics, Peking Union Medical College & Chinese Academy of Social Sciences, Xi'an, 9–12 September 2008; Bionet, *Biobanking & Personal Genomics: Challenges and Futures for EU–China Collaborations*, fourth workshop report, Beijing Genomics Institute at Shenzhen, Shenzhen, 27–29 April 2009; Bionet, *Recommendations on Best Practice in the Ethical Governance of Sino-European Biological and Biomedical Research Collaborations*, Bionet Expert Group Report, London: London School of Economics, 2010; and Bionet, *Ethical Governance of Biological and Biomedical Research: Chinese–European Co-operation—Final Report*, London: London School of Economics, 2010, all available at http://www2.lse.ac.uk/BIOS/research/BIONET/.

10 N Rose, *The Politics of Life Itself: Biomedicine, Power, and Subjectivity in the Twenty-first Century*, Princeton, NJ: Princeton University Press, 2006.

11 I have chosen not to identify the persons from whom the quotes that follow are taken. Information on the composition and participation of Bionet workshops can be found in the various workshop reports, at http://www2.lse.ac.uk/researchAndExpertise/units/BIONET/. What I am analysing here are the contours of the negotiations that I observed and recorded during these events as opposed to ascribing a certain 'view' to an individual or institution. It is the *negotiations* that are the object of my analysis here.

12 See Bionet reports at footnote 9.

13 K Sunder Rajan, 'The experimental machinery of global clinical trials: case studies from India', in Ong & Chen, *Asian Biotech*, pp 55–80.

14 A Jack & A Yee, 'China overtakes India in drug testing', *Financial Times*, 27 August 2007.

15 Reubi, 'The will to modernize'.

16 A scandal surrounding the faking of data in the development of Motorola-chips at Jiaotong University.

17 A Petryna, 'Clinical trials offshored: on private sector science and public health', *BioSocieties*, 2(1), 2007, pp 21–40; and Petryna, 'Ethical variability: drug development and the globalization of clinical trials', *American Ethnologist*, 32, 2005, pp 183–197.

18 See also Sunder Rajan, *Biocapital*.

19 See, for example, A Petryna, *When Experiments Travel: Clinical Trials and the Global Search for Human Subjects*, Princeton, NJ: Princeton University Press, 2009; P Geissler, KA Wenzel, B Imoukhuede & R Pool, '"He is now like a brother, I can even give him some blood"—relational ethics and material exchanges in a malaria vaccine "trial community" in The Gambia', *Social Science and Medicine*, 67(5), 2008, pp 696–707; and CS Molyneux, DR Wassenaar, N Peshu & K Marsh, '"Even if they ask you to stand by a tree all day, you will have to do it (laughter)!"—community voices on the notion and practice of informed consent for biomedical research in developing countries', *Social Science and Medicine*, 61(2), 2005, pp 443–454.

20 US Government, 'Trials of War Criminals Before the Nuremberg Military Tribunals Under Control Council Law No 10', Vol 2, Nuremberg, October 1946–April 1949, Washington, DC: US Government Printing Office, 1949, pp 181–182.

IDENTITY, INEQUITY AND INEQUALITY IN INDIA AND CHINA

21 This observation is not unique to China as similar points have been made in other countries, especially where research takes place in rural areas or so-called 'resource-poor' settings. See P Geissler, KA Wenzel & C Molyneux (eds), *Evidence, Ethos and Experiment: The Anthropology and History of Medical Research in Africa*, New York: Berghahn Books, 2011.
22 An important component of the Bionet project was an Expert Group co-chaired by Prof Christoph Rehmann-Sutter and Prof Qiu Renzong, whose remit it was to prepare recommendations on best practice in the ethical governance of Sino-European biomedical research collaborations. See Bionet, *Recommendations on Best Practice in the Ethical Governance of Sino-European Biological and Biomedical Research Collaborations.*
23 *Ibid*, pp 46–47.
24 Escobar, *Territories of Difference*, pp 310–311.

Notes on contributor

Ayo Wahlberg is Asian Dynamics Initiative Postdoctoral Research Fellow at the Department of Anthropology, University of Copenhagen. He is co-editor (with Susanne Bauer) of *Contested Categories—Life Sciences in Society* (2009) and (with Laurence Monnais and C Michele Thompson) of *Southern Medicine for Southern People—Vietnamese Medicine in the Making* (2012). His current project is focused on reproductive technologies in China, for which he is the recipient of a Sapere Aude Young Researcher Award from the Danish Council of Independent Research.

Post-colonial Renaissance: 'Indianness', contemporary art and the market in the age of neoliberal capital

MANUELA CIOTTI

ABSTRACT *Arjun Appadurai has argued that 'the materiality of objects in India is not yet completely penetrated by the logic of the market'.[1] However, the entry and the visibility of modern and contemporary Indian art into the circuits of the global art world increasingly challenge this argument. The story of modern and contemporary Indian art is one of the inscription of local objects and their 'Indianness' into the above circuits, with market value being created in the process. If the globalisation of the art world provides a conceptual and material arena where objects are circulated, displayed and bought and sold through auction houses, exhibitions, biennales and art fairs, this article analyses an event that epitomises some of the forces at play in this arena: the contemporary art exhibition 'The Empire Strikes Back: Indian Art Today' held in 2010 at the Saatchi Gallery, London. An artistic cum business instantiation of 'India in Europe'—and one that challenges the visual and aesthetic canons 'traditionally' associated with India—this article examines this exhibition as an entry point into the analysis of how neoliberal capital produces 'culture', and into the tension between the commodity form and the infinite possibilities, and unintended consequences, opened up by this very status.*

Introduction

On the occasion of the fiftieth anniversary of India's independence from British rule in 1947, Aijaz Ahmad wrote about the contradiction between India's distressing social development indicators versus promising cultural trends:

> India is one of the few countries of the world, certainly the only country of considerable size and claim to world distinction, that will enter the 21st century with half of its people illiterate and its women facing a dowry death every one hour and 42 minutes, a rape every 54 minutes, a molestation every 26 minutes.

Manuela Ciotti is Assistant Professor in Global Studies at Aarhus University, Denmark.

India also produces an impressive cross-section of the world's technical personnel and some of the world's most celebrated novelists in the English language; *exhibits and auctions organised by such illustrious agencies as Christie's would suggest that an increasing number of Indian painters and other artists are now selling at very good prices in the global art market*. How are these contrasting facts related to the state of culture in India half a century after Independence? (emphasis added).[2]

An analysis of the correspondence between phenomena such as widespread illiteracy or sexual violence *vis-à-vis* that of the artistic production that expanded established auction houses' business horizons would most likely return the 'India-as-a-land-of-contrasts' argument.[3] Development's unevenness notwithstanding, an attempt to evade such an argument—and delve into the complex nexus between societal and cultural trends occurring within the same national boundaries in times of globalisation and neoliberalism—would require disjoining heterogeneous phenomena from the 'embrace' posited by the above argument, investigating their respective aetiology, and, only then, attempting an explanation of their interrelations.

For over a decade now, the promising cultural trends mentioned by Ahmad—that is modern and contemporary Indian art auctions and the entry of Indian artists into the global art world—have become even more enticing.[4] These trends are substantiated by flows of objects travelling across and out of India and its diaspora, which—often through the mediation of global actors and institutions—are exhibited, valued and sold *back to* or onto a largely Indian clientele in India and abroad. Art objects, their makers and collectors in an emergent market such as India are captured in a network connecting them physically or ideally with the global art world. These flows, and the business infrastructures sustaining them, point to the rise of the modern and contemporary art commodity form to a scale which had not existed before the 1990s, and to the presence of collectors of Indian art who also, elites aside, did not previously exist. Although Indian art is not solely confined to the actors and circuits of the global art world and market, these influence the art that is exhibited, circulated and traded at the local level. That is, the mediation of such actors and circuits might be physically or ideally present. A digression into these global dynamics as part of the emergence and visibility of modern and contemporary Indian art is necessary at this point.

In 1995, both Sotheby's and Christie's held their first contemporary Indian art sales in New York. In the same year, Christie's opened an office in Mumbai.[5] Increasingly, Indian art was exhibited by western museums and galleries. In 2000, the Indian online auction house Saffronart was founded: labelled 'the Sotheby's of India', 10 years on it has become the largest online auction house in the world. Over time, the volume of Indian art sales has steadily grown: according to Saffronart, 'The Indian art auction market has shot up from $3 million in 2000 to an estimated $120 million this year[2010]'.[6] Since 2005, works by Indian modernists have broken selling price records. As a result of the financial crisis, sales experienced a downfall between 2008 and 2009. Currently, the market appears to have recovered—and it seems to be sharing the more general buoyancy present in the global art market in times of economic crisis. Estimated at up to $400 million, the value of the modern and contemporary Indian art market represents only a small fraction of the global art and antiques market, which was set in 2010 'at 43 billion euros ($60 billion), up 52 per cent from 2009 when values slumped as a result of the financial crisis'.[7] If the share of the Indian art market is likely to grow, it is hardly comparable with the spectacular performance of the Chinese market: for the first time in 2010 'China overtook Britain to become the biggest art market in the world after America'.[8]

Modern and contemporary Indian art is an emerging presence in global art, and is being created, displayed and purchased in many different world locations—including online ones. The epicentre of this market is not Europe and the US—despite the 'west' still playing a major role in this story. At the same time, this is not a fully Indian story either; it is in fact a truly global one made up of galleries, auction houses, art fairs, business enterprises, buyers and artists operating at several geographical nodal points. In addition to prominent galleries in locations such as New Delhi, Mumbai, London and New York, among others, Indian art is shown at international fairs such as Art Dubai, Art Basel, Art Hong Kong, Art Basel Miami, while the growing popularity of the India Art Fair (previously Art Summit), held in New Delhi since 2008, testifies to art's appeal at home. Moreover, after some three decades of absence, in 2011 India has made a comeback as a national pavilion at the 54th Venice Biennale, responding to the need to showcase Indian art at this venerable venue.[9] According to experts, emerging art markets such as India can be divided between those whose governments support art and those that do not receive such support.[10] Although the Indian pavilion at the Biennale has shown the presence of government support, overall, Indian art falls into the latter group, so that private museums and patrons are mainly fostering art and its market.[11]

This article analyses an example of an out-of-India high-profile private enterprise promoting contemporary Indian art at a particular geocultural juncture: this consists of the exhibition 'The Empire Strikes Back: Indian Art Today' held at the Saatchi Gallery, London, in 2010. Opened in 1985, since 2008 the gallery has been situated at the Duke of York's Headquarters, an imposing complex in the upmarket London neighbourhood of Chelsea. The gallery has hosted many successful free-entry exhibitions: 'The Empire Strikes Back' featured among the top 10 most visited exhibitions in London during 2010.[12]

While in recent years 'Empire' seems to have returned as a heuristic tool, for example under the guise of the pervasive power conglomeration of the present,[13] or as the political institution governing much of world history,[14] the exhibition's *leitmotiv* lends itself to further reflections on the analysis of the fiftieth anniversary of India's independence offered by Ahmad.[15] If some of the artwork at the Saatchi Gallery gestures towards Empire, its revisiting only covers part of the exhibition's spirit and production. The art exhibited at the gallery no longer appears to be under the compulsion of looking 'at the world from an Indian way, not a British way', that is the manifesto of the Progressive Artists' Group founded in 1947—according to one of India's eminent modernists and member of the group, Sayed Haider Raza.[16] The contemporary Indian artists exhibiting at the 'Empire Strikes Back' appear to be firmly looking at the world in an Indian way—albeit not necessarily displaying 'Indian elements' in all their productions—and they are showing this art to the world without a 'counter-optic' in mind. In fact, the exhibition far exceeds the cultural perimeter of an 'East–West' encounter, rather, it can be conceived as a 'contact zone'—to borrow Pratt's powerful trope[17]—where India is articulated, re-narrated to and transformed in the 'cosmopolitan eyes' of the diverse publics traversing London.

To transpose Benedict Anderson's work to the world of materiality, the exhibition could also be conceived as connecting presences of (modern and contemporary) Indian art in the world in an 'imagined community' of objects.[18] This community rests on the above-mentioned network of actors (artists, business enterprises and galleries), which forms its indispensable infrastructure. India is, to a large extent, the location where most of the production of contemporary art takes place. And India is very often—but not always—the cultural reference for art objects. This might well point to one of the latest avatars of 'artistic nationalism' as coined by Winther-Tamaki. In his words:

> artistic identity is fundamentally contingent to national identity. Many individuals construct meaningful places for themselves in the world by participating in the creation, interpretation, and dissemination of works of art or by belonging to the social and economic networks that collectively manage these tasks. Although such communities, discussed as 'art worlds' [...] often encompass considerable diversity, they also predict a set of values, canons, and goals shared by many of their members. In short, art can function as a kind of identity.[19]

If Indian art exudes 'identity'—a proposition which does not foreclose its global reach and universal aspirations—contemporary artistic nationalism in India is shaped by at least two features: the infinite circulation possibilities engendered by media and technology, and artworks increasingly turning into asset values.[20] Where these features are widely shared across the world, an interesting example of the combination of the two in India is the recently held 'The India Art Collective', the country's first online art fair, which took place in November 2011. An article that appeared in *Tehelka Magazine* reporting on the fair produced the following manifesto of commodification and transnationality: 'Forty one galleries. Around 900 art works. A thousand visitors a day. Indian art is available to art collectors, appreciators and curious visitors alike, from New Jersey to Austria to Surat.'[21] This event was set to attract a global audience, but the media have also reported on the opening of galleries in Delhi shopping malls, testifying to efforts to lure local buyers.[22] This trend contrasts with the concept of gallery districts—existing in many metropolises—as distinct spaces for the art trade, with the charm and exclusivity which connotes them. More importantly, placing galleries in malls makes art objects equal to other commodities available for purchase. This 'commodity convergence'—an attempt to overcome customers' hesitation

Buying oneself?

The imagined community of art objects brings together another globally dispersed, imagined community: that of Indian buyers of modern and contemporary Indian art. In 2010, an interview with Saffronart CEO Minal Vazirani revealed that:

> 'About 80 per cent [of the clients] are still of Indian origin, whether [in India] or diaspora.' Twenty-five per cent are American. 'They've gotten slightly younger over time. Initially, it was mostly long-term collectors, but now we have several buyers and bidders coming in at different price points. Typically, it's someone who travels quite a bit, someone who is reasonably well informed about Indian art or jewellery.' Though it might seem surprising, many of the buyers make their purchases sight unseen—at least half of Saffronart's top 10 works were sold to people who had never physically been near their artwork.[23]

Although western actors have promoted Indian art in the global market, as discussed earlier, it is Indian-owned capital—at home and in diaspora—which has played a crucial role. And this is very different from the forces that initiated and fostered the Chinese art market up until a few years ago. A media article published in 2008 and featuring the views of Melissa Chiu, the Director of New York's Asia Society Museum, states: 'Unlike Indian art, which is mostly bought by South Asians and non-resident Indians, the majority of buyers for Chinese art were in the US and Europe, until about three years ago. This has influenced Chinese art, Chiu says, as much as government censorship.'[24] Today, younger Chinese buyers acquire modern and contemporary Asian art, while wealthy and older investors, among other purchases, pay large sums to bring Chinese antiquities back to China.[25] An emerging-markets professor at Sotheby's Institute of Art, Joe Lin-Hill, recently observed: 'Someday soon a Chinese ink painting is going to outsell Picasso'.[26]

If it is Chinese buyers that fuel the Chinese art market today, it would not be far-fetched to say that they are 'buying themselves', and given that a great deal of the artwork that Indian artists produce is *about* India, it follows that Indians too are 'buying themselves'. In turn, 'India'—as a *feature* shared by artists, art objects and buyers—has emerged both globally and locally as a desirable 'brand'. Where the correspondence between Indian art and Indian buyers points to the creation of a new layer of affect in addition to the consumption of other (Indian) commodities, 'buying local art' is a feature of emergent art markets cross-culturally. As reported by Adam in *The Art Newspaper*,[27] in Philip Dodd's view: 'Typically, people from recently emerged economic regions start by buying their own art, often 19th century; they then move to local contemporary art, and then on to international contemporary; fairs are crucial in this process.'[28] On the one hand, whether Indian buyers will diversify their collections by 'internationalising' them along the lines outlined above is too early to say—nor is a teleological view predicting the development of the Indian art market being endorsed here. On the other hand, an interview with Peter Sumner, the Indian art specialist at Phillips de Pury, reveals that:

> The buyers for Indian contemporary art are becoming increasingly global. Without question, there is always a strong trend among collectors to buy art from their own country as this art is often most relevant to their background, society and context. However, top Indian contemporary artists such as T.V. Santhosh, Atil Dodiya, Thukral and Thagra and Jitish Kallat employ techniques and explore themes that appeal to the global western audience, whilst maintaining an inherent Indian quality.[29]

Sumner goes on, saying that 'Indian art is collected mainly locally and by western art collectors and institutions' testifying to a degree of heterogeneity of the buyers.[30]

Where in the art objects' virtual and physical traffic it is their features of 'Indianness' which make them valuable locally and globally, it is suggested that this feature per se is not striking: rather, it is what this Indianness is the vehicle for in times of globalisation and neoliberal capital that is worth deciphering—that is the contents underneath Indianness *as* a representation of self and difference. Concerning the contemporary dynamics between capital investment and culture that emerge from a post-colonial context, the alignment of nation, commodity and buyer under the rubric of 'Indianness' is also suggestive of the avenues through which objects may acquire agentic power. Such an alignment places (Indian art) objects *in-between* Hicks and Beaudry's delineation of analytical paths conceiving objects either 'as fully agentive (Latour 1993a) or as the "indexes" of human agency (Gell 1998)'.[31] Understanding this *in-betweenness* requires a digression into the creation of modern Indian art as a market category (a creation which has subsequently also benefitted con-temporary art)—that is the ways in which objects produced by artists at a particular historical juncture are 'given agency' in the global art world—while gaining financial value in the market through their association with 'India'. In turn, understanding the relation between the agency of objects and makers through the mediation of large entities (India, nation) helps towards the understanding of how the relationship between art and market has engendered an *aesthetic of social and economic change*.

'The birth of a subject': a new commodity enters an old market

'Objects from India were used to construct an ecumene that went beyond national boundaries, though its cultural forms facilitated the reification of the nation-state.'[32] While the objects that Breckenridge refers to in her renowned article are those displayed in world exhibitions, there is a degree of resemblance with the ways modern and contemporary Indian art performs in the now global ecumene[33] and its possible reverberations on the nation-state. As suggested earlier, the core of the success of art objects lies in the marketing of their

Indianness. Following Appadurai, this article suggests that the construction and marketing of art objects are inscribed in the ways 'materiality and abstraction may inhabit one another in societies like India, in which the social life of things is both rich and undisciplined enough to allow a fuller analysis of their relationship'.[34] Appadurai then adds that:

> India, in spite of a growing and status-hungry middle class, is not yet a 'consumer society' in the Western sense. Thus, the materiality of objects in India is not yet completely penetrated by the logic of the market. That is to say, objects are not yet seen primarily as material repositories of monetary or exchange value. In the most advanced industrial economies, of which the United States is still in many ways the leader, objects have become fairly thoroughly colonized by the market.[35]

While India is not a consumer society in the western sense, as Appadurai states above, the 'yet' signals it is becoming one and is a promise for the future. However, with particular categories of commodities in view, such as art, India might be 'approaching' the condition of consumer society in the western sense. This article argues that the affirmation that 'the materiality of objects in India is not yet completely penetrated by the logic of the market' is being challenged by the very commodity status of modern and contemporary Indian art. But how did such art enter the global market scene?

Given the fast-shifting relations between the symbolic and financial value of Indian art objects, systematic investigations of this phenomenon in both the humanities and the social sciences are still largely missing. Unsurprisingly, however, modern and contemporary Indian art has attracted the attention of business academics—while business media closely follow art market trends. In 2010, two US-based management scholars, Khaire and Wadhwani, co-authored an article explaining the transformation of modern Indian art into a market category. These scholars argued that the Indian art which is now viewed as modern was produced from the early twentieth century until the 1980s, and was 'usually classified and traded (if at all) as part of the traditional or provincial art of the Subcontinent'.[36] The real change took place not so long ago: Khaire and Wadhwani contend that at the heart of Indian art's emergence lies the combined efforts of art historians and critics, who, between 1995 and 2007, re-classified twentieth century Indian art from being viewed as 'provincial or decorative' to 'modernist'.[37] These scholars also argued how auction houses built on this new classification to apply the same conventions which were used to assess western modernist works to Indian ones. In turn, this laid the foundations for Indian art's judgment of aesthetic value and price and aligned it with the global art world's standards. Subsequently, 'journalists, museums, and critics, institutionalized both the new categorical understanding of the art and the new criteria by which it was to be judged'.[38] By virtue of the creation of this market category, works by the generation of Indian painters labelled as modernist began to command large sums of money at auctions and other sales. Contemporary artists benefitted from the establishment of the category at the time of entering the art market.[39]

The creation of a market category took place within an established market system symbolised by the auction house. Like the case of Mumbai-based Saffronart, the institution of the auction house was to be appropriated and re-embedded locally.[40] In an interesting re-circulation of market institutions, Saffronart set up its offices in art market strongholds such as New York and London.[41] This phenomenon also points to the issue of time compression, by which the centuries-old western history of the art market and collecting has been appropriated in record time in a different geographical context.[42] The analysis of the appropriation of art market institutions is intimately connected to that of the relation between buyers and consumption. Drawing on the observation that 'consumption' is now used to name nearly all representations of self-expression or enjoyment, David Graeber has recently advocated the view of consumption, not as an analytical function, but as an ideology, and to:

> start looking at what we have been calling the 'consumption' sphere rather as the sphere of the production of human beings, not just as labor power but as persons, internalized nexes of meaningful social relations, because after all, this is what social life is actually about, the production of people (of which the production of things is simply a subordinate moment) [...].[43]

How Indian art consumption—as an extension of consumer culture—'produces people' and how this production differs from that arising from the consumption of other commodities will be probed through ethnographic investigation. Art complements the 'new sites of consumption' of housing property (for the development of gated communities), leisure and wellness in India, as analysed by Brosius.[44] In turn, if art and cultural consumption legitimise social difference,[45] research is needed to understand how art consumption performs as a novel status-production strategy among the Indian middle classes. More specifically, Bourdieu contended that:

> Of all the conversion techniques designed to create and accumulate symbolic capital, the purchase of works of art, objectified evidence of 'personal taste', is the one which is closest to the most irreproachable and inimitable form of accumulation, that is, the internalization of distinctive signs and symbols of power in the form of natural 'distinction', personal 'authority' or 'culture'.[46]

Where the art Bourdieu referred to consists of 'priceless works' in the context of French society at the time of writing, how art consumption works in a post-colonial context, and in times of the globalisation of the art market, how this squares up with the mass creation of artistic taste among Indian buyers, and whether art consumption is accorded the same power in terms of symbolic capital accumulation is largely unknown. As in the case of the appropriation of art market institutions, temporality issues are very relevant here too: the above phenomena are taking place at a very fast pace. Moreover, the megacity appears to be an additional important feature as it hosts new collectors and part of the infrastructure that allows Indian art to exist on a global scale as well as to be circulated and traded locally.

Research into the consumption of art objects as the 'production of people' will also shed light on the ways modern and contemporary Indian art 'rebrands' India, which, as stated previously, given the lack of government support, is being carried out by private enterprise. Rebranding would not have taken place without the process of liberalisation of the Indian economy that has been vigorously pursued since the 1990s, with the emergence of the new middle classes, and the subsequent creation of a market category which has turned existing artistic expressions into global commodities. India's entry into the art market has signalled the country's economic growth and its global modernity. This raises different questions from those surrounding the anxieties about the preservation of national cultural boundaries against contamination by Euro-American culture which enlivened early debates on globalisation in India. The phenomenon of modern and contemporary Indian art suggests the need for a more plural reading on the ways the global conjugates the post-colonial and vice versa. The art brought together by the 'Empire Strikes Back' exhibition is an entry point to explore this nexus in conjunction with that between materiality and contemporaneity. Concerning the latter, not only does the exhibition address Empire, but a large section of it portrays India's new social, economic and political conjuncture: a journey into the exhibition will look at the interplay between the encompassing national container and its representational devices.

India as a catalogue?

World Fairs mixed commerce with culture in a mode that was then innovative, even radical.[47]

As expectations were built around the exhibition for its potential to revitalise the downturn in the fortunes of Indian art, 'The Empire Strikes Back: Indian Art Today' could well be considered as a post-Empire 'commerce cum culture' enterprise.[48] At the Saatchi Gallery 'The Empire Strikes Back' was preceded by exhibitions such as 'The Revolution Continues: New Chinese Art' (2008–2009) and 'Unveiled: New Art from the Middle East' (2009), in which new artistic production was anchored to national backgrounds. This has not only been the case for non-western art however. 'The Empire Strikes Back' is an ensemble from the personal collection of Charles Saatchi[49] who personally curated the exhibition.[50] This included art by a new generation of artists, 27 in total, of whom some were born in India, some had never travelled outside the country, while some were born in the diaspora as well as in Pakistan. Both established contemporary artists and emerging ones were present—the former and their artwork forming a now familiar visual landscape symbolising contemporary art from India.

The author of the exhibition catalogue, Zehra Jumabhoy, has pointed out Indian artists' changing relation with India:[51] she observed that famous artists are no longer based full-time in India, while artists from the diaspora are setting up their exhibitions in South Asia and are boasting of their links with this region.[52] Jumabhoy also remarked on the transformation of the Indian art world during the early 2000s: art has benefitted from the creation of gallery spaces[53] and the possibility to produce large-scale art within India. The figure of the contemporary artist and art-making as a new profession—with ateliers and teams of assistants firmly established as a global practice—also invokes comparative reflections *vis-à-vis* the long-standing history of art-making in India. Jumabhoy also offered reflections on the crucial question of identity: 'It is difficult to know now what makes an artist "Indian"'.[54] On the one hand, the world-famous Mumbai-born British artist Anish Kapoor—who was not part of the exhibition at the Saatchi Gallery, and who has resisted the association of his oeuvre with 'Indian identity'—exhibited his work for the first time in India in November 2010. A BBC article states 'He pointed out that an artist should be defined by ability to create and invent and not by country of origin.'[55] On the other hand, in 'The Empire Strikes Back', a sense of imminent teleology is generated between the artist's Indian (and South Asian) identity, her/his engagement in representing India and the charged exhibition theme. Reflecting on whether the artwork could have been made by an Indian artist, an Indian diaspora artist or one who has never set foot in India, an exhibition reviewer asked '[...]how Indian is their art?'.[56] Another reviewer depicted the exhibition as follows: 'It's modern art, but not as we know it: imagery in a strictly localized dialect, which offers a heart-warmingly honest and erudite depiction of an India for the twenty-first century.'[57]

If the reviewer's collective speaking subject 'we' does not seem to place this exhibition of Indian art within the 'universal' domain of contemporary art,

FIGURE 1. Pushpamala N. and Clare Arni. From the ethnographic series Native Women of South India: Manners & Customs, 2000–2004 (supported by an Arts Collaboration Grant from the India Foundation for the Arts).
Notes: Medium: set of 45 sepia-toned silver gelatin prints; Dimensions: variable.
Source: Image courtesy of Saatchi Gallery, London. (c) Pushpamala N. and Clare Arni, 2010.

the themes dealt with in the exhibition engage with universal themes as mediated through the life in the subcontinent. Wrapped by Jitish Kallat's vibrant representation of street children (see Figure 6), the exhibition's catalogue offers images of the colonial era—ranging from post-1857 mutiny to imperial durbars—in lieu of overture. As mentioned earlier, the exhibition was as much about revisiting colonialism as visiting the present: in addition to Empire, the themes of poverty, migration, democracy contested national boundaries, labour, urbanisation, religious violence, gender roles, among others, were 'talked about'. The ways in which they were talked about offer a powerful visual shift to the public:

FIGURE 2. Pushpamala N. and Clare Arni. From the ethnographic series Native Women of South India: Manners & Customs, 2000–2004 (supported by an Arts Collaboration Grant from the India Foundation for the Arts).
Notes: Medium: set of 45 sepia-toned silver gelatin prints; Dimensions: variable.
Source: Image courtesy of Saatchi Gallery, London. (c) Pushpamala N. and Clare Arni, 2010.

'They are certainly not purely decorative works which fit in with our notion of Indian art, which is of beautiful miniature paintings, for example', said Rebecca Wilson, associate director of the Saatchi Gallery. 'This is showing a whole other side of India and it's not surprising that the artists are engaging with things to do with migration, poverty, slums and refuse', she added.[58]

What follows is a selection of the representation of a number of the above themes. The first is a photograph by Pushpamala and Arni (Figure 1).

The photograph shown in Figure 1 teases the colonial anthropometric projects, which—together with the institution of the census—profoundly reshaped the sociology of the subcontinent, with the consolidation of caste boundaries and the construction of social categories. From the same series, Figure 2 showcases a playful subversion of gender roles: while a woman dressed in a sari would never be seen playing cricket in India, the intentional creation of the 'social mismatch' between an image of Indian femininity and playing this sport opens up alternative spaces for gendered agency.

It is highly symbolic that 'The Empire Strikes Back' exhibition took place at the heart of the former Empire. Place fills the following art piece with much evocative power: 'Public Notice 2' (Figure 3) by Jitish Kallat refers to the famous speech that Gandhi made in 1930 just before embarking on the protest march against the British salt tax, at the height of the anti-British struggle. An example of re-narration of historical events through art, the

FIGURE 3. Jitish Kallat. Public Notice 2, 2007.
Notes: Fibreglass sculptures; Dimensions variable.
Source: Courtesy of the Saatchi Gallery, London. (c) Jitish Kallat, 2010.

speech is composed of 4479 fibreglass bone-shaped letters. Here, the message of non-violence and civil disobedience preached by Gandhi emerges against the violence of colonial rule.

FIGURE 4. Mansoor Ali. Dance of Democracy, 2008.
Notes: Installation with discarded chairs; Dimensions variable, approx. 427 x 244 x 244.
Source: Image courtesy of Saatchi Gallery, London. (c) Mansoor Ali, 2010.

FIGURE 5. Subodh Gupta. U.F.O., 2007.
Notes: Brass utensils; Dimensions 114 x 305 x 305 cm.
Source: Image courtesy of Saatchi Gallery, London. (c) Subodh Gupta, 2010.

Made with discarded chairs, 'Dance of Democracy' by Mansoor Ali (Figure 4) is a representation of the largest democracy in the world, but also of its complexity and realpolitik. In common parlance, *kursi*, chair in Hindi, is a metaphor for the pursuit of political power.

FIGURE 6. Jitish Kallat. Eclipse 3, 2007
Notes: Acrylic on canvas, triptych; Dimensions 274 x 518 cm.
Source: Image courtesy of Saatchi Gallery, London. (c) Jitish Kallat, 2010.

FIGURE 7. Jitish Kallat. Death of Distance, 2007.
Notes: Black lead on fibreglass, rupee coin and five lenticular prints; Dimensions: Sculpture 161 cm diameter; Prints 46 x 60 cm.
Source: Courtesy of the Saatchi Gallery, London. (c) Jitish Kallat, 2010.

Assembled with brass water vessels, 'U.F.O.' (Figure 5) is a creation by Subodh Gupta, an artist famous for, among other things, turning everyday stainless steel objects, which are so much part of the quotidian in India, into art. 'U.F.O.' is a statement on 'the Indian migrant worker's dream of escape'.[59]

If 'U.F.O.' evokes outer space, 'Eclipse 3' by Jitish Kallat (Figure 6) depicts street children and takes the viewer back to the realities on the ground. The exhibition also hosted a large-scale sculpture by the same artist of a child with a bloated stomach because of hunger selling books at traffic lights—evoking a common sight in urban India.

While poverty becomes the inspiration for aesthetic production, Jitish Kallat's 'Death of Distance' (Figure 7) points to the tragedy of development in neoliberal India versus the benefits of affordable technology offered by corporations. Looking at the prints from one angle, the viewer reads about a phone company offering one rupee a minute call charges, which would connect far ends of the country with one another. When the viewer looks at the prints from the opposite angle, these narrate the suicide of a girl who needed one rupee to pay for her school meal: scolded by her mother who could not give her the meal fees as a result of poverty, the girl hanged herself.

Conclusions

Could 'The Empire Strikes Back' exhibition be read as a post-Empire vendetta? Whether this exhibition can be conceived so—or whether it was ever envisioned as such—is uncertain. One of the exhibited sculptures, 'The Orientalist' by Huma Bhabha, is described as conveying 'ideas of exoticism, difference, and otherness. Equally primitive and futuristic, Bhabha's figure theatrically poses as an ominous king or deity. Cast in bronze, it sits as an imposing relic from a fictional history.'[60] And surely the orientalist feels as such. But even with her/his demise and that of the orientalist project, and the re-narration of the agency of the colonial powers shown by the artwork discussed above, vendettas might not take place without a veil of ambivalence. In her exhibition review, Joanna Pitman asks: '[...] who is this politically motivated art for? In a flash contemporary gallery on London's King's Road, you wonder whether these artists are shouting at the already converted'.[61] Combine the above with the following statement from the Saatchi Gallery and additional aspects of this ambivalence will come to light: 'The rapid flourishing of this art scene on one hand and the recent economic downturn on the other have prompted critical questions about Indian culture and globalisation in a country torn between a proudly independent mindset and a dependence on global consumption'.[62] Concerning the tension within the nation, the permeability of its cultural boundaries and globalisation, if the 'west' might not be a central concern when artists engage with India or other visual landscapes, 'west' has often provided the infrastructure for Indian art to scale up to a global level, while artists have capitalised on its schools and material resources and have been legitimised by their relation with it and by their ties with galleries and auction houses. However, the horizons of the global art world increasingly encompass much more than the 'west' alone, with art fairs, biennales and exhibitions being organised in Asia and the Middle East for example. In addition, where Indian art's portrayal of India departs from previous aesthetic canons, the artists are representing India for audiences different to those of previous historical periods. Saloni Mathur has finely captured the process through which representations of India were made to suit western taste in the cultural domains of Empire.[63] By contrast, even if a number of western collectors purchase modern and contemporary Indian art, this appears to be mainly appealing to buyers from India and of Indian descent living abroad.

What does this node of complex trends suggest about the relationship between distressing social development indicators and Indian art auctions introduced at the beginning of this article? Interestingly, the socio-political and cultural engagement present in the art exhibited at 'The Empire Strikes Back' goes hand in hand with the growth of gross domestic product—even with its figures being revised downward—and with the widening gap between the poor and the middle classes. Art objects insinuate this scenario both as a new commodity and as a novel narrative device of socio-economic change. Where the exhibition showcases forms of artistic production engendered by economic growth within India and the Indian diaspora, the representational agency displayed at the Saatchi Gallery shows a number of elements at play: first, the exhibition viewer is not in the presence of a 'counter-gaze', that is, art is not about India looking outwards and offering representations of the other other-than-self. It is actually the former 'other', India, portraying itself. Like a great deal of contemporary Indian art, 'The Empire Strikes Back' is an introspective lens on India and South Asia—with histories, people and objects being represented and presented to global audiences—for a price of course. Second, the former 'other' appears to be portraying its contemporary 'others': the child at the traffic light, the casual labourer and the migrant, among others. Thinking of the multitude of forms of identity politics within India and transnationally—gender, caste and religion-based—these cultural others seem strikingly 'identity-free'.

In the exhibition, the socio-economic indicators that Ahmad had pointed to as going hand in hand with the promising cultural trends of Indian art's entry into the circuit of the global market may be rejoined through the commodification of art:[64] it suffices to envision Indian buyers of Indian art deploying their capital to acquire representations of child poverty in India, for example, and showcase them in their homes. Object, representation and buyer come together in an act of consumption. As images of the 'Third World' enter the homes of those who benefitted from development and economic liberalisation, the aestheticisation of poverty and its end result might lead to a capitulation in favour of the 'India-as-a-land-of-contrasts' argument. However, if the 'Third World' is recast under new aesthetic semblances, phenomena such as sexual violence, to recall Ahmad's passage, know no class, religion or community. Dowry deaths and female foeticide are actually phenomena associated with rising wealth.[65] So the land-of-contrasts argument appears to be defeated on this very ground—or rather, wealth has opened up new grounds for the multiplication of inequality and violence, its beneficiaries included among the victims.

'The Empire Strikes Back' exhibition, and more broadly contemporary Indian art, are sites for self-representation and soul-searching about what is 'India' and 'Indianness' today. And given its nascent status as a market category and the relatively young career of the objects journeying to exhibitions, as well as other cultural and business manifestations both in India and globally, whether 'Indian art' re- or de-exoticises 'India' in the eyes of its diverse constituencies of buyers and viewers—and what this ultimately says about the production of new post-colonial difference(s)—is a question that only time will be able to answer. For the time being, what is unmissable is the artistic renaissance that neoliberal capital has engendered.

Acknowledgements

Earlier versions of this article were presented at the workshop 'Asian countries as exhibited at World Expositions: revisited in a global historical perspective' at the International Institute for Asian Studies (IIAS), Leiden, 2 July 2010; at the panel 'Governing difference' at the conference 'Asian diversity in a global context', University of Copenhagen, 12–13 November 2010; at the SERIS seminar on 25 October 2011 and at the 'Visual culture in contemporary India' workshop, 8–9 December 2011, both held at Aarhus University. I wish to thank YoungSoo Yook and Ravinder Kaur and the audiences at the above events for they all provided invaluable comments and suggestions. Moreover, I would like to express my deepest gratitude to the Indiana University Center for the Study of Global Change for the award of a Framing the Global Fellowship (2011–2014) for the project entitled 'Modern and contemporary Indian art and the global: culture, capital, and the development of post-colonial taste': research for this project will allow me to take further the questions developed in this article.

Notes

1 A Appadurai, 'The thing itself', *Public Culture*, 18(1), 2006, p 18.
2 A Ahmad, 'Cultures in conflict', *Frontline*, 14(16), 1997, at http://hinduonnet.com/fline/fl1416/14160760.htm, accessed 18 September 2010.
3 I am not implying that Ahmad endorses this argument.
4 This article focuses on an exhibition of contemporary Indian art. However, as discussed later in the text, its entry into the global art world is linked to the rise in visibility and market value of modern Indian art. Moreover, as a specialist in modern and contemporary Indian and Southeast Asian art at Sotheby's, Priyanka Mathew has stated: 'The distinction between modern and contemporary South Asian art is not a formal one, but rather a qualification created by galleries to catalogue artists who worked in different time periods' (P Mathew, 'State of the art', *India Today*, 25 March 2011, at http://indiatoday.intoday.in/site/story/state-of-the-art/1/133354.html, accessed 8 August 2011).
5 IndiaArtConnect, Vol. 1, June 2009, at http://www.karmayog.org/info/upload/24709/India%20Art%20Connect-Newsletter-June%202009.pdf, accessed 14 June 2010.
6 R G Shah, 'India's online auction pioneers', 2010, at http://www.nytimes.com/2010/09/08/arts/08iht-rartsaffron.html?_r=1, accessed 7 September 2010.
7 M Collett-White, 'China overtakes Britain in art market: report', 2011, at http://www.reuters.com/article/2011/03/14/us-market-china-idUSTRE72D5EW20110314, accessed 10 December 2011.

IDENTITY, INEQUITY AND INEQUALITY IN INDIA AND CHINA

8 *Ibid.*

9 I analyse the presence of the India pavilion at the Venice Biennale in a separate article.

10 See J Boloten 'The state of the global art market 2011', public lecture at the London School of Economics, 23 February 2011, http://www2.lse.ac.uk/newsAndMedia/videoAndAudio/channels/public LecturesAndEvents/player.aspx?id=898, podcast accessed on 24 February 2011.

11 One of first private art museums in India, the Kiran Nadar Museum of Art (KNMA), opened in New Delhi in January 2011 (http://www.knma.in/about.asp). It hosts an impressive collection of modern and contemporary art. Concerning public museums of contemporary art, there has been a delayed response to the new artistic wave in India.

12 Between 29 January 2010 and 8 May 2010, the exhibition recorded 407,796 visitors (http://www.saatchi-gallery.co.uk/, accessed 3 December 2011).

13 M Hardt & A Negri, *Empire*, Cambridge, MA, Harvard University Press, 2000.

14 J Burbank & F Cooper, *Empires in World History: Power and the Politics of Difference*, Princeton, NJ, Princeton University Press, 2010.

15 Ahmad, 'Cultures in conflict'.

16 R G Shah, 'Not just modern art, but Indian', 2011, at http://www.nytimes.com/2011/03/04/arts/04iht-rartindia04.html?pagewanted=all, accessed 20 March 2011.

17 M L Pratt, *Imperial Eyes. Travel Writing and Transculturation*, New York/London, Routledge, 2008 [1992].

18 B Anderson, *Imagined Communities: Reflections on the Origin and Spread of Nationalism*, London, Verso, 1983.

19 B Winther-Tamaki, *Art in the Encounter of Nations: Japanese and American Artists in the Early Postwar Years*, Honolulu, University of Hawaii Press, 2001, p 7.

20 If this form of investment is relatively new in India, elsewhere it has been a standard practice, see D Harvey, *The Enigma of Capital and the Crises of Capitalism*, London, Profile Books, 2010, p 21, on post-1980s investments in asset values including art.

21 J Ganesan, 'Let your mouse take you on an artistic journey', 2011, at http://www.tehelka.com/story_main51.asp?filename=Ws231111Art.asp, accessed 27 November 2011.

22 A Sawhney, 'Mall-titude of artworks', 2010, at http://www.hindustantimes.com/StoryPage/Print/637898.aspx, accessed 27 November 2011.

23 C Howorth, 'The Sotheby's of India', 2010, at http://www.thedailybeast.com/blogs-and-stories/2010-11-06/indias-online-auction-house/, accessed 7 November 2010.

24 N Susan, 'Another cultural revolution?', 2008, at http://www.tehelka.com/story_main40.asp?filename=hub081108another_cultural.asp, accessed 19 May 2010.

25 K Crow, 'The China factor', 2011, at http://online.wsj.com/article_email/SB100014240529702034768045766130503736962701MyQjAxMTAxMDAwNzEwNDcyWj.html?mod=wsj_share_email, accessed 20 October 2011.

26 *Ibid.*

27 G Adam, 'Starting local, going global', *The Art Newspaper*, 2011, at http://www.theartnewspaper.com/articles/Starting%20local,%20going%20global/23996, accessed 4 November 2011.

28 *Ibid.*, accessed 9 November 2011.

29 H Suroor, 'Indian art goes global', 2010, at http://beta.thehindu.com/opinion/columns/Hasan_Suroor/article405538.ece, accessed 23 April 2010.

30 *Ibid.*

31 D Hicks & C M Beaudry, 'Introduction. Material culture studies: a reactionary view', in D Hicks & M C Beaudry (eds), *The Oxford Handbook of Material Culture Studies*, Oxford, Oxford University Press, 2010, pp 1–21, at http://weweremodern.blogspot.com/2010/05/material-culture-studies-introduction.html, accessed 20 May 2011.

32 C Breckenridge, 'The world on exhibition. The aesthetics and politics of colonial collecting: India at World Fairs', *Comparative Study in Society and History*, 31(2), 1989, p 214.

33 U Hannerz, 'Notes on the global ecumene', *Public Culture*, 1(2), 1989, pp 66–75.

34 Appadurai, 'The thing itself', 18.

35 *Ibid.*

36 M Khaire & R D Wadhwani, 'Changing landscapes: the construction of meaning and value in a new market category—modern Indian art', *Academy of Management Journal*, 53(6), 2010, p 1289.

37 *Ibid.*, p 1282.

38 *Ibid.*

39 For a study of the performance in online auctions of both Indian artists classified as established (born in the first quarter of the twentieth century) and emerging ones (born after 1955), see S K Reddy & M Dass, 'Modeling on-line art auction dynamics using functional data analysis', *Statistical Science*, 21(2), 2006, pp 179–193.

40 In China, the houses Poly Auction and China Guardian Auctions were created.

41 Shah, 'India's online auction pioneers'.

IDENTITY, INEQUITY AND INEQUALITY IN INDIA AND CHINA

42 This appropriation needs to be analysed *vis-à-vis* the broader cultural economic context of the art trade in Indian history, of the status of art as a commodity, its relations to capital, princely patronage and the colonial era.

43 D Graeber, 'Consumption', *Current Anthropology*, 52(4), 2011, p 502.

44 C Brosius, *India's Middle Class. New Forms of Urban Leisure, Consumption and Prosperity*, New Delhi/London, Routledge, 2010.

45 P Bourdieu, *Distinctions: A Social Critique of the Judgement of Taste* (trans. R Nice), New York, Routledge, 2003 [1984], p 7.

46 *Ibid.*, p 282.

47 Breckenridge, 'The world on exhibition', 212.

48 See C Gleadell, 'Indian art: a taste for Saatchi's hot favourites', 2010, at http://www.telegraph.co.uk/culture/art/art-reviews/7078106/Indian-art-A-taste-for-Saatchis-hot-favourites.html, accessed 25 May 2010.

49 For a market analysis of the artwork acquired by Saatchi and later exhibited at 'The Empire Strikes Back', see *Ibid.*

50 Email communication from the Saatchi Gallery, London Press Officer, 23 July 2010.

51 Z Jumabhoy, 'Introduction', in *The Empire Strikes Back. Indian Art Today*, London, Jonathan Cape Random House, 2010, p 56.

52 *Ibid.*, p 64.

53 *Ibid.*, p 74.

54 *Ibid.*, p 64.

55 P Pinglay, 'First Anish Kapoor exhibition is staged in India', 2010, at http://www.bbc.co.uk/news/world-south-asia-11868762, accessed 2 December 2010.

56 M Hudson, 'It's modern India, but it's not all Indian', 2010, at http://www.saatchi-gallery.co.uk/current/india_reviews/Empire-SundayMail-7Feb2010.jpg, accessed 20 May 2010.

57 K Weir, 'The Empire Strikes Back at the Saatchi gallery', *Indian Art News*, 2 February 2010, at http://www.indianartnews.com/2010/02/empire-strikes-back-at-saatchi-gallery.html, accessed 20 April 2010.

58 M Collett-White, 'Indian art show tackles Gandhi, war and poverty', 2010, at http://in.reuters.com/article/2010/01/29/exhibition-india-saatchi-idINLDE60R2F620100129, accessed 30 May 2010.

59 A M Di Brina, 'Visions of India', 2010, at http://www.newstatesman.com/blogs/cultural-capital/2010/02/india-art-saatchi-women, accessed 30 June 2010.

60 http://www.saatchi-gallery.co.uk/artists/artpages/huma_bhabha_orientalist3.htm, accessed 25 June 2010.

61 J Pitman, 'Caste in the bleakest of lights', 2010, at http://www.saatchi-gallery.co.uk/current/india_reviews/Empire-Times-29Jan2010.jpg, accessed 20 June 2010.

62 Press Association, 'UK gallery holds Indian art expo', at http://www.pressassociation.com/component/pafeeds/2010/01/29/uk_gallery_holds_indian_art_expo?camefrom=india, accessed 30 June 2010.

63 S Mathur, *India by Design. Colonial History and Cultural Display*, Berkeley, University of California Press, 2007.

64 Ahmad, 'Cultures in conflict'.

65 Judging by the preliminary data released from Census 2011, these trends continue unabated.

Notes on contributor

Manuela Ciotti is Assistant Professor in Global Studies at Aarhus University. Her research interests range from modernity, gender and politics, and subaltern communities (Dalits) in India to art and the global. She is the author of several articles in leading journals and of *Retro-modern India. Forging the Low-caste Self* (2010), *Political Agency and Gender in India* (forthcoming) and *Femininities and Masculinities in Indian Politics* (forthcoming).

Making Gujarat Vibrant: *Hindutva*, development and the rise of subnationalism in India

TOMMASO BOBBIO

ABSTRACT *A significant aspect of India's postcolonial history has been the rise of subnationalism—popularly addressed as the challenge of regionalism—which has often pitted the Indian state against the regional centres of power. In fact, the organisation of Indian territory along linguistic lines favoured the emergence of regional movements challenging the authority of the central government in arguments typical of nationalist rhetoric, such as the specificity of language, territory and traditions. This notion of subnation, however, has taken a new turn during the past two decades of neoliberal reforms as regional states compete with each other to attract greater foreign and domestic investment and to secure higher growth rates. Taking as a point of departure the case of 'Vibrant Gujarat', this article proposes rethinking the emergence of subnational cultures in the past two decades in the light of the effects of the neoliberal economic reforms and the rise of Hindu extremist movements in the political arena.*

From 1991 onwards the progressive opening of India's economy to foreign and private investment, and the further devolution of competences to the single governments in terms of economic policies, enhanced a competition among states to secure the highest share of private investment and capital.[1] In this context Gujarat came forth as one of the model-states for this type of development pattern. In applying neoliberal directives, the government of Gujarat emphasised aspects such as the deregulation of the labour market, the creation of special economic zones (SEZ), and forms of tax relief to companies choosing to invest in the state. In this way it secured high levels of private investment, and became the state recording the highest rate of growth of per capita income among the 16 major states in the post-1991 reforms period. Such patterns of economic growth underpinned the creation of a discourse around 'progress' and 'modernisation', in which the middle classes were seen as the protagonists of a sort of social and economic revolution that projected Gujarat in the global world. In particular, since the early 2000s, the rise of the Bharatiya Janata Party (BJP) leader Narendra Modi to the chief

Tommaso Bobbio is an independent scholar from Italy.

ministership of the state marked a turn both in the way development projects were enacted and in the way these were advertised to the general public and the media.

When he inaugurated the first 'Vibrant Gujarat Global Investors' Summit', in September 2003, Chief Minister Modi outlined the main political lines through which he sought to lead the state of Gujarat in a new era of economic development and growth. The launch of the Summit was conceived as part of his new political strategy. The initiative represented the effort, on the part of the state government, to carve out a role for Gujarat in the competitive landscape of India's post-reform economy. At the same time it was meant to focus public and media attention on the economic and development policies enacted by the government of Gujarat.

The timing of the summit is noteworthy. In 2003 the state was still shaken by the consequences of the anti-Muslim pogroms that had taken place, with the complicity of the local government, one year before. The Assembly Elections in November 2002 had been fought entirely around the alleged responsibility of the BJP government for allowing widespread massacres of Muslim civilians all over Gujarat. In this scenario the party obtained a landslide victory, which represented also a tremendous personal success for Narendra Modi. The Chief Minister, who was known to be a *Hindutva* hard-liner, had toured the state extensively, holding rallies in hundreds of villages and towns. During the campaign, named the *Gaurav Yatra* (Procession for Pride), Modi turned upside down all the arguments that the media, opposition parties and human rights associations had thrown at him and his government. According to his rhetoric those who pointed the finger against the brutalities perpetrated against Muslims were in fact accusing the whole population of Gujarat of being murderers, religious fanatics and the like.[2] While setting up a defensive argument for himself and his party, Modi sought to address 'the people of Gujarat' as a whole, implicitly enclosing in this group only the Hindus.

While this kind of propaganda proved effective in terms of electoral results, soon after the election Narendra Modi apparently shifted the scope of his political agenda from a blatant communal platform to a more inclusive, development-oriented one.

The summit was to be the store-window to advertise the state as the best place in India to invest capital. In order to do this, the government shaped a campaign around three main points: first, Modi's cabinet was a model of good governance, so all procedures for allowing private investment were simple and secure; secondly private investors would be granted fiscal benefits for investing in the state; thirdly thanks to the inherited attitude to business and to social harmony of the Gujarati population, private investors would find Gujarat the ideal environment to start new economic activities.

Thanks to the success of the first Vibrant Gujarat event, the summit has been repeated on a biennial basis, with increasing success in terms of participation from both institutional and private subjects, and in terms of the amount of investment determined through memoranda of understanding (MOU). Over the years Modi's rhetoric has increasingly centred on an argument that tends to emphasise cultural and social elements as determinant in making Gujarat the best place to invest in. In this frame, the idea of a so-called 'Gujarati ethos' emerged as a pivotal element to describe the local society as naturally oriented to business: 'Gujarat is a land of entrepreneurs', as Modi claimed during his inaugural speech to the 2011 summit.[3]

At several times in postcolonial India local politicians have made an assertive use of local, or subnational, feelings to gather electoral consent.[4] What makes the construction of an idea of 'Gujaratiness' unique is its equation with propaganda around economic development in the frame of the rise of Hindu extremism in the state.[5] This gave to the subnational idea an intrinsic exclusive character, deriving from two different elements. On one side, the 'natural orientation to business' of the Gujarati population referred to the traditional milieu of high-caste Hindu and Jain traders of urban Gujarat, thus conferring on the subnational idea a defined Hindu tint. On the other side, fashioning the Gujarati identity in the light of a neoliberal conception of economic development referred directly to an imagined model of a globalised middle class milieu, while implicitly endorsing a culture of intolerance towards those sectors of society which are left behind by this economic model.[6]

This article explores the historical roots and contemporary success of the subnational Gujarati culture, in relation to rise of the BJP as the undisputed political force in the state since the 1990s. Through a historical investigation of the elements that contributed to delimiting the boundaries of present-day Gujarati subnationalism, the following analysis highlights the role that this kind of rhetoric had in fostering the emergence of an aggressive, self-assertive public culture in urban Gujarat.

Origins of Gujarati subnationalism: Maha Gujarat *Andolan* (1956–60)

Although regional stereotypes have been encapsulated in rhetoric around economic development and the so-called upper-caste Hindu traditions of the Gujarati culture, the emergence of subnational ideas in the political arena is not a phenomenon confined to the last two decades of the twentieth century. Strong echoes of the political use of regional cultural stereotypes can be found in the early days of India's independence, when Gujarat was still part of the Bombay state and urban middle classes started demanding the creation of a separate state enclosing the Gujarati-speaking communities.

The movement advocating the creation of a state of Gujarat, which took the name of 'Maha Gujarat Andolan' (Movement for a great state of Gujarat), became part of the controversy involving the Union Government and the Congress Party over the territorial reorganisation of the Indian territory, in the wake of Independence. At that time the territory of present-day Gujarat was split between the Sauhrashtra princely states, including the Saurashtra peninsula and Kachchh, and the state of Bombay, which merged part of Gujarat with Maharashtra and part of present Karnataka.

The controversy started within the Congress Party, soon after the formation of the first Nehru government in 1947, as the administrative organisation of the Indian state was to be resettled, either along linguistic or territorial lines. According to the first principle, linguistic divisions would have granted equal access to jobs in the public services as well as the creation of an administrative system that was comprehensible to most citizens. Conversely, the criterion of organising the territory in wider regions, merging together areas with different linguistic groups, and thus establishing a common language for the whole administrative system, would have simplified the reorganisation of the political map of India by dividing its territory into five or six states. This organisation would also have answered the fear that, in the long run, a division along linguistic lines could foster separatist or autonomist feelings among local elites.[7]

Within the bilingual Bombay State, controversy over the reorganisation of the territory increasingly focused around the destination of the city of Bombay after the supposed division of the state. While belonging 'traditionally' to a Marathi-speaking area, the city was the headquarters of a strong community of Gujarati and Parsi traders and businessmen. The Samyukta Maharashtra Samiti (United Maharashtra Committee) had started organising agitations in the late 1940s to ask for the creation of a Marathi-speaking state, with Bombay as its capital.[8] In 1952 a group of intellectuals and professionals representing the Gujarati-speaking people organised the first Maha Gujarat Conference in Ahmedabad: meant to be a public answer to the agitation in Maharashtra, the conference became the first moment in which leading personalities in the city advanced the request for a state of Gujarat.[9]

At the end of 1955 Nehru announced the decision to implement a plan to divide Bombay state into two monolingual units, Gujarat and Maharashtra, and to grant the city of Bombay the status of Union Territory, under the direct administration of the central government. However, this plan triggered off large protests in Bombay: leaders of the Samyukta Maharashtra Samiti were immediately arrested and the police opened fire over the demonstrators, killing more than 80 people.[10] Partly as a consequence of the riots, and partly as the result of cross-party parliamentary opposition, Nehru's government withdrew the three-state resolution and, on 8 August 1956, sanctioned the maintenance of a bilingual Bombay state, as part of the States Reorganisation Act.[11] This date marked the beginning of the agitations in Ahmedabad and other cities of Gujarat. Students, workers and political activists from the Praja Socialist Party and the Communist Party started a series of demonstrations in the streets.

During the peak of the agitation (8–13 August 1956), leaders from the various groups formed a united front under the banner of the Maha Gujarat Janata Parishad (Maha Gujarat People's Association), with the intent of giving an organised form to the protests. The Association concentrated its activity in direct opposition to the central government and the Congress party, especially against the figure of Morarji Desai, the 'supreme leader' of Gujarat Congress. At an organisational level the Parishad sought to mobilise the Ahmedabad citizenry using a highly symbolic vocabulary. The Parishad appealed to the collective emotion generated by the death of young students and workers from the police shooting. In the language of the agitators the victims became 'martyrs' (*shahid*) and the celebration of a 'martyr's day' (*shahid din*) had a central role from the beginning of the movement. The decision to create a bilingual state was challenged on the ground that the Gujarati-speakers comprised roughly 33 per cent of the total population of the bilingual state. The language issue was then channelled into people's fear of becoming marginalised in their own territory, as if a second type of foreign rule would be imposed upon the Gujarati population.

When the emotional wave of the protest faded, under the leadership of Indulal Yagnik, the Maha Gujarat Janata Parishad entered a new phase, in which it focused more on an institutional strategy, oriented at transforming people's support into votes and then at bringing the protest onto the official ground of parliamentary politics, both at the state and at the national level. Such a strategy, which eventually led to the creation of the state of Gujarat in 1960, was characterised by a lower level of violence and sanctioned the emergence and consolidation of a new class of politicians, either drawn from the lines of dissident Congressmen and from the leftist parties, or from the milieu of young middle-class college students. Behind the presence of a leader like Indulal Yagnik, whose moral authority among the people of Ahmedabad had consolidated during the struggle and remained unaffected until his death in 1972, many activists of the Parishad emerged as future leading figures in the state's political arena. People like Chimanbhai Patel, who became president of the Gujarat branch of the Congress (I) and controversial chief minister of the state (1973–74 and 1990–94), and Ashok Bhatt, one of the leaders of the BJP and a *Hindutva* hardliner within his party, took their first steps in the political life of Gujarat as members of the Maha Gujarat Janata Parishad.

The Maha Gujarat movement fostered the consolidation of subnational symbols in the political rhetoric of Gujarat. Many of the seeds planted during that movement can be seen in the kind of subnational rhetoric that emerged in the political life of Gujarat towards the end of the past century. The ideological platform of the movement consolidated the notion, widely shared among urban middle classes in the state, of a Gujarati identity defined through language, territory and history. From the creation of the state onwards, the memory of the movement has been thoroughly institutionalised, as for instance through the construction of a monument in the centre of Ahmedabad city, or through the institution of a memorial day which is widely attended by local politicians. Thus, if Maha Gujarat represents the first step in the assertion of a specificity of local people within India, the present claim for a Gujarati *ethos* can be seen, in continuity with the previous movement, as the revival of a local identity in a 'globalised', Hindu version.

From 'Maha' to 'Vibrant' Gujarat (1980s–2000s)

During the 1980s the impact of the crisis that laid waste to the whole textile industrial sector in Ahmedabad and Surat had the proportions of a catastrophe. Nearly one-third of the population of Ahmedabad was dependent on the mills for its income and resided in areas that had grown up around the industries.[12] Moreover, the industrial crisis forced local and state administrators to redesign economic and planning strategies in order to favour the establishment of new private enterprises in the city. In this context the 1991 New Industrial Policy (NIP), adopted by the central government and applied differently by single states, provided the opportunity for the Gujarat government to plan economic development through the privatisation of services and the liberalisation of investment in the state.[13] By the end of the 1990s, projects of urban development and new infrastructure building sought to transform Ahmedabad in the state's storefront for promoting private investment. In the political and public debate the image of a globalised city was gradually substituted for that of an industrial city.

As a result of this process, during the 1990s the state of Gujarat improved its economic record, climbing up the national rankings relating to economic growth and average income to consolidate its image as one of the healthiest economies in the Indian Union, although its ranking with regard to social indicators, such as literacy (especially for women), infant mortality and child labour, remained poor.[14] For large sectors of the urban middle class, which had more access to higher education and could enter the labour market as a highly skilled workforce, the economic reforms opened new chances and better paid jobs. For these sectors privatisation and liberalisation became opportunities for upward mobility.[15] Large cities attracted the largest share of investment and developed as economic centres based on financial and service-based activities. Being the largest city of Gujarat, Ahmedabad attracted consistent investment in the industrial (mainly pharmaceutical and chemical), the financial and the construction sectors. The image of an economic success thus began to overcome the shadow of the textile industry crisis. Political forces and mass media depicted the reconstruction of the city's economy in the 1990s, from an industrial to a financial base, as a positive strategy that was dragging the city out of the crisis of the previous decade. Such elements consolidated in a narrative about the success of Ahmedabad and its population in overcoming the crisis, and created an image of the city as a globalised urban centre with a large and dynamic middle class. 'From mills to malls' became a recurrent motto that well summarised the rhetoric of progress entrenched in this narrative: a commercial sector flourishing on the ashes of the old decaying textile industry; the redefinition of the urban territory and the emergence of new poles of commercial activities; the city conforming to a supposed globalised model of urban development; the rise of an urban middle class that was in line with a 'westernised' imaginary based on consumerism.

From the early 1990s most political forces in the state, as well as in India as a whole, appropriated such elements in the construction of a propaganda discourse that equated the implementation of neoliberal economic reforms with a positivistic idea of 'progress' and 'modernity'. By understanding concepts such as globalisation and modernity in 'purely technological terms', political actors filled their discourses with a rhetoric that considered technological progress as the driving force of innovation at all levels of society, from communication to industrial organisation. Economic indicators assumed increasing importance as mirrors of social progress, and this equation contributed to creating a public culture that progressively identified economic growth with social welfare at large, and in which commodity production and consumption became cultural phenomena.[16] Arguments advocating economic growth as the primary objective of 'modern' politics (as against the previous phase of a centrally planned economy) constituted the undisputed core of a political culture that permeated the public debate in the state. In this idea of progress high GDP growth rates in the long run would benefit all sectors of society, leading to a progressive 'eradication' of poverty all over India.

In Gujarat the emergence of such a political culture assumed peculiar features and went along with the rise of the BJP as a dominant electoral force, particularly in large urban centres, towards the end of the 1980s. The party took the basic elements of neoliberal economic propaganda—liberalisation, privatisation of services and infrastructure management, deregulation of the labour market, globalisation of investment—and enclosed them in an ethno-nationalist frame. By associating economic progress and religious bigotry, the Sangh Parivar contributed to producing a political culture aimed at addressing an imagined urban, Hindu middle class. The main targets of the Hindu political propaganda were those sectors of the urban milieu that were striving to modernise and to adopt the symbols of a lifestyle that was at the same time globalised (in its adoption of consumerism) and typically 'Indian' (in its allegiance to the exterior canons of religious devotionalism). In this sense, in delineating the guidelines of a political ideology that interwove the call for economic liberalisations with strong ethno-nationalist propaganda, the Gujarat branch of the BJP in the early 1990s was a precursor of the programme that the party was to adopt at a national level.[17]

This strategy has proved successful in bringing the BJP to power in Gujarat since 1995 (in Ahmedabad it was already the largest party in 1990) and, more importantly, it contributed to the emergence of the cliché of a 'middle class ethos' in narratives of self-representation for large sectors of the urban population. The construction of such a culture borrowed typical elements of a so-called Gujarati cultural tradition, specifically from an upper-caste Brahmin and Bania fold, mixing them with the stereotypical features of a globalised society, in order to create the image of the Gujarati population as more predisposed to entering global economic markets and doing business in a 'modern', post-industrial, economy.[18] Modernity, globalisation and development became keywords to represent the economic miracle of Gujarat.

The claimed success of economic reforms in the state was inscribed in figures that showed Gujarat as the fastest growing economy among Indian states in the early 2000s. Implicitly recalling an imaginary of positive, endless progress, from both an economic and social perspective, such a narrative glorified the new course in economic policies and, at the same time, referred to a specific—although indefinite—social group, the urban middle class, as the actors of process. The model of a traditional mercantile culture formed the cultural background that made Gujarat a natural environment for economic development. Such a narrative, taking from widely shared traditional stereotypes, depicted mercantile elites of Ahmedabad as traditionally peaceful and tolerant. Interestingly, the common practice of vegetarianism among Brahmin and Bania groups (both Hindu and Jain) recurred frequently as a sort of proof of the peacefulness inherent in the upper caste social milieu of Ahmedabad.[19] At the same time industrial peace, the heritage of the Gandhian culture of peaceful trade unionism in the city, became another element in the construction of an image of Ahmedabad as a peaceful environment, as a place where 'even late at night a woman can move around and walk alone without fear'.[20]

In line with the emerging dominant narrative mercantile traditions, industrial past and peaceful environments became the elements that justified the emergence of Gujarat as a fast growing economy in the post-1991 reforms years. These features contributed to portraying a stereotypical Gujarati businessman (sic) as the model entrepreneur in the globalising economy. While Gujarat as a peaceful state represented the ideal environment for private investors to install new activities, the Gujarati population was naturally oriented towards business. In this perspective, the equation between peace and business in the name of globalisation aimed to project 'Gujarat and Gujaratis' as 'more westernised and modernised than the rest of India and Indians'.[21]

Economic recovery was thus depicted as a mixture of spontaneous initiative and entrepreneurial spirit of large sectors of the population, who sought new economic opportunities in establishing commercial activities and other private initiatives. Such a vision called for a notion of a Gujarati ethos that has become a widely-shared cultural stereotype in present-day Ahmedabad. According to this perspective, the ethos defined a sort of inborn inclination towards business that most Gujarati people were supposed to have.[22] Hence, economic growth came as many people reacted to mill closures by starting small businesses and other activities. In the words of a prominent leader of the BJP in the city, the economic recovery was mainly ascribed to people's 'courage' and self-initiative.[23]

The rise to power of Narendra Modi in the state (2001) exacerbated the main arguments of such a cultural construction in the public debate. A staunch advocate of economic reforms, Modi used the narrative of a Gujarati ethos to promote his economic policies and to project the state, and himself, as in the forefront of good governance and progress in India.[24] The launch of the 'Vibrant Gujarat Global Investors' Summit' must be understood against this background.[25] Addressing the conference in several public speeches, Modi adopted all the symbols that consolidated the equation between Gujarati culture and business in the name of 'modernity'. In his speeches during the summit Modi clarified the programmatic idea that lay behind the initiative, at the same time showing how his government understood economic growth at a cultural and social level.

> On the launch of this function I want to apprise you all of our achievements, of the potential that is available in Gujarat, on the possible wealth generating

partnerships that exist, on how global entrepreneurs can join us in our march towards progress, and how investors can reap rich dividends in Gujarat. I would say if you plant a rupee in the Gujarati soil, you might be able to get a dollar in return! Such is Gujarat's entrepreneurial spirit.[26]

Themes of modernity and globalisation recurred in Modi's speeches as constant reminders of the positive effects that economic growth would almost naturally produce in society. Privatisation and modernisation would bring an 'infusion of modern technology' in the state's economy and this would eventually benefit all sectors of society.[27] Modi traced the lines of a peculiar development pattern that appeared to combine modernity with traditions as, according to his arguments, the local cultural heritage made Gujarat the best place to start new economic activities. In this way, cultural stereotypes entered the political arena to define the traits of a supposed uniqueness of Gujarati society. The relationship between 'commerce and culture, trade and tradition, entrepreneurship and entertainment' would make Gujarat competitive 'in the modern times of the World Trade Organization'.[28]

Such a narrative underpinned the construction of the image of a Gujarati ethos, which supposedly represented the rise of the middle class. Discourses of this type formed part of a public culture which conferred legitimacy to the BJP on different levels. The party could present itself as the champion of the state's economic recovery and as the sole representative of the Gujarati spirit of entrepreneurship. It also managed to gather support from all those sectors of urban society that represented themselves as the middle class and that sought to protect their interests and social status. On another level, such arguments relied on the promise of upward mobility and welfare for all those backward groups that were in fact penalised by the reformed economic system.

However, at a social level, the consolidation of a middle class culture took the form of an increasing intolerance towards the circumstances of the urban poor and a further marginalisation of the Muslim minority groups in the city. In this sense, if in the political arena the BJP tried to build the image of a secular party in the name of economic growth and globalisation, as a cultural phenomenon the idea of a Gujarati ethos consolidated a reality of social exclusiveness, shaped on communal lines. Behind the positivistic image of progress and modernisation, the consolidation of such culture among large sectors of urban society concealed a further polarisation of that society, and legitimised politics of exclusion and discrimination as a common practice.

Subnational chauvinism and cultural exclusion

The emergence of a 'middle-class culture' in the public representation of urban society was largely based on symbols calling for a regional cultural specificity of the Gujarati identity. Interestingly, political leaders and the mass media referred to the so-called economic recovery of Ahmedabad city always through the mediation of the idea of Gujarati ethos. Relating the city's economic growth mainly to the people's attitude towards business proved a successful political argument. In this sense every single citizen was entitled to be part of the city's aspirations to modernity through individual initiative, spirit of entrepreneurship and 'courage'. At the same time, while embodying the positive outcomes of modernisation, the idea of 'Gujaratiness' created a defined rift between the rich, those who could afford modernity and globalisation, and the poor, who lagged behind in the construction of a global economy.[29]

Hence the idealisation of so-called Gujarati traditions as the base of a middle-class culture became a first, powerful element of cultural discrimination. The idea of a Gujarati ethos referred directly to the cultural and social environment of traditional mercantile elites in the city, mainly upper caste Brahmin, Bania and Jain. Elements such as vegetarianism, peacefulness and business orientation belonged to a specific imaginary found in the Jain and upper caste Hindu traditions, as well as in Gandhi's legacy in the city's social milieu. These references proved instrumental, in the discourses of Hindu extremist associations, in strengthening their position as representative of the supposedly original traditions of the state. As Ashis Nandy noted in a controversial article, soon after Modi's re-election to the Gujarat chief ministership in 2007, 'Gandhi himself has been given a saintly, Hindu nationalist status and shelved'.[30]

The rhetoric about the peace-loving and non-violent Gujarati people defined the boundaries of cultural and social exclusion in a city like Ahmedabad, which had grown largely over a lower-caste, migrant labour force. When discussing the relationship between the representation of Gujarati people as non-violent and the frequent occurrence of riots, Ashok Bhatt, senior BJP leader from Ahmedabad, declared that '*we* never have problems with *other* people, and this is a long lasting tradition of Gujarat'.[31] In this case, the distinction between 'we' and 'other people' reveals the disruptive potential of a narrative based on subnational stereotypes. On the one hand, the apparently inclusive character of this rhetoric encompassed all those 'courageous people' who reacted to the industrial crisis by starting individual businesses and commercial activities. Such a category implicitly included all those tens of thousands of former mill labourers who were forced to reinvent themselves as self-employed, street vendors or casual labourers.[32] In fact, for these sectors of informal and insecure workforce, the transition from an industrial to a service economy can be better considered as a symptom of their utter lack of contractual power and helplessness, rather than the outcome of a business mentality. On the other hand, the continuous reference to subnational symbols acted as a reproduction, on a local scale, of the Hindu extremist propaganda at the national level: arguments equating the Indian nation with the Hindu population of India were transposed to a regional dimension, with the direct effect of projecting the local branch of the BJP—and its leader Modi—as the true representative of the traditional Gujarati culture both internally, towards the non-Hindu and non-Gujarati religious minorities, and externally, asserting the specificity of Gujarat within the Indian nation.

Subnational chauvinism proved a powerful argument in the hands of local Hindu extremist leaders to project their political propaganda into a broader cultural frame, and became an essential element designed to mask intolerant and sectarian feelings behind the smokescreen of an urban, middle class ethos, combining a strong traditional heritage with attention to development and modernisation. As emerged from the testimony of many social workers and activists, in Ahmedabad the equation between Hindu and Gujarati identities became so rooted among certain sectors of society that native Gujarati Muslims were automatically classified through their religious affiliation instead of their regional origins, or mother-tongue.

In this perspective the subnational discourse underpinned what has been defined as a process of 're-imagination' of the state, based on the interrelation of ideas and values at different levels, from the religious to the economic, in order to include *Hindutva* within an ideology of development and modernisation. The consolidation of a regional identity as a widely shared culture in the city represented the success of the Hindu extremist associations in their 'battle for control of the culture of the state, and especially of Ahmedabad'.[33] The mixture of religious, cultural, political and economic issues, which merged in the broader reference to a Gujarati ethos and subnational identity, constituted a seductive ideology for large sectors of the urban population, and proved a powerful tool for political organisations and extremist groups to mobilise masses of people around religious issues.[34]

In 1990, from the moment the BJP took control of the state's administration, subnationalism became a hegemonic discourse that constantly informed the party's political rhetoric. Subsequently Modi's rise to power marked a further increase in the political use of these symbols, in strong association with a Hindu extremist rhetoric. Modi projected himself as a model of the Gujarati ethos, making business a pivotal element of his political image. In doing so, he projected himself as a leader with strong roots in the local community and culture, but at the same time strongly committed to leading the state's economy in the global market. Consequently, after consolidating his popularity in the state, Modi exploited his image as a strong local leader to renegotiate the boundaries of his personal political power both within the state and in the relationship with the centre.[35]

The massive wave of anti-Muslim violence in 2002 represented a watershed in terms of the political debate within the state and in the balance between the state and the central authority.[36] As Indian media gave almost complete coverage to the riots, and as human rights organisations and activists came to investigate the events early on during the violence, large sectors of public opinion, within and outside Gujarat, openly questioned the state government's attitude during and after the violence. In light of this situation the state government, and the chief minister in person, set up an aggressive propaganda campaign against the press, the opposition parties and all those sectors of civil society that had mobilised to denounce the various abuses that public agents had committed during and after the riots. This counter-propaganda represented a further step in the consolidation of a subnational idea among large sectors of the Gujarati population.

In the months preceding the election (November 2002), Modi toured Gujarat extensively, seeking to aggregate the electorate around his figure and in defence of the people of Gujarat against the attacks of media and opposition parties. The name he gave to the campaign, *Gaurav Yatra*, clearly highlighted the emotional over the political intention of the whole operation. The *Yatra* was meant to represent the pride of the entire Gujarati population, and Modi appointed himself the defender of local people's culture and ethos from 'the unprecedented criticism ... following the post-Godhra violence'.[37] During the two months of campaigning the chief minister sought to transform the electoral competition into an ideological battle in defence of the culture and traditions of Gujarat. The main narrative underlying the campaign described Gujarat using national attributes, thus allowing the BJP to reframe the debate around the pogroms in antagonistic terms. Media coverage of the violence and political attacks against Modi and his government were portrayed as examples of a propaganda discourse aimed at vilifying the people of Gujarat. In this frame the debate was not about whether or not Modi's government was somehow involved in the eruption and expansion of the conflict all over the state, but called the whole people of Gujarat into question for all being considered 'rapists and murderers'. In rally after rally Modi developed his discourse by constantly labelling all accusations against his government as anti-Gujarat:

> [Congressmen say that] Gujaratis are violent people. They say that here people stab passers-by with knives. You must have heard all this. The Congress says that Gujaratis keep petrol bombs with them in their pockets. And then they use them to burn people alive in the streets! They [Congressmen] have played with Gujarati pride. Who are the culprits of Godhra? You tell me. Had nothing happened in Godhra, would anyone have hurled a single stone?[38]

The election results showed that this propaganda paid high dividends in terms of votes. The BJP obtained more than two-thirds of the seats in the Legislative Assembly (and 49.85 per cent of the votes), testimony that an aggressive propaganda campaign, based on two forms of identity, religious and cultural, had reached wide sections of the electorate, both in rural and urban areas. While the campaign was still going on, many commentators denounced Modi's decision to embark on the *Gaurav Yatra* as an attempt to reap electoral benefits from the carnage, and from this point of view the chief minister achieved his goal.[39] However, from a different angle, the battle that Modi fought during the electoral campaign was not limited to the forthcoming election—the *Gaurav Yatra* was in fact aimed at consolidating a sense of 'unity' and 'self-respect among fifty million Gujaratis'.[40] In this sense the propaganda discourse that accompanied the *Yatra* was in line with the whole rhetoric around the ethos and uniqueness of the Gujarati people that had informed BJP politics in the state from the previous decade. After their victory in the 2002 election, Modi and the BJP gradually abandoned anti-Muslim slogans in favour of propaganda that emphasised the achievements of the government in terms of economic growth and development. The launch, in September 2003, of the Vibrant Gujarat Global Investors' Summit sanctioned a new phase for the state's government. In this effort to clean up the party façade in the face of public opinion, Modi resorted even more frequently to the vocabulary of subnationalism instead of to blatant anti-Muslim slogans.

The reorganisation of the state's economy acted as a further element that strengthened a sense of unity and cohesion among Gujarati people. Under the blanket of Gujarati identity, such rhetoric proved successful in representing the aspirations of large sectors of the urban population to be part of a 'modern' middle-class fold. Narendra Modi personified the success of these politics as he represented the most powerful stereotypes related to the Gujarati ethos: success as an economic reformer, religious devotionalism, capability to secure social peace.

Revisiting secularism

Paradoxically, in Gujarat the space for a debate about secularism has shrunk considerably shrunk since 2002. As a moral value and a political practice secularism was reframed and gradually entrapped within the context of economic policies.[41] As a by-product of the consolidation of the BJP as a dominant political force in the state, development-oriented arguments also assumed a hegemonic role within a debate over secularism. In fact, the political and cultural agenda summarised in the 'Vibrant Gujarat' slogan affirmed the notion that high GDP rates and economic growth were the only elements that could foster equality in India.

In recent years the idea that true secularism comes with economic development has become a key point in the political culture of Gujarat today. According to this perspective, economic growth is the only factor that can lead to a general improvement of people's life conditions, and thus curb social inequalities in the long run. Thus a liberalised and privatised economy provides the possibility for everyone, irrespective of their social or religious affiliation, to succeed and move up the social ladder. The relationship between secularism and economic growth in a liberalised market represents a powerful argument in the hands of Hindu extremist political leaders, who elevate economic indicators as the sole argument by which to measure equality of opportunity and respect for all religious groups.[42]

Moreover, it has been convincingly argued that the construction of a secular ideology based on economic arguments functioned as a smokescreen to conceal communal politics behind the realisation of 'development programmes'. While on paper neoliberal reforms granted equal opportunities to all citizens, in fact religious inequalities emerged in terms of real access to economic resources and to government-funded development project.[43]

The debate around secularism was thus reframed as a discussion about economic growth and development strategies. The construction of a subnational rhetoric based on the idea of 'ethos' constituted a powerful form of exclusion of religious minorities. The definition of a strong subnational identity shaped on typically Hindu, upper-caste elements became the background for the emergence of a development-oriented idea of secularism. Following from this perspective, shifting the balance of the secular principle to economic arguments can be seen as the end point of two decades of identity politics in Gujarat. As we have seen, the call for a Gujarati 'ethos' functioned as an ideological cover to conceal communal feelings and a deep intolerance towards religious minorities and backward groups. In this sense the equation between economic development and secularism represented a further step.

In September 2011 Narendra Modi launched a new campaign, named the *Sadbhavana Mission*, to 'further strengthen Gujarat's environment of peace, unity and harmony'. During the following three months, Modi toured the state with the aim of promote a message of social peace based on economic and development arguments. The success of Gujarat in terms of GDP growth and income has become the main argument to counter allegations against the chief minister and his government of being communally biased.

> The unhealthy environment created by the unfounded and false allegations made against me and the Government of Gujarat, after 2002 riots, has come to an end. For the past ten years, it has become fashionable to defame me and the State of Gujarat...Every citizen of Gujarat has internalized peace, harmony and development. Gujarat has experienced an unparalleled phase of peace, harmony, and development in the last decade. Gujarat is committed to march forward on this path only.[44]

As sociologist Shiv Vishwanathan has pointed out, development has become the pillar of a new discourse on secularism: 'Secular-speak is always in the language of economic rationality. Investment can be calculated, so it is rational. Anything outside this is subjective, ethnic and irrational.'[45] The political connotation of subnational arguments has thus become an element in legitimising the politics of exclusion in the name of progress and development.

Acknowledgements

I thank everyone who has read and commented on the early drafts of this work, and particularly Dr Ravinder Kaur, who has endured numerous revisions. I alone am responsible for any remaining inconsistencies.

Notes

1 I Hirway, 'Dynamics of development in Gujarat; some issues', *Economic and Political Weekly*, 26 August–2 September 2000, p 3111. See also D Mahadevia, 'Interventions in development: a shift towards a model of exclusion', in A Kundu & D Mahadevia (eds), *Poverty and Vulnerability in a Globalising Metropolis: Ahmedabad*, New Delhi: Manak Publications, 2002.

2 See, for instance, the documentary *Final Solution* by Rakesh Sharma (2004), in which the director shows long clips of the speeches Modi delivered in rallies during the *Gaurav Yatra*.

3 'Narendra Modi's speech at Vibrant Gujarat', at http://ibnlive.in.com/news/narendra-modis-speech-at-vibrant-gujarat-2011/140214-53.html, accessed July 2011.

IDENTITY, INEQUITY AND INEQUALITY IN INDIA AND CHINA

4 RD King, *Nehru and the Language Politics of India*, Delhi: Oxford University Press, 1997; and S Nag, 'Multiplication of nations? Political economy of sub-nationalism in India', *Economic and Political Weekly*, 17–24 July 1993.

5 The rise of Hindu extremism in Gujarat is a well researched theme. See O Shani, *Communalism, Caste and Hindu Nationalism: The Violence in Gujarat*, Cambridge: Cambridge University Press, 2007; A Yagnik and S Sheth, *The Shaping of Modern Gujarat: Plurality, Hindutva and Beyond*, New Delhi: Penguin, 2005; A Yagnik and S Sheth, *Ahmedabad, from Royal City to Megacity*, New Delhi: Penguin Books, 2011; A Nandy, S Trivedy, S Mayaram and A Yagnik, *Creating a Nationality: the Ramjanmabhumi Movement and Fear of the Self*, New Delhi: Oxford University Press, 1995; G Shah, 'Caste, Hindutva and Hinduness', *Economic and Political Weekly*, 13 April 2002; J Breman, *The Making and Unmaking of an Industrial Working Class; Sliding Down the Labour Hierarchy in Ahmedabad, India*, New Delhi: Oxford University Press, 2004; H Spodek, 'In the Hindutva laboratory: pogroms and politics in Gujarat, 2002', *Modern Asian Studies*, 44(2), 2010. However, few authors have sought to analyse the cultural effects of a political rhetoric combining religious and economic propaganda. This article aims to fill this gap within the debate over identity politics and neoliberal reforms in present-day Gujarat.

6 Mahadevia, 'Interventions in development', p 80 ff, 120 ff.

7 In the 1920 session in Nagpur, the Congress had adopted the linguistic principle to organise its internal structure and, in the 1945–46 elections, the party's electoral manifesto included the objective of redrawing the political map of India along linguistic lines. This notwithstanding, Prime Minister Nehru, fearing the divisive potential of politics based on language, started favouring the non-linguistic option. See 'States merger proposal', *Economic Weekly*, January 1956.

8 TB Hansen, *The Saffron Wave: Democracy and Hindu Nationalism in Modern India*, Princeton, NJ: Princeton University Press, 1999, p 41 ff.

9 My reconstruction of the events is based mainly on the autobiographical accounts of two leaders of the then Maha Gujarat Janata Parishad, Brhamkumar Bhatt and Indulal Yagnik. The events referred to by these authors, and their interpretation, have been cross-checked with newspaper articles from the *Times of India* (Bombay edition), and the *Economic Weekly*. B Bhatt, *Lé Ké Rahemgé Mahagujarat* (in Gujarati), Ahmedabad: Dasharat Gandhi, Sarangpur, 1987; and Yagnik, *Atmakatha*.

10 TB Hansen, *Wages of Violence: Naming and Identity in Postcolonial Bombay*, Princeton NJ: Woodstock; Princeton University Press 2002, p 42.

11 'Opportunist solution' (editorial), *Economic Weekly*, 11 August 1956.

12 A Varshney, *Ethnic Conflict and Civic Life: Hindus and Muslims in India*, New Haven, CT: Yale University Press, 2002, p 249.

13 Hirway, 'Dynamics of development in Gujarat', p 3110.

14 M Nussbaum, *The Clash Within: Democracy, Religious Violence, and India's Future*, New Delhi: Permanent Black, 2007, pp 133–134.

15 Shinoda has noted that traditional economic elites and upper class/caste groups, mainly Bania, Brahmin and Patel, had much higher access to state concessions for small-scale industries than did backward groups, Dalits and Adivasis (tribal peoples). T Shinoda, 'Institutional change and entrepreneurial development: SSI sector', *Economic and Political Weekly*, 26 August–2 Semptember 2000.

16 F Jameson, 'Globalisation and political strategy', *New Left Review*, 4, 2000, pp 49, 53.

17 G Patel, 'Narendra Modi's one-day cricket: what and why?', *Economic and Political Weekly*, 30 November 2002, p 4832.

18 F Ibrahim, 'Capitalism, multiculturalism and tolerance: a perspective on "Vibrant Gujarat"', *Economic and Political Weekly*, 25 August 2007, pp 3446–3447.

19 Gujarat Chief Minister, Narendra Modi, in a speech to a summit of international investors, defined vegetarianism as the 'main strength' of Gujarati people, and a 'native' feature of the Gujarati culture. Modi, 'Speech delivered to the Vibrant Gujarat Global Investors Summit', 2 October 2003, at http://www.gujaratindia.com/media/media4.htm, accessed 14 January 2009.

20 KN Raval, 'Law and order in Ahmedabad', paper presented at the seminar 'Is Ahmedabad Dying?', Centre for Environmental Planning and Technology and Gujarat Institute of Civil Engineers and Architects, Ahmedabad, 1987, p XIV. The argument about girls moving about safely in the city in the evenings has become a recurrent *topos* in middle class narratives about the city, which people from higher social groups often presented to me as proof of its 'modern' character.

21 V Joshi, 'Cultural context of development', *Economic and Political Weekly*, 26 August–2 September 2000, p 3165.

22 Hirway, 'Dynamics of development in Gujarat', p 3106.

23 Interview with Ashok Bhatt, Member of the BJP, May 2008.

24 N Sud, 'The Nano and good governance in Gujarat', *Economic and Political Weekly*, 13 December 2008, p 13.

25 For a presentation of the initiative, see the official website at http://www.vibrantgujarat.com/.
26 N Modi, 'Speech delivered to the Vibrant Gujarat Global Investors Summit', 28 September 2003, at http://www.gujaratindia.com/media/media4.htm, accessed 14 January 2009, p 1.
27 *Ibid*, p 5.
28 *Ibid*, p 1; and Modi, Speech 3 October 2003, p 5.
29 Mahadevia, 'Interventions in development', p 80.
30 A Nandy, 'Blame the middle class', *Times of India*, 8 January 2008. After this article was published, the Gujarat Branch of the National Council of Civil Liberties filed a case against the author charging him with exciting communal feelings and tensions in the state.
31 Interview with Ashok Bhatt, May 2008, emphasis added.
32 M Chatterjee & M Shah, *Organising Street Vendors: SEWA's Experience in Ahmedabad City*, Ahmedabad: Self Employed Women's Association, 1997.
33 H Spodek, 'In the Hindutva laboratory', p 33.
34 A Prakash, 'Re-imagination of the state and Gujarat's electoral verdict', *Economic and Political Weekly*, 19 April 2003, pp 1602–1609.
35 Particularly since 2004, when the Congress-led United Progressive Alliance gained power in the central government.
36 For detailed accounts of the pogrom, see S Varadarajan, *Gujarat, the Making of a Tragedy*, New Delhi and New York: Penguin Books, 2002.
37 'Gaurav Yatra: Phase IV commences from Saturday', *Indian Express*, 4 October 2002.
38 N Modi, addressing a meeting during the *Gaurav Yatra*. The meeting was recorded and reported in Sharma, *Final Solution*.
39 See, for instance, *Communalism Combat*, special Issue, March–April 2002, p 110.
40 Sharma, *Final Solution*.
41 S Ganguly, 'The crisis of Indian secularism', *Journal of Democracy*, 14(4), 2003, p 16.
42 For a typical example of the use made by BJP leaders of the concept of secularism, see the interview with LK Advani, 'Advani goes back to future vowing to protect Hindu India', *Indian Express*, 25 November 2004.
43 N Sud, 'Constructing and contesting a Gujarati–Hindu Ethno-religious identity through development programmes in an Indian province', *Oxford Development Studies*, 35(2), 2007, p 137ff. See also R Sachar, *Social, Economic and Educational Status of the Muslim Community of India: A Report*, New Delhi: Prime Minister's High Level Committee, Cabinet Secretariat, Government of India, 2006, pp 149–150.
44 *Letter From Gujarat CM Narendra Modi to Citizens*, 13 Septmeber 2011, at http://narendramodi.in/news/news_detail/1622, accessed September 2011.
45 A Yadav, 'The truth behind the stage show', *Tehelka*, 1 October 2011.

Notes on contributor

Tommaso Bobbio holds a PhD in the history of India from Royal Holloway, University of London (2010). His thesis was on *Collective Violence, Urban Change and Social Exclusion: Ahmedabad 1930–2002*. His research interests focus mainly on the dynamics of urban transformation in post-colonial India, with a special interest in the relationship between social and structural changes of the city and the development of group tensions. While carrying on research independently, he works as Coordinator of the Events Office of the Asiatica Film Festival, the festival of Asian cinema and literature of the city of Rome.

Between Egalitarianism and Domination: governing differences in a transitional society

SWAGATO SARKAR

ABSTRACT *This article presents the problem of governing differences as a problem of constituting a social whole out of the play of antagonistic elements like class, caste, gender, religion, etc, which is essentially a modernist political project in its normative grounding. The problem is explored here vis-à-vis the trajectories of global capitalism and the options for development (that is, the transition from an agrarian economy to an industrial one) for the smaller federal states. The experience of the Left Front Government in West Bengal, India is analysed to understand the issues at stake. The narrative presented in the article shows that questions of land ownership and freedom from oppression and bodily toil remain the fundamental political problem which determines the course and dynamics of governance of differences, particularly its egalitarian mode. This problemat also points towards the limits of agrarian modernity, which many post-colonial countries have tried to constitute.*

The transition to industrial capitalism is the dominant narrative in post-liberalisation India. Although the Bharatiya Janata Party (BJP), which launched the 'Shining India' campaign,[1] lost the 2004 general election, the dream articulated in that campaign survived: 'Shining India' has transformed into 'the India story'. Economic growth, which has always been the economists' and policy-makers' intellectual pursuit, has now become the creed of the nation. The federal states are the stage where this theatre of growth is enacted. However, economic growth in India has been a chequered regional phenomenon. There are a few star performing states and many laggards. Almost all the star performers—Gujarat, Tamil Nadu, Maharashtra and Andhra Pradesh—have witnessed the flourishing of the native business communities along with their ability to attract investments from foreign and domestic corporations. At the same time every state is confronted with the problem of increasing inequality. The overwhelming reaction to such growing inequality is to advocate social welfare

Swagato Sarkar is in the Jindal School of Government and Public Policy, OP Jindal Global University.

programmes—a monolithic political imagination. Yet it is pertinent to enquire after the fate of other narratives of progress and freedom that have existed in India and to explore the difficulty of articulating an alternative vision in the current political economic context, the difficulty of managing differences and contradictions within an agrarian modernity and its transition to an industrial one.

A case in point is the experience of the Left Front Government in West Bengal—the world's longest running popularly elected government formed by the Communist and leftist parties. During the 2006 Assembly Elections it coined and advertised a slogan: 'Agriculture is our foundation, industry our future'. This slogan embodied the tension of transition: what is to be done with the stagnating agrarian economy which supports the livelihood of the majority of the people in the country? The Left Front won the 2006 elections convincingly and (mis)understood this as a mandate to embark on a fully fledged industrialisation programme at the cost of agriculture. It promised massive subsidies, and incentives like tax holidays, cheap loans, land and water, etc to private companies. Some companies were attracted by the 'policy package' and planned to invest in the state. But what the state government did not have at its disposal was land. Land acquisition for industrialisation became a political flashpoint: people's resistance movements against land acquisition spread around southern and western Bengal. Within a span of two years the Left Front was politically cornered and finally was routed in the State Assembly Elections in 2011.

The rise and the fall of the Left Front Government in West Bengal provides an invaluable insight into the process of constituting an (agrarian) modernist project, into managing differences and contradictions within it and into the difficulty of transition to industrial capitalism in a globalised world.

In this article I look at the leftist political imagination, its normative basis and the itinerary of its agrarian modernity in West Bengal over the past 35 years or so. I try to detect the contradictions and antagonisms which developed within the agrarian economy, but which could not be resolved in the given context. Instead, paradoxically, certain structural conditions emerged which resisted the dissolution of the agrarian society in favour of an industrialised one. I also present the fragments of memories of the historically marginalised people, in an attempt to understand social changes from their point of view. The data used in writing the article have been collected over the past 12 years from the districts of North and South 24 Parganas. The method of participant observation was practised in following the proceedings of the *Panchayats*, *Gram Sabha* and political rallies. I conducted semi-structured interviews with political leaders, *Panchayat* officials and villagers, and group interviews with self-help groups and women. I analysed the texts in publicity materials, political communiqués and newspaper reports.

Inter alia I directly or indirectly raise the following questions here: is it possible to manage both the transition to industrial (corporate) capitalism and the differences in a society? What are the limits of this process? What are the contradictions within this process? The 'development narrative' was perceived as limitless, as an ever-unfolding narrative of accommodation and emancipation. Have we reached a moment where this narrative is disrupted— the movement is no longer guaranteed? This, I believe, is an interesting enquiry because we are in a paradoxical time: on the one hand, the Western economies are in crisis and, on the other hand, 'the India story' is simultaneously triumphant and faltering. Parallel to this, I understand that the management of difference is successful when it ultimately finds a normative basis for the project. Now, if we are indeed in a paradoxical time, where and how does a project find its normative basis and ideological certitude?

The leftist agrarian modernity

The districts of North and South 24 Parganas are located in the southern-most part of West Bengal, the delta area of the Hooghly River. The land in this area used to be marshy and was forested a century ago. The *zamindars*, feudal landlords, brought people to this area to clear the forests and to build bunds to recover and reclaim land and to check the soil salinity through the use of their physical labour. Gradually the land became arable, but those who made it so remained landless. Instead, their body became bonded to the feudal landlords.

The landless people used to work as domestic helps, shepherds, agricultural labourers and sharecroppers. While working as domestic helps and shepherds they were directly under the surveillance of the employers, in everyday contact with the latter. As agricultural labourers and sharecroppers they did not have daily interaction with their employers and such relation-ships were primarily seen as economic. Mostly young people were employed as shepherds and domestic helps; they were provided with food, clothes and medical attention in case of severe illness by their employers.

In this feudal society land emerged as the pivot of social existence; land acquired meaning beyond its function as a means of production. Land ownership was not just an assertion of an economic independence—a minimum security of food and an asset for mortgaging in the time of personal crisis—it also acquired the status of a cultural symbol. The desire for home, pond, hen, duck, cow, a few trees—a good life—were all spun around this land. Land was the island where dreams were anchored. Land was a symbol of social status, imparting an identity to the residents, a sense of belonging and the promise of a stable life.

The political discourse of the pre-land reform era was constructed around the nodal points of land, body and freedom: freedom from subjugation and oppression, and the security of land tenure or property. This discourse was invariably modern as it was premised on securing the conditions for the emergence of a new Man (sic), with the promises of stability, security and dignity, ie the conditions for being free. The emergent leftist politics were founded on such a discourse, albeit selectively.

The leftist agenda of restructuring feudal land relations was based on a modernist teleology, that is, the transition from feudalism to capitalism.

A technocratic imagination informed the political programme of the leftist parties: land was a means of production which supplied 'food for the millions, raw materials for the growing need of... industries and [created] the market essential for the development of the secondary and tertiary sectors of... [the] economy'.[2] The primitive accumulation from the agrarian economy would provide the capital necessary for industrial development and growth and to feed the working class in the urban areas cheaply.

On the other hand, surplus, whether surplus labour or value, was generated by the workers, by their bodily capacity to labour. The absolute emancipation required and heralded when the worker fully controlled his or her body and the product of labour was co-operatively and collectively appropriated. Within this horizon one strand of political activism was directed towards lessening the 'load' on the body, towards securing better working conditions and statutorily limiting the working day. In a feudal society the workers' bodily capacity was not only exploited, it was also subjugated and oppressed; the female workers' body was many a time appropriated by the landlord for sexual gratification. The political intention to free the body was visible in the interventions aimed at abolishing the intermediary landlords who exploited and oppressed the labourers' body and in establishing a direct link between land and labour, that is, the creation of self-cultivators.

The leftist parties and the central government converged on the aims of the land reforms: '(i) abolition of intermediaries; (ii) imposition of ceiling on [the] size of ownership-holding; [...] and [iii] regulation of share tenancy'.[3] However, in Bengal, the incumbent Congress Government hardly undertook any land reform. There was less support from the judiciary 'with its sympathy for the principles of inviolability of private property' and the 'former landowners continued to enjoy the usufruct of their former land by assigning it to dependent tenants, who, for a couple of years, would be allowed to remain on the land as the rightful allottees of the *patta* [land deeds]'.[4]

The Communist Party of India (Marxist) (CPI (M)) and its farmers' wing, Kisan Sabha, organised and mobilised the peasants in the state, identified the potential surplus land held by landlords and resisted the eviction of sharecroppers. The movement 'reached a height in 1969 when spontaneous seizure of illegal holdings of land became a mass phenomenon'.[5] The mobilisation of peasants and violent actions brought the individual experience of exploitation into the public sphere as common experience under the *jotedari* system.[6] The *jotedari* system was constructed as a malicious force and the landlord was the 'Common Principal Enemy' and the Left Front an agent of social change. This movement of the late 1960s and 1970s led to the ascendancy of the Left Front to the state legislative power in West Bengal in June 1977.

When the Left Front came to power in West Bengal, it constructed an agrarian modernist project around land reform, securing tenancy of the sharecropper and the *Panchayat* (local, decentralised, self-governance institution). This project sought to address social inequality and differences, and thereby to transform society.

The Left Front government started to distribute land 'to enable [people] to "walk on two legs": the minimum security of land, and food income from it, would enable them to press for higher agricultural wages'.[7] In the face of bodily toil and the threat of eviction in the feudal era, the agrarian programme of the Left Front brought a sense of stability and security in rural Bengal, and provided people a haven. The implementation of, and amendments to, the Minimum Wage Act promised wherewithal for a family's survival. The Food-for-Work programme was oriented towards providing food security during the lean seasons.

The Left Front government rejuvenated the *Panchayati Raj* institution and institutionalised and decentralised the exercise of power.[8] The *Panchayats* were no longer the privy of upper caste and class people. This institutionalised power of the party and *Panchayat* helped the peasantry to negotiate with the powerful sections of society through an informal dispute-settlement process, '*salishi*' or '*bichar*'. It also helped them to bargain over wages with the landowners.[9] The land reform programme not only restructured land relations, but also the caste composition of the villages. The body politics of the village were redefined.

The contradictions in the modernist project

The exit of the big landlords from the villages after the land reform programme produced a situation where the very rich people were absent from the social and political life of the village. The provision of land converted a large section of landless labourers and marginal farmers into small peasants, although a substantial number of them still remained landless. A new class of supervisory cultivators emerged, having access to income from government jobs (often as school teachers), business, agri-input businesses, etc. This class also cornered the best agricultural plots, in terms both of productivity and location, distributed by the government. The earlier polarised and tighter class-structure in the society became diluted and dispersed, engendering a band of intermediary classes.

As the land reform programme was broadened and intensified, two unique situations arose. First, as most of the surplus land was redistributed over a period of time (although the process involved certain anomalies), after a point, no more land was available for distribution to the remaining landless labourers; any further lowering of the land ceiling would result in the loss of land by the middle and rich peasants. Second, an increase in the minimum wage would also go against the interest of the middle-class (and rich) farmers, who were dependent on daily wage labourers for cultivating their lands. The land reform consolidated the hold of the middle-class farmers and made them the dominant force in the rural areas.

The middle-class farmers started to control the party apparatus. In the first *Panchayat* election under the Left Front government the total number of party members, mostly based in the urban centres, was around 30 000, whereas the number of constituencies in which the Left Front fielded candidates was above 80 000. This saw a rapid induction of members from the middle peasantry who had not actively participated in the earlier leftist movements. By assuming a leadership position in the party, the middle-ranking peasantry protected their interests. Most of the *Pradhans* [chiefs] of the *Panchayats*, the secretaries of the Local Committee (LC) and the Zonal Committee members of CPI (M) were from such families. Very soon, the conditions for social mobility required familial connections in the party and sufficient affluence to provide an education, which in turn would create a new articulate class.

In order to obtain a majority, the party had to include different peasant classes whose interests could not be in harmony with each other. In the process it relegated the contradictory inter-class interests to a secondary level. Ashok Rudra noted: 'If a political party aims at majority support among the agricultural population, it cannot but in the ultimate analysis betray the most exploited and the most oppressed sections of the rural masses'.[10]

By the late 1980s it was becoming clear to the leftist critics of the Left Front that the latter had failed to translate land reform into a broader framework of agrarian reform and social transformation. The slowing down of 'Operation Barga' and the retreat of the Food-for-Work programme and credit facilities were pointers to this.[11] They understood it as a problem of the state, that is, the failure of institutional intervention. From a modernist standpoint the failure of rural/agrarian transformation was attributed to the inability to start a co-operative movement, to promote non-farm businesses, and of the non-functional agricultural extension services. Registration of sharecroppers gave security of tenancy, but the promised two-thirds share of the harvest for cultivators was not realised in most of areas. The Minimum Wages Act was not amended to raise the minimum wage. The Block Office housed various departments for agricultural development. A separate *Krishi Prajukti Sahayika* (Agri-technology Assistance Centre) and the *Gram Sevaks* (village-level workers) were of no help to the farmers. These extension departments and their staff rarely visited the villages; on a few occasions they provided them with advice and seeds. However, these critics ignored the emerging contradictions in leftist politics and their forms of exercise of power.

The restructuring of class relationships in favour of middle-class farmers and the marginalisation of small peasantry and landless labourers were not acknowledged or noted as the Left Front won election after election and farm productivity, particularly rice output, increased. This increase in rice production could not be attributed to any public policy initiative as such, but rather to the market forces. The rural areas witnessed gradual inroads of chemical fertilisers, hand-driven mechanical tillers, pesticides and private exploitation of ground water through the use of shallow tube-wells. These markets were controlled by the middle-class farming families and the peasants purchased the inputs on credit. The school teachers, with a regular salary, became the new money lenders and investors in small businesses like fishing.

The late 1980s also saw the advent of Boro rice cultivation in the dry period, which increased the total rice production in the state. It opened up the market for land-lease; a section of the landowners started to lease out land to others in the winter for Boro cultivation. Some small farmers and landless labourers would take this land on lease, provided they had some working capital and personal relationship with the landowners and were thereby trusted. By the mid-2000s, the leasing out of land was done on upfront cash payment and the dealers were reluctant to supply chemicals on credit.

This arrangement of farming was different from the earlier sharecropping system, because, first, the entire exchange process had been monetised: no exchange of crops as in the feudal period was practised. Second, land-lease was available on contract only for one season instead of an indefinite period of contract. Third, the land-owner got a certain fixed amount as rent instead of a share of the harvest, and the risk of crop failure was solely borne by the lessee.

With the waning of the land reform programme and the restructuring of the social through the formation of a new dispersed band of classes, the party had to restructure its political discourse. The focus of leftist politics shifted from the *exploitation* of the body to the *management* of the body.

'Development' as a means of managing the social

The discourse and practice of development redrew the boundaries of the private and the public, with the public, as usual, being the political. Legally any relations of production are an interpersonal affair between the worker and his/her employer, and hence are also private. With the rise of the CPI (M) and Kisan Sabha, these relationships and the oppression and exploitation therein were brought into the public sphere, into the domain of public discussion, where the right of the *jotedar*s to own a large tract of land (above the land ceiling) as private property was challenged. The exploitation of the labourers' body by non-working supervisory large landowners was no longer a private matter but a generalised 'social malevolence'. Thus the land relationship became significant in the political rhetoric, agenda and programme. After the land reform programme, the issue of exploitation could no longer be sustained, as it would indicate the existence of exploitation and inequality, and hence the failure of leftist politics and its interventions into that social. The discourse accordingly moved onto the management of the body, which the 'developmental' schemes supported.

The Left Front subscribed to the discourse of development and proposed that it was a form of 'class struggle', a position which was later officially articulated by the late Anil Biswas, the then member of the party's Polit Bureau: 'The task of organising development was not alienated from the concept of class struggle since the task was to identify the target group for whom the developmental tasks were being orchestrated and mark out the process of development itself'.[12] The Front reinvented the *Panchayat* as an apparatus of this discourse of development and constructed 'the people' as a political subject (the term 'target-group' was later borrowed from the NGO vocabulary). The earlier programme of social justice and freedom through the transformation of production relationships was replaced by a *populist* developmental agenda.

The *Panchayat* was described in the public meetings as a democratic and free space for exercising people's will and power. Rhetorical claims about 'holding regular elections', 'divesting power in the hands of the people', 'people are the partners in the development', 'people could do development with their own hands', 'people are the real owner' were set in motion to project 'the people' as the real agent of development. The *Panchayati Raj* system was presented as an effective form of governance, which was transparent and participatory, accountable to the people. The publication, presentation and distribution of an annual income–expenditure report to the electorate was emphasised. A *Panchayat Pradhan* explained: 'through struggles and movements, we are trying to transform this *Panchayat* and make it a people's *Panchayat*'.

The politicians and government officials constructed and defined 'development', which had emerged as the new field in which to practise politics. The concept of 'development' appeared in three different contexts: in implementing the available government programmes and schemes, in collaborating with the donors/sponsors (eg UNICEF) in specific projects where the *Gram Panchayat* was an executing agency, and in demanding certain improvements of the area. 'Development' in these three contexts appeared as an instrument with the potential for change or inducing some action. These actions took place in response to perceived deficiencies, deprivation or absence of certain parameters of 'quality of life'—they operated with the concept of absence and lack. 'Development' was an act of creating certain objects which were not present before. The objects were mostly physical and literal, visible to the spectators. This visibility was essential in electoral politics: it was evidence or proof of 'work-done' by the elected representatives, which would fetch the necessary mandate to stay in power. The reorganisation of the visual field provided an aesthetic experience of development as well.

The practice of 'participatory development' and the negotiations took place within the framework set by the party. The agenda of the meetings was drawn up and moderated by the party leaders. Discussions took place over the type, location and length, etc of a project (eg for roads, whether to be brick-laid, earthen or metalled). But the very episteme of 'development' remained unquestioned and unproblematised in this practice of 'participatory development'. It consequently worked towards maintaining the status quo and the *Panchayat* appeared as a supplier of roads, tube-wells, canals and other infrastructure to the villagers.

In the biannual *Gram Sansad* (ward-level) meetings of the *Panchayat*, mostly in the second meeting held in the month of October/November every year, the planning was always done in excess: the listed works to be done or demanded were more than the total resource allocated to the *Gram Panchayat* under various schemes. Perhaps one of the reasons for adopting this practice was to sustain the rhetoric of deprivation, a gap between demand (for development at the local level) and supply (of resources from the central government). This logic also supported the filing of various petitions and deputations for development to the Block Development Office and the District Magistrate, which was a way to continue to mount pressure on the supply side and a cause of continuous 'struggle' and 'movement'. Thus, like the earlier deprivation of land during the feudal period which precipitated a mass-mobilisation, a strategy of deprivation was again deployed to mobilise people against the new 'enemy', identified in the opposition party(parties)-led central government. Earlier the enemy was within the local society and hence the social appeared fragmented and plural in the discourse, which made mass mobilisation possible. But now, with the identification of the enemy outside local society, the plurality and social fragmentation was inverted to make it appear a coherent force resisting the outside enemy. The political discourse thus foreclosed the possibility of enunciation of exploitation and inequality within the given society.

One of the objectives of infrastructure development schemes was to support the lowest strata of society during the lean (agricultural) seasons. These programmes were supposed to create and provide wage-work to marginal farmers and landless workers. The schemes were directed towards individuals or groups with an explicit objective of 'helping' the 'beneficiaries' and 'target groups'.

As the number of 'beneficiaries' who could be supported by these schemes was limited as a result of scanty resource allocation by the central government, so the selection of 'beneficiaries' became an important political activity. It was of little surprise that the people who were close to the party leaders had a better chance of being selected. Sukhada Sardar's husband got both a house under the *Indira Awas Yogna* (a free housing scheme for the poor) and a loan under the Integrated Rural Development Project (IRDP) scheme; when asked how he had availed himself of both these schemes, she replied: '*party-r dada-der kichhu dite hoi*' (the political leaders need to be paid a percentage).When a *Panchayat Pradhan*'s uncle could not arrange the necessary dowry for his daughter's marriage, the *Pradhan* provided him with a loan of Rs 5000 for poultry farming. The poultry, as expected, never materialised, and the sum was utilised in the marriage ceremony.

In this form of political discourse the issues of exploitation and social inequality were again pushed to the *private* sphere, to be dealt with solely by the individual. An emphasis was put on the individual's capacity to work as the 'engine for bringing change' in his/her personal life. This work was gendered. The individual initiative, capacity and success in mitigating adverse forces were projected as the qualities of a person and were celebrated in public lectures. Amjad Amin (name changed), a Zonal Committee member, cited the example of a 'girl', whose 'husband was an alcoholic', but who had the 'vision and ambition' to 'marry her daughter off'. She used to sell earthen pots in the local market and saved money from her profits. This made it possible for her to pay a dowry of Rs 10000 to marry her daughter off. Since even a woman had the capacity to work (that is why the example of a woman was cited), so men, in this patriarchal society, should be more able to perform their duties of self-sustenance. One could only blame oneself for the inability to improve one's socioeconomic condition. The question of social change had thus been privatised, and become a matter of private initiative.

On the other hand, the implementation of 'developmental' programmes required the display of the disciplining dimension of power. A UNICEF-sponsored sanitation programme was presented as a 'very good project'. A diarrhoea epidemic in the area was supposed to have broken out as villagers excreted in the open fields. The villagers were persuaded to install a low-cost latrine in their houses. This line of persuasion soon turned into a language of command and regimentation. The people who dared to continue to defecate in the open were 'shameless like the *Biharis*' and they were engaged in 'polluting the environment'. If anyone was found doing the same, he or she would be 'caught and tied with rope'. People were asked to change their habits and regularly use the latrines.

Institutionalised power was no longer the medium by which to contest the powerful in the villages, rather it provided the party cadres with an instrument to manage and control the micro-events and processes of rural life. The very participation which constituted the movements and unleashed the processes of social change in rural areas was replaced by mechanical attendance. 'Development' was converted into a language of command; the party leaders 'spoke in a scolding tone' ('*dhamak-er sure kotha bole*') to the 'subjects of development'. There was resentment about the party's leaders' and cadres' 'arrogant behaviour' ('*oudhotto-purno achoron*').

The possibility of creating a hegemonised society, a whole, gave way to a condition which Ranajit Guha would have described as 'dominance without hegemony'[13]—wherein persuasion never manages to outweigh coercion; coercion becomes explicit in the formation and operation of power relationships. It is important to explore how the dominated and marginalised people lived in this condition of 'dominance without hegemony'.

Living under 'dominance without hegemony'

The dispersed social positions that emerged in post-land reform rural Bengal might seem to offer, hypothetically, social mobility within it. But this was not the case. The marginalised families, who did not have any 'social capital' or any working capital, as expected, found it difficult to 'participate in the market'. On very rare occasions they might have got small amounts of credit from the self-help groups, which would allow them to lease a piece of land. They continued to depend on earning daily wages, ie on selling their bodily capacity to labour.

The Mahatma Gandhi National Rural Employment Guarantee Act (MGNREGA) makes it mandatory for the local governance institutions, the *Gram Panchayat* and the Block Office, to provide 100 days of wage-employment in a financial year to a rural household whose adult members want to do (unskilled) manual work. Shankar had obtained a job-card to get his '*Eksho diner kaaj*' ('100 days-of-work', the name by which MGNREGA is known in the villages). He would arrive at the job-site around 7 am (mostly to do earth-work), work there until 12 noon or 1 pm, and then would come back home for a meal. After taking a rest, he would again go to work in the fields of a land-owner and work till 5 or 6 pm. He said: 'If one is willing to work, there is no dearth of work'. Yet he found it difficult to 'run' his family. Why? 'Prices have increased so much.' In a high-inflation economy, wages earned did not necessarily meet household expenditure and relieve the body; the intensity of labour increased and the body remained the only asset to sell in the market.

During my interview with a group of women, one of them described her family as 'poor'; others also supported her. The reason provided by the woman herself and others for being poor was that her husband was 'paralytic and invalid'. So, because of the absence of an able-bodied male in the family, who could have had earned, they were 'poor'. Mannan Sheikh, having lost his vision, was not considered as a worker any more. Nobody wanted to employ him and he received less attention from his relatives, villagers and politicians. To the villagers he was a 'beggar' living on 'alms', and the monetised society bestowed residual sympathy on him. As the sole male member was invalid, the villagers and Mannan did not consider his daughters, who worked as agricultural labourers and kept the fire in the kitchen alive, as wage-earners.

The body is a machine, which is a personal property of an individual, so any 'failure' of it and its 'repairing' is the responsibility of the individual. When the state is negligent and the social services are weak and inadequate, conventional biopolitics is never practised. The successful practice of biopolitics requires strong governmental and non-governmental interventions, particularly through social care and welfare services, which can convert the body into a space to exercise power. In their absence, the development discourse structures the field of power in a skewed way. 'Development' articulates a (technological) imagination (along with institutions, practices and desires) which frames life in a particular way and displaces the older ways.

The new frame of life required material resources to realise it. Since such resources were in short supply from governmental and non-governmental agencies, people had to make their own arrangements; they were forced to increase their out-of-pocket expenditure to arrange private tutor's fees, books, medicine, etc. 'Development' accelerated the commodification of everyday life and created a 'market for welfare commodities'. Thus, this new framing of life opened up a paradoxical political field: it showed the escape routes to the marginalised, but at the same limited them.

The desire of the asexual body of the labourer had always been to reduce the pressure on the mechanised body; that is, social mobility was perceived as a movement from labour-intensive work towards less labour-intensive work. Along with the uncertainty of work, health problems and old age, the desire for a less labour-intensive life was linked to the societal attribution of higher status to 'intellectual' activity, and to the higher wages that the latter received.[14] Amulya Sardar lamented: 'I can't work anymore...while others are living happily... I am working in this old-age. If my son and daughter-in-law had earned enough, I would have sat back at home and relaxed . . . but that's never going to happen'.

The education of children appeared as an instrument to overcome exploitation and a way to make one's children free from dependency on physical labour. Shakila asked: 'Why our children should also become labourers like us and spend the rest of their life working for others? No, they should go to the school and be educated; after that, they will do what they want.' They sent their children to the nearest school and strived to arrange and pay for private tuition for them, even if only before school examinations. Often the family would support one (male) child to study up to college level and would expect that person to find a job and, in turn, support the family.

However, the privatisation of social change limited the exercise of power. While the political and governance apparatus had set up an elaborate capillary network for exercising power, it did not necessarily constitute 'the whole', a completely hegemonised space. Since they had to fend for themselves, the marginalised people broke away from that structure or maintained a distance; they were suspicious of any contact with that network. When Mannan Sheikh was approached for an interview, he was alarmed: 'Now you will land me in trouble . . . I don't know what to say and what not to say . . . and by slip of tongue if I say something I will be in trouble (*jhamela*)'. Jamila Bibi followed her father's advice:

> My father was a very good person, he never used to mingle with the rich. He never used to join the [political] party; he was scared that they would kill him by taking his thumb impression [that is, he would get involved in an uncomfortable legal hassle]. He had a great fear; he used to tell, 'be very careful in life; don't go to anybody else's place. We are poor; so if they spit on us, don't say anything. Be careful when you walk on the *aal* [narrow path through the field, here used as a metaphor]; it is full of snakes'. My mother was also like that.

Padma said: 'We are Hindu, so we never get involved in any risky affair'. They hardly attended the *Gram Sansad* meetings where the development discourse was set into action; but at the same time, they did not have a radically alternative vision of development.

The self was constructed as naïve, docile, apolitical—always having the tendency to withdraw, to maintain a de-linked and non-partisan social relationship with the elite; at times, accepting and submitting to the latter's whims to avoid any kind of 'trouble'. These strategies of submission and withdrawal were a part of their broader strategy to negotiate with the context of their everyday life. It is a modality of minimising the spheres of domination, restricting it to the economic relationships only.

The strategy of the marginalised people to orient themselves within the given social setting operated on three planes: mimicry of the elite (eg sending their children to school and supplementing this by providing private tuition), creation of a negative image of the local political leaders and elite and withdrawal from 'politics' and 'society' (as seen in avoiding the *Gram Sansad* meetings), and expecting the intervention of an external agency (like the government or 'god') to solve their problems. These skewed strategies (selective participation, withdrawal and external help) placed them at a tangent to the dominant power relationships. It was within these multi-prong ambiguous strategies that they left a trace of their agency, 'the capacity to manage actively the often discontinuous, overlapping or conflicting relations of power'.[15] But they did not thereby become an autonomous agent. This tangential relationship or the strategy of subversion did not change their location in the socio-political space; rather it appeared as a contingent arrangement in perpetuity. They remained exploited and marginalised, always dependent on external agencies to guide them to bring a change in the system. On their own, they had little scope for manoeuvre.

The Left Front's end game

By the mid-1990s the Left Front realised the limits of agrarian modernity and its incapacity to form capital to spur industrialisation in the state. Unemployment in the state was very high, the small peasants were squeezed, many landless workers started to migrate to other parts of the country, income growth for middle-class farmers was plateauing and the state's exchequer was almost empty. The Left Front had to do something.

In the meantime the rest of India had started to embrace the policies of liberalisation and privatisation of the economy, which brought an end to the Licensing Policy. In other words, industries could be set up without seeking permission from the central government. The Left Front government wanted to take this opportunity to attract private investment in the state and drafted an industrial policy in 1994. The government argued that land reform had vastly improved the rural economy and increased the purchasing capacity of people in the state, and hence a consumer- and worker-base was available for heavy and medium industries. To make the state capital, Kolkata, aesthetically pleasant and attractive to investors, several 'operations' were undertaken to evict hawkers and slum-dwellers.

The government appointed the management consultancy firm, McKinsey & Company in 1999 'to assist the single-window facility' (for investors) of the West Bengal Industrial Development Corporation.[16] Later the firm was approached to suggest a plan to restructure agriculture in the state. It drafted the Agribusiness Vision 2010 for West Bengal, which recommended contract farming and a shift to agribusiness, which would attract 'a number of participants across the food value chain [to] play an important role, viz input, extension, storage, marketing, processing and retailing'.[17] The *Panchayat* would 'act as a liaison between the farmer and the agribusiness company and help to build farmers' confidence in the contract relationship'.[18] McKinsey also suggested that the state government should adopt a relaxed labour regulation and provide exemption from the Land Ceiling Act. The state government should develop non-forest waste land and gradually build infrastructure such as green houses, irrigation, cold rooms, facilities for grading/packaging, mobile refrigerated trucks and equipment. It should also provide a capital subsidy, up to 20 per cent, to fruit and vegetable industries, and financial support to certain large-scale projects, such as a cinchona plantation.[19] This proposal for contract farming met with enormous resistance from CPI (M)'s partners in the Left Front because they perceived that the farmers would be tied or bonded to big corporations, and the local market for agricultural produce would be affected or destroyed.

The state government also tried to open up the retail sector to large corporations like Metro, Reliance, etc, which was again violently resisted by small traders and the Left Front's partners like the Forward Block. With the failure of large-scale vertical integration of peasant production with industrial and financial capital, the Left Front dived into industrialisation. But any attempt to industrialise a densely populated state with mostly fertile land and small landholdings would require a violent transformation of the agrarian base.

In the mid-2000s the government embarked on acquiring land for industrialisation and urbanisation. While many of the middle-class and rich farmers were willing to sell their land to the government for compensation, as was the case in Singur and Rajarhat, the smaller peasants and landless labourers violently resisted any such land transfer. The resistance movement against the Tata car factory in Singur was the first spark; when the government proposed to set up a chemical hub in Nandigram, the fire spread rapidly. Quite a few peasants lost their lives at the hands of the CPI (M)'s armed cadres (*Harmad Bahini*) and the police. Memories of the violent 'land grab' movement were revived. The leftist political imagination in West Bengal had reached its limit.

Conclusion

The experience of the Left Front in West Bengal shows that any political project that tries to govern difference successfully has to be dynamic in nature. Agnes Heller argued that modernity moves forward by destroying the existing foundations, but at the same time it promises greater freedom.[20] A political project therefore needs to be both dynamic and to secure freedom; however, this possibility of progress and securing freedom is fraught with tension.

The leftist politics in West Bengal successfully restructured class relations by distributing land and securing tenancy contracts. This in turn changed the caste composition and relations in the rural areas. There was a significant improvement in people's purchasing power and agricultural productivity increased. Political stability was re-established after the tumultuous years of the 1960s and 1970s. However, the restructuring process created a new dominant class and the initial emancipatory role of the *Panchayat* in negotiating social power in the rural areas soon faded away. The new society became very much embedded in the market, yet there was hardly any intervention to help the marginalised people to negotiate with this new set-up. People were largely left to fend for themselves. The discourse of 'development' was deployed to reconstitute the social, but it remained supplementary and could hardly cover the antagonisms which had developed as time went on. 'Development' became the new language of discipline and command.

The possibility of creating hegemony, understood as the constructed whole based on consent, co-optation and co-operation, through which differences can be governed, was never obtained. Rather, the ruling party focused on congealing its constituency by becoming a constituting element in the construction and negotiation of power in the rural areas—power relations became transactional, incentive-driven, bereft of any normative basis. The fragility of these power relations was overlooked because the Left Front remained unchallenged. The marginalised people developed various covert strategies to survive in these conditions. But the move to prioritise industrial development by destroying a section of the agrarian economy created the conditions for a collapse of the power relations (the limits of agrarian modernity had already been reached). Arguably, what West Bengal witnessed and experienced were limits of the egalitarian modes of governing differences in the globalised world.

Notes

1 The 'Shining India' campaign was launched to project the positive effects of the liberalisation, globalisation and privatisation of the Indian economy and to showcase the developments that had apparently spread out through the country.

2 N Bandyopadhyaya, '"Operation Barga" and land reforms perspective in West Bengal: a discursive review', *Economic and Political Weekly*, 16(25–26), 1981, p A-38.

3 *Ibid*, p A-41.

4 GK Lieten, 'Depeasantisation discontinued: land reforms in West Bengal', *Economic and Political Weekly*, 25(40), 1990, p 2265.

5 Bandyopadhyaya, '"Operation Barga" and land reforms perspective in West Bengal', p A-41.

6 *Jotedars* were relatively small landholders compared to the *zamindars*.

7 Lieten, 'Depeasantisation discontinued', p 2268.

8 BK Chandrasekhar (ed), *Panchayati Raj in India—Status Report 1999*, New Delhi: Rajiv Gandhi Foundation, 2000.

9 K Bag, 'Red Bengal's rise and fall', *New Left Review*, 70, 2011, p 80.

10 A Rudra,'One step forward, two steps backward', *Economic and Political Weekly*, 16(25–26), 1981, p A61.

11 R Khasnobis, 'Operation Barga: limits to social democratic reformism', *Economic and Political Weekly*, 16(25–26), 1981, pp A43–48; S Bandopadhyay & D Von Eschen, 'Agricultural failure: caste, class and power in rural West Bengal', in D Gupta (ed), *Social Stratification*, Delhi: Oxford University Press, 1991; Rudra, 'One step forward, two steps backward'; and Bandyopadhyaya, '"Operation Barga".

12 B Prasant, 'No barrier exists between class struggle & development', *People's Democracy*, 23 October 2005, at http://pd.cpim.org/2005/0925/09252005_bengal-1.htm, accessed 4 October 2011.

13 R Guha, *Dominance with Hegemony: History and Power in Colonial India*, Cambridge, MA: Harvard University Press, 1998.

14 A Beteille, 'Introduction', in Beteille (ed), *Equality and Inequality: Theory and Practice*, Delhi: Oxford University Press, 1983.

15 L McNay, *Gender and Agency: Reconfiguring the Subject in Feminist and Social Theory*, Cambridge: Polity, 2000, p 16.

16 K Mandal, 'West Bengal seeks McKinsey help on single-window plan', *Indian Express* (New Delhi), 6 November 1999, at http://www.expressindia.com/fe/daily/19991106/fec06041.html, accessed 4 October 2011.

17 McKinsey & Company, 'Immediate action required to catalyse investment in the agribusiness sector', Memorandum to the Agriculture Minister, 6 May 2002.

18 McKinsey & Company, 'Contract farming: agribusiness for the future', Memorandum to the High Power Committee (Agribusiness), nd.

19 McKinsey & Company, 'Encouraging crop diversification in West Bengal', discussion document, 8 May 2002.
20 A Heller, *The Three Logics of Modernity and the Double Bind of the Modern Imagination*, Public Lecture Series No 23, Collegium Budapest, Institute for Advanced Study, Budapest, 2000.

Notes on contributor

Swagato Sarkar is Assistant Professor and Assistant Dean (Academic Affairs), and Assistant Director, Centre for Equitable Development, Jindal School of Government and Public Policy, OP Jindal Global University. His publications include the book-length monograph *The Limits of Politics: Capitalist Development, Land Acquisition, and the Crisis in the Logics of Indian Democracy* (forthcoming); 'Populism and the anti-corruption movement of Anna Hazare', *Indian Journal of Human Development* (forthcoming); 'The impossibility of just land acquisition', *Economic and Political Weekly*, 8 October 2011; and 'Political Society in a Capitalist World', in A Gudavarthy (ed), *Re-framing Democracy and Agency in India: Interrogating Political Society* (2012).

Rule through Difference on China's Urban–Rural Boundary

JESPER ZEUTHEN

ABSTRACT *In both the academic debate as well as in Chinese politics urban–rural difference is a frequently used categorisation. Policies addressing previous neglect of rural China have been the official top-priority of China's current leadership since it came to power in 2003–2004. This article argues that we need to nuance the distinct dichotomy between urban and rural, and look into the specifics of how differences are actively mobilised when claims are made. The article builds on extensive fieldwork on the claims made by land-losing peasants and local political leaders on the urban–rural boundary in one of the front posts of the current regime's refocus on rural development, Chengdu, appointed as an experimental zone of Urban–Rural Integration (cheng-xiang yitihua) along with Chongqing in 2007 and, as a result of this, subject to massive restructuring of land use. Instead of a clear-cut urban–rural boundary that would have the potential to split the country in two, I find a much more finely masked form of differentiation based on where people are from. Both local leaders and citizens in each locality may bend and interpret rules and regulations considerably as long as their claims do not go beyond their locality.*

'My daughter can marry whoever she wants, as long as he is not a peasant', the taxi driver told me when we arrived in what used to be a village but was now a densely populated entity, described by another taxi driver as the 'wild west', the home of thousands of rural–urban migrants living in what used to be farmhouses, and of a few former local peasants.[1] The urban taxi driver thus reproduced the urban–rural boundary as a boundary between different types of human beings, a way of understanding the urban–rural boundary widely discussed within the China literature, presenting Chinese peasants as massively despised (through, among other things, discourses on personal quality (*suzhi*) presenting rural subjects as uncultivated) and discriminated against (through, among other things, the *hukou*-system), 'non-citizens' with 'nothing but their labour to sell'.[2] The way rural subjects continue to see discrimination as an inescapable faith is regarded as an essential part of China's growth-engine and continued stability.[3] The political refocus on rural development, with an

Jesper Zeuthen is in the Department of Cross-Cultural and Regional Studies, University of Copenhagen.

ongoing, surprisingly open debate on the problems of rural China, however, appears to suggest that the disciplining function of China's urban–rural boundary might be endangered. The boundary might even become a reference point for political mobilisation from below.[4]

This article argues that analytically dividing China into a rural and an urban China, be it for the sake of studying exploitation by the urban strata or for examining political mass mobilisation, neglects 1) how much more finely masked differentiation is; and 2) the fact that boundaries applied in differentiation are not always only in the interest of rulers or elites, but may be just as important in claims making by non-elites. It does so by examining how local leaders and citizens engaged in some of the many different urban, industrial and agricultural development projects making up most of the diffusely defined Urban–Rural Integration Policy mobilise differences to work the system in the politically tense context of resettlement.

Boundaries and claims making

In a village on the outskirts of Chengdu city proper, a few hundred metres from the border with a suburban county, I met a middle-aged woman living in a house planned for expropriation.[5] Both sides of the border were undergoing massive resettlement. In her village almost everybody was to be resettled. She told me how, in the neighbouring village in the suburban county a few hundred metres away, 'everybody took stuff out to the highway and sat on it' because all the land of two sub-villages (each of a few hundred households) had been occupied. 'Those places are all creating trouble these days', she continued: 'There has been beating. Those leading on were arrested by the police and the unrest was suppressed... They take away your house and give you 150 yuan per month to go rent a house.'

A village party secretary had informed me that the monthly pay in the district the woman lived in was 500 yuan. When confronted with this, she replied:

> The 500 yuan is only for the five city districts. There it is Xindu District. The state says that it compensates so much money, but when it comes down to members of the collective, you don't get this amount of money... If compensation were made according to Property Law, they would be properly compensated... Those who don't have any connections, except a few of them, can't make any noise... When those with connections make some noise, and you find someone well connected, then they are not alone and it becomes a matter of several thousand yuan. As an ordinary citizen [*laobaixing*], many don't want to do like this, but what can you do? In the end you'll have a lot of money in your hand. Those at the top have no chance of knowing of it.

The woman showed an interest in what happened on the other side of the border, and she had clear sympathies towards the protests. Yet the protests were none of her business. She was likely to become part of a similar protest, but her protest would be directed towards her local authorities and based on the well-connected noise-makers she would be able to find once her sub-village was to be developed.

The form of claims making the woman refers to resembles very much what O'Brien and Li call 'rightful resistance'. Here, protesters attempt to find allies higher up in the system, or in other departments of the fragmented authoritarian system, who can help them work their very specific and localised claim through the bureaucracy. This form of claims making requires a popular belief that, if only the top leadership knew, things would be just, and it requires clear boundaries defining the scope of claims. The zoned nature of 'rightful resistance', along with the fact that it requires allies close to the political top, means that it does not pose a threat to regime resilience. If claims were made along the urban–rural boundary, this would seem to be a break with 'rightful resistance', and to open up for protests that could potentially split the nation in two.[6]

In his life-long work on boundaries Tilly argued that they either work to define categories of bounded individuals more or less silently accepting each other's very different sets of opportunities (opportunity hoarding), or they may be used as reference points in mobilisation.[7] Opportunity hoarding is a non-elite strategy to protect privileges. Here a prerequisite for all privileges of each category is a perception of the boundaries defining this category as 'natural'. In mobilisation boundaries work quite differently. Here, the ideal is that opportunities should be equal. Boundaries justifying unequal opportunities are perceived as unjust and exaggerated in order to increase mobilisation in very open networks, including different strata of society. Clearly the borders between small localities with different sets of opportunities for negotiation and networking seem like arenas for opportunity hoarding. The urban–rural boundary, on the other hand, seems like a boundary against which people might mobilise across the nation; and indeed were mobilised during both the 1949 revolution and the Cultural Revolution.[8]

In the following sections this article seeks to identify how the urban–rural boundary and borders between localities are controlled and exploited at different administrative levels as well as among ordinary citizens outside the state system. I find a very strong zoning created from the top but, equally, maintained from below.

State control and zoning

A view traced throughout Chinese history is that zoning enables authorities to blame lower levels, intervene whenever needed, and accept high degrees of autonomy for local elites in prosperous zones not posing any treat to the overall stability, while simultaneously contributing to national prosperity (what Ong refers to in its present form as variegated sovereignty).[9] There seems to be agreement on this basic structure. Disagreement starts when it comes down to explaining how well the centre is able to intervene and how intended the zoned structure is. Views range from Cai Yongshun and Wang Fei-ling agreeing that intervention is really only a matter of whether the centre wants to intervene or not to O'Brien and Li's concept of rightful resistance that would seem to be a view of a political centre in which at least some elements want to do good.[10] A third view is that there is no master plan. Local cadres implement the policies they select, and only occasionally may a higher-level cadre attempt to mobilise lower-level cadres in social engineering projects, with little or no base in the demands of the people or consideration of social stability.[11] The zoning between different localities, I argue, means that it is of less importance to regime resilience whether claim makers believe in the virtues of the top leadership. As long as claims by local cadres and citizens are kept within a single locality, they do not pose a real danger to overall stability. The zoned structure, I further argue, is enforced through claims made from below. In such claims maintenance and expansion of the opportunities hoarded in a locality require that the zoned structure is maintained.

The infrastructure for the zoned structure is the *hukou*-system with roots in imperial times. In its present form (or something more amenable to its present form), it was properly in place from 1958.[12] A *hukou* was assigned to everybody. The *hukou* system regulated access to land, occupations, housing, food, education and medical care. A major characteristic was the *hukou*'s distinction between agricultural and non-agricultural occupations. These were the formal occupations that persons were supposed to have, and possibly did have when the system was initiated. An agricultural *hukou* guaranteed usage-rights to land and the provision of resources from the rural self-supplying collective. A non-agricultural *hukou* guaranteed access to non-agricultural occupations, without land, but with the provision of food rations directly from the state; thus hoarding opportunities were different between these two categories. When the system was initiated during the Great Leap Forward (1958–59), the ration system ensured food supplies to non-agricultural *hukou*-holders, while millions of agricultural *hukou*-holders starved to death.

Since the 1980s the *hukou* system has been altered. Especially in Western media, but also in parts of the more serious China literature as well as Chinese media, the *hukou* system has in recent years been portrayed as having been almost abandoned.[13] Chan and Buckingham argue that such reports are based on a misunderstanding of the introduction of uniform *hukou* in several metropolitan areas. The uniform *hukou* refers to abolishing the distinction between agricultural and non-agricultural occupations, and only note the place of registration in the *hukou*. Services provided for individuals not holding a local *hukou* are as limited as always, while peasants from already fairly well-to-do villages under the jurisdiction of the city prefectures get access to more extensive urban welfare. Abolition of the agricultural/non-agricultural element of the *hukou*, according to Chan and Buckingham, does not mean that the urban–rural boundary becomes less significant, at least when it comes to entitlement to urban welfare. The big picture of the rural as poor and the city as rich remains the same; the cities merely absorb some of their frontiers. The introduction of a uniform *hukou* is part of the many disputes over land issues near large cities. Peasants do not want to replace their usage-right to valuable land with the declining services attached to an urban *hukou*.[14]

Wang Fei-ling argues that the agricultural/non-agricultural divide primarily enabled opportunity hoarding along the urban–rural boundary, with a growing domestic market in the cities, and agricultural *hukou*-holders accepting underpaid jobs. I argue that it is now mainly the rank of localities of registration that enables this mechanism, while the agricultural/non-agricultural divide appears to be anything but silently accepted in the way that it would be in opportunity hoarding. Chan and Buckingham's view of the system as instituting a metropolitan/non-metropolitan divide, I argue, does not fully appreciate the fact that zones are much more finely ranked than merely as metropolitan or non-metropolitan.

Chengdu's urban–rural integration policy

The keyword for the reordering of land under the integration policy was 'three concentrations' (*san ge jizhong*), ie the concentration of residential land, agricultural land and industrial land. As one of the architects behind the policy, originally started as a city prefecture policy in 2004, has argued, through concentration specialised zones would become more competitive and more easily manageable.[15]

In China peasants usually have usage-right of around one *mu* (666 m^2) per family member. Normally this land is placed close to the family's home. Concentrating land in areas that used to be rural for large-scale projects is thus by implication a massive change in the physical space. Concentration of land also implies a major change of who controls land. In principle, all land in China formally classified as agricultural belongs to collectives. These 'collectives' are the lowest administrative units in the Chinese state system (referred to here as villages and sub-villages). Chinese legislation in principle ensures that sub-letting agricultural land to larger projects can only take place if a clear majority of such a village collective agrees. Such collectives can become strong organised enterprises when sub-letting land, or the sub-letting agreement may be manipulated by a few local leaders or private elites. By changing the formal status of land from rural to urban, higher-level governments and elites connected to these may take over control of the land. Urban and rural hence become important categories deciding who can possibly claim control over land use.[16]

An important element of the Urban–Rural Integration Policy was *hukou*-reforms. The city prefecture government divided the city (12 000 km^2, 14 million inhabitants in 2010) into three different zones forming rings around the city (see Figure 1). Targets for land use in each zone differed. The most central zone consisted of the already almost built out city districts. Here urbanisation would reach 100 per cent. The counties furthest away were supposed to reach a much lower degree of urbanisation, and considerable agricultural production would be maintained. Rights to social welfare and books used in schools differed between these zones. The monthly social welfare for the handicapped was around 70 yuan in the outer counties and around 500 yuan close to the city, so differences were very real to individual citizens. It was the intention that all citizens within each of the ring-zones

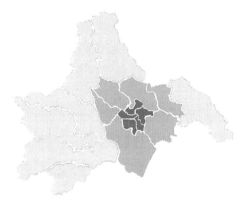

FIGURE 1. Chengdu's ranked districts and counties.
© Mette Willaing Zeuthen.

should have the same rights to social welfare, etc, irrespective of their status as holders of agricultural or non-agricultural *hukou*. In the most rural zone county towns had a special status as local urban centres. Transfer of *hukou* to a more attractive ring was heavily regulated, leaving residents from the external rings in essentially the same situation as rural–urban migrants from outside the city prefecture when entering the central city districts. The city prefecture was to abolish the agricultural/non-agricultural divide for locals within each zone and maintain rural–urban migrants (be they from far away or from a neighbouring district) as non-locals. In this way the *hukou*-policy had many similarities with those studied by Chan and Buckingham; the major difference was the ranking of counties and districts of registration on an urban–rural continuum, where getting a *hukou* was less attractive the further one moved from the city, but without a distinct metropolitan/non-metropolitan divide.[17]

Claims by local leaders

With the city's policy of appointing specialised zones, the competition to become a special zone and thereby attract political goodwill as well as funding and career opportunities was tense. As a head of a county-level department put it, 'each township had its own speciality, so I needed to visit all of them in order to really know what the Urban–Rural Integration Policy was about'.[18] In this section, I study how local leaders used the urban–rural boundary to justify policies by adding content to special zones in localities with different distances from the urban centre.

You-tien Hsing divides her analysis of urbanisation in contemporary China into different types of zones, very similar to the rings defined by Chengdu's government. Far from the city centre, in what she calls the rural fringe, land has a limited value, and local authorities often have quite a free hand to override legislation on land use. Closer to the urban centre, land is more valuable and the many actors interested in the land there make the citizens' influence larger, often with sub-village or village organisations as their representatives. Below, I apply Hsing's terminology and look for similarities.

The rural fringe

Huaqiu village was one of the most distant villages still under the jurisdiction of the city prefecture. The now legendary village party secretary, Liu, had a few years before I met him in 2007 single-handedly encouraged his fellow villagers to build the steep, paved mountain road we had arrived on. After the road had been built, a tea company was established, financed by loans channelled through a company run by the county government to the party secretary who owned it. Pictures of the building of the road were now exhibited in a newly built exhibition hall next to the company headquarters.[19]

By manifesting a good story of hardship endured, Secretary Liu had *de facto* monopolised the usage-right to land in the village, and he was an important figure for more highly placed authorities to display. When national inspections arrived, county officials staffed a nearby closed down factory, supposedly ensuring that peasants without usage-rights to land had a source of income for the duration of the inspection. Everybody within the local state had an interest in preserving this story of the poor but hard-working mountain village and its success. Secretary Liu, now also one of the county's only two members of the provincial party committee, as the hero of the story had more or less a free hand to do as he pleased. The county government would find almost anything justified, and displayed the success of Huaqiu village to cadres at the city-prefecture, province and national level in order to illustrate how it more than met the demands of the central leadership. The hard-working and entrepreneurial party secretary had made Huaqiu a model village. Other villages on the rural fringe had their specialities. In some villages the speciality, as in Liu's mobilisation of villagers to build a road, had its origin in something that had been truly successful, such as the establishment of a successful collectively-owned agricultural company in one case; and in another the attraction of urban industries (the party secretary's own factory on remarkably cheap land). In other cases, models developed by one village were copied, often with less promising results. In all rural fringe cases the low status of the localities made it possible for local leaders with an entrepreneurial spirit to justify bending and bypassing the regulations by exemplifying a technique to fight for rural development. Although there was a resemblance to what Scott might call social engineering, the zoning of experiments made consequences less disastrous, and many projects were only a thin veneer justifying land seizure for local elites, which, while often putting some at a vast disadvantage, might also contribute to local development.

The urban fringe

In a county town with a formally higher rank than the surrounding rural fringe townships, the entrepreneur Li Yongkang almost succeeded in becoming the *de facto* single ruler of a new town district through his visions for urban planning.[20]

In 2002, when rural tax reforms had taken away a substantial part of the county funding, Li Yongkang's private enterprise Ruiyun Group was allowed to more than double the area of the town with around 150 000 inhabitants. Scholars, who quickly became aware of this process, called it the C-BOT-model. Also written C-BOT in Chinese, the C was short for 'city' and B, O and T were abbreviations for 'build, operate and transfer'. The system meant that services were to be operated by the company and fees were to be paid to it. The new city area would *de facto* be run by Ruiyun for 50 years.

This quite unorthodox way of leading a town was only politically possible because it was presented as new, innovative and necessary in order to develope the backward town and make it meet the new requirements of a modern city. Director Li continuously pointed at how backward the town was, and made sure to ally himself with university intellectuals who had come up with the C-BOT term. He had made a study trip to England in order to ensure that the new town district would look extraordinarily appealing. In this way he had convinced local authorities of the benefits of developing the town according to his ideas. He needed to convince these authorities, because his ideas were on a scale where going through a village would not be feasible, unlike many of his other projects. However, after an inspection by the State Council in 2004, the experiment was halted and the county party secretary fired. This was probably because the state council could not accept letting a private enterprise run a county town. Yet by arguing for the special need of his home town, Li Yongkang almost made Beijing waive some of its cardinal legislation.

When I visited the county town, some years after Director Li's project, the mapping of land use was extremely detailed, and interviews seemed to confirm that continued resettlement was being carried out according to regulations. The room for manoeuvre of local elites and political leaders to mobilise each other through difference had been considerable, and the mobilisation had had very few links to ordinary people. Development after Li Yongkang's project suggests more focus from above on control, and less room for bypassing regulations by being creative.

Closer to Chengdu, in a more central zone with much higher levels of compensation for lost land, the tendency seemed to be similar, yet with somewhat quicker shifts between the selected development models. Here, a large 13-storey compound built on rural land that had made the collective economy grow from 100 000 yuan to 23 million per year in just three years, was no longer presented as a model project, probably because of concerns following a central government focus on the illegal selling of agricultural land. During my fieldwork the ownership structure of the compound did not change. The strategy seemed to be to hush it up while the neighbouring street committee, where land had been converted to urban land, became the model and was praised for resettling according to the regulations. Until recently both places had been dominated by oversized farmhouses partly illegally occupying all available land and mainly inhabited by rural–urban migrants renting rooms from local landlords, as in the taxi-driver's description of 'the wild west'. So strategy shifts were very fast.[21]

In these examples we see a tendency towards more freedom for local cadres and well connected local elites to engage in projects that manifest development technologies (or what Scott might refer to as 'high-modernist ideology') the farther the distance from the city. This is quite similar to Hsing's observations. On the urban fringe merely mobilising difference did not work. It seemed that citizens' influence in urbanisation had been considerable when locals expanded their farmhouses to host rural–urban migrants, yet authority was in the process of being transferred to higher-level government. This was partly justified by a belief that they could protect the interests of resettled residents better. Citizens may have become protected by this manoeuvre, but village organisations clearly had not. The zoning enabled variegated sovereignty, where regulations could be more easily overridden in some localities (rural fringe) while heavily enforced in others (urban fringe).

Claims from below

As in local governance, particularities and special conditions of a small locality were also frequently applied in the claims of those targeted by resettlement. I found that claims made might in some cases go directly against central politics, but since they usually do not involve large categories such as 'all peasants' in China, the sometimes high degree of social mobilisation locally against such projects involving resettlement remains possible to control.

I divide my analysis of public claims between three different categories that were treated considerably differently by the local state: 1) locals with an agricultural *hukou*; 2) locals with a non-agricultural *hukou*; and 3) non-locals. On the outskirts of the city proper the per capita compensation offered for resettlement depended almost exclusively on this formal status: 51–60 m^2 of new housing for locals with an agricultural *hukou*, 30 m^2 for local urban residents (non-agricultural *hukou*-holders), and nothing for non-locals, because in principle they could not have rights to local agricultural land. In each of these three categories a number of citizens had good jobs, and had already bought housing at market prices. These individuals might also make claims, and probably had a better chance of succeeding with them. Here, however, I choose to focus on citizens for whom the claim was vital to their life chances. I do so because I am concerned with how boundaries can justify politically created or maintained inequality (opportunity hoarding) and how they may be applied to target allegedly unfair inequality (mobilisation). I keep this a major concern by focusing on citizens for whom rural land, a politically assigned good, is essential, rather than citizens whose opportunities are largely decided by market forces less directly under political control.

Close to the city the three categories of citizens lived next to each other. All the local urban residents I interviewed were laid-off workers, who were either registered in a township seat (*zhen*) and had worked in local industry instead of having access to land before economic reforms, or had been compensated with a state sector job in an earlier urbanisation process. Many of them were not resettled, because they already lived quite densely and occupied little space. These urban residents might feel bypassed by the, in their eyes, over-compensated peasants. Local peasants had often built quite large houses, parts of which they sublet to the many rural–urban migrants. In most villages farther away from the centre the vast majority consisted of local peasants. Since access to interviews without local cadres present was much easier when persons were not yet resettled in a gated community, most of my data cover peasants in the process of negotiating their deal or anticipating how negotiation will go. During my fieldwork, the resettled-to-be was a much larger group than those already resettled. The three categories represent different types of divides. Each of the three categories has boundaries with the two other groups. All these boundaries have the potential to be understood as urban–rural boundaries, while only the boundary between locals and non-locals is also a boundary between citizens administratively assigned to different localities. I argue that this boundary between different localities and citizens from different localities plays a great role not only for individuals' real opportunities, but also for the way individual citizens believe their opportunities should rightfully be; this boundary is not seriously contested. The boundary between locals registered as peasants and urban residents, on the other hand, is seriously contested, and not accepted by increasingly marginalised laid-off workers. In my view this is because the boundary is not based on where citizens are from.

Local peasants

I first analyse the restructuring of land from the viewpoint of local peasants, both close to the city and farther away.

As illustrated by the woman in the farmhouse about to be expropriated discussed earlier, peasants' distrust of the local administrations was widespread. This was not least the case for a young widow in a village on the rural fringe. She was much more socially challenged than most others, since she had a small child and only one income. She now earned a very small income by working for watermelon growers invited from Zhejiang province, more than 1000 kilometres away, by the local authorities to till land leased from the village collective. She was one of very few informants who hinted at a possible conflict with outsiders:

> The government doesn't want us locals to rent the land, so people from outside come and rent the land, because there's a profit involved. Here it is not like other places. If the government lets locals rent the land, the market price is transparent, and they [officials] will get no profit. With people from outside, they get a profit. The logic is that easy... People say that development is for ordinary citizens, to develop agriculture... But the government doesn't do it like that; like here it just reports to the upper level government the planned production quantity, but never cares about the life or death of ordinary citizens.

Although she saw the watermelon growers as outsiders, her real dissatisfaction was directed towards the village leadership, not at the melon growers, nor at the central leadership, which was seen as at least partially well-intended. When I interviewed other peasants far away from the city, they all knew about the much higher level of compensation for land in places closer to the city, but in claims, references were to neighbouring villages. They believed that they should have the same opportunities as villagers living in places similar to their own, but saw no chance of reaching the same level as those closer to the centre.

Almost all peasants interviewed believed that they as peasants had to work hard. A peasant in his 40s who had lost land and a house very close to the centre and was waiting for resettlement explained how hardship was part of being a Chinese peasant, as opposed to being a former state employee:

> Often unemployed workers don't want to do jobs that make them lose face. Peasants, on the other hand, can do all kinds of jobs. They do it thoroughly, because they need food... Laid-off workers always believe they are workers and a level higher than peasants...; it used to be like this, but now peasants are a bit higher, so now many urban residents want to become peasants, and don't want to be workers. Peasants have land which they can let out and earn money by.

Although hardship was perceived as an integral part of being a peasant, it was also clear that peasants were believed to have to work harder the further away from the city they were. Rural–urban migrants were believed to have to work very hard. This perception of geographically differentiated opportunities was most clearly expressed by an elderly married couple close to the city. When talking about the many rural–urban migrants in their village, they explained:

> A district party secretary from a mountainous area couldn't even be like a sub-village leader [three administrative levels lower] here. Our sub-village leader here gets several hundred yuan per month. A party secretary of a mountain district only gets a bit more than one thousand per year.

Both cadres and subjects were perceived as having fewer opportunities the further they were from the centre. These differences were perceived as, if not just, then more or less 'natural', as in opportunity hoarding, while differences within localities of the same rank were understood as the result of more and less successful local leadership and hence subject to public claims. Rural–urban migrants in this respect were understood as belonging to their places of registration.

Most of the informants above were neither particularly well-to-do nor particularly poor, but they all seemed to identify themselves very much as ordinary citizens (peasants) who were having a hard time. However, they were also aware that some, like laid-off workers or peasants from further away were having a harder time, but this fact in no way made them incapable of making claims against their local authorities. Though there was to some degree a notion of China's ordinary citizens (peasants) against the elite around the state, when making a claim it was important to present a case as particular and draw a line distinguishing it from other cases.

It seemed that the continued mobilisation for campaigns for proper resettlement schemes in connection with the very long lasting and massive resettlement had given local peasants some sense of resistance that went beyond a single case and went beyond their narrow locality. In some situations, this was leading to a situation where it was almost as if the major authority trusted was not the local administration, but potential protesters with proper allies. By having somebody well connected approach higher political levels, there was a chance of getting a more just treatment. Whether this belief implied a belief that higher-level politicians were truly just or simply wanted to avoid 'noise', however, was not clear. What was clear was that claims and the network of people backing the claims were extremely place- and case-specific. Claims were made in extremely small units with reference only to nearby localities with similar rank on the urban–rural continuum. While much was disputed within localities of the same rank, the ranking was surprisingly little questioned. The ranking was a prerequisite for making claims of a scope limited enough to succeed with them.

Local urban residents

Attitudes found among holders of non-agricultural local *hukou* were quite different, and references were considerably less place-specific. One old urban resident, living in a single leftover house between several large development projects, explained how the state (*guojia*) had betrayed her several times through changes of her *hukou* status. First, she had been sent down to the country during the Cultural Revolution and had got a rural *hukou* when it was more attractive to be urban. Then, during early economic reforms, she had become an urban resident. Thus she could only get half the compensation given to everybody else. She thought that China's overall progress was all very fine, but she had been unfortunate and had not enjoyed any of it.[22]

The old woman's point of view was quite similar to that of two laid-off female workers approaching fifty years of age. They lived in small, badly kept rented rooms at the compound of the former state-owned enterprise at which they had worked. When asked to compare peasants and urban residents, they explained:

> A: Now, really, laid-off workers are the most miserable. Peasants aren't a bit miserable any more.

> B: Peasants have land. Their land is money. The working class neither has a tile over their heads nor a speck of land. It all belongs to the state, right?

> A: [The state] hasn't mentioned those laid off, they all talk about peasants.

> [...]

> B: We have fought for the state, all [our] youth and hot blood was given to the Communist Party, and the result is that it is very miserable now.

In both cases the state was identified as the reason for the misfortune rather than merely its local arms. The old woman in the last house standing was not able to blame the local government for misinterpretation of regulations; her ill fate had its root in central politics both during the Cultural Revolution and under the reforms. The two women interviewed above understood economic reforms as continually taking away privileges from them, especially with the latest focus on rural development. They all saw their opportunities as considerably worse than those of local peasants, but they blamed the state, not the more privileged local peasants themselves. Many former state-employed workers might, when explicitly asked, claim that they were more cultivated (had a higher *suzhi*) than local peasants and that they were also harder-working than local peasants; many saw themselves as being in the same boat as the migrant workers. They did not see themselves as having a higher *suzhi* than rural–urban migrants. Informant B noted: 'When they leave their homes, it is also to work, we also work, it's all for making a living. It's the same there's no difference.' Local peasants, on the other hand did not need to work hard since they had land and houses.

The urban residents had quite strong perceptions of themselves as having been mistreated, and frequently returned to almost archaic political paroles, like 'I represent the laid-off workers of China'. In Tilly's terms, there was clearly no silent acceptance of their faith. These laid-off workers blamed the political centre rather than local authorities for their misfortune. The group of laid-off workers clearly illustrated the fact that maintaining an urban/rural divide between citizens registered at the same place severely challenged local state authority. Once compensated, urban and rural residents would, however, have the same rights to public service, so the divide was probably a transitional phenomenon and, although they questioned the authority of the entire political system, the fact that their rights were subject to locally defined regulations, and their limited number, ensured that they were no true danger to the regime.

Non-locals

During an interview of an otherwise quite well informed interior decorator from around 200 km from Chengdu, who had lived in Chengdu for decades, I asked whether there were any plans to demolish the farmhouse on the outskirts of Chengdu in which he rented a room. He was not able to answer the question and had to turn to his landlord. She could then answer the question. The question of resettlement did not matter to him. When his present locality was demolished, he would rent a room slightly further out of town. One of the watermelon growers from Zhejiang, described by local peasants as really well connected with the local authorities, seemed to be doing good business. Even so, he lived with his family in a tent and was not planning to buy any other accommodation in the village. Like the interior decorator, he did not reveal any signs of a long-term spatial affiliation to the area to which he had moved.[23]

In the 20 interviews with migrants to central Chengdu conducted, I only came across one case in which expropriation seemed to have been an issue. A group of sellers of Chinese medicine had rented land from a local sub-village leader (and now husband to one of the migrants) more than a decade ago, and then built their own housing on this piece of land. These migrants would get compensation for the building materials used to build the houses, but nothing more. Unlike most of the locals, they were satisfied with their compensation.

Migrants perceived their stay as temporary, and their expectations towards local authorities were extremely modest. Migrant informants might occasionally claim that they worked harder than locals, but there was no real disdain directed towards locals. The only group singled out of by a rural–urban migrant as a danger were the 'blind floaters' (*mangliu*), ie migrants migrating without a proper job. Interviews with local authorities and reports written by local authorities revealed slight problems with registering migrants, family planning, and ordinary crime among some migrants, but the big issue of social unrest was clearly that involving local peasants in land appropriation.

The rural–urban migrants stood in vast contrast to a group of immigrants (*yimin*) resettled (with *hukou* transfer) from a very large dam project to various villages on Chengdu's rural fringe. The project had caused severe unrest, reportedly the largest incident since the Tian'anmen incident. The military had been used, and Premier Wen had had to deal with the problems personally. The high degree of political attention now placed on their resettlement gave them a considerable negotiating power against local authorities. This was a negotiating power that local peasants knew they could not get and did not even attempt to get. Claims remained isolated between locals and non-locals.[24]

It was clear that rural–urban migrants were regarded as role models of rural hardship by both local peasants and urban residents. This is quite different from findings in studies of the middle class, where rural–urban migrants are rather regarded as the materialisation of anything it does not want to be.[25] Hu and Wen's rhetoric on rural China may have contributed to this.

Claims were made in isolation among different groups. Differentiation between people from different localities was not disputed, while maintaining differentiation between locals categorised as urban and rural seemed to be regarded as unjust. The boundaries between localities were an accepted part of the opportunity hoarding taking place; urban–rural boundaries were not. Boundaries between localities may have been enforced by the explicit zoning part of Chengdu's Urban–Rural Integration Policy.

Conclusion

When I studied in China in the 1990s I frequently heard myself telling my urban friends how similar Chinese cities were to Denmark and how different the Chinese countryside was from the cities. I had never set foot in rural China but still firmly believed in this image of the Chinese countryside and was frequently reassured by urban Chinese friends that I was right. To me at least, the urban–rural boundary was extremely manifest. Yet, when I physically went to places where the urban–rural boundary appeared to be, the boundary was not manifest to the people there, and the boundary itself was a belt stretching more than 50 kilometres from the centre of the city, far beyond the sign at the fourth ring-road not allowing dirty cars to enter the city proper.

The physical urban–rural boundary was hard to identify. The ranking of zones defined by the *hukou* system reflected this gradual urban–rural boundary. When the boundary was referred to, it was mainly by leaders at various levels, either with the intention of making their power penetrate more deeply (the city government), or in order to please the higher levels and justify local projects (local leaders). Ranks and borders based on the *hukou* system fixed claims to places so they almost never got beyond these boundaries. This meant that social-engineering-type projects in one locality could be contained, and it meant that government could control claims from below even if, as in the dam case, they were to blame high-ranking levels within the state system.

Although boundaries and ranking were constructed by the state (city prefecture), the maintenance of the zoned structure was only possible because this was equally crucial in claims made from below. Heavily compensated land-losing peasants on the urban fringe would have a weak case if they were to include peasants from the rural fringe in their claim. A prerequisite for the claims made was that each category of citizen had certain privileges based on the status of the locality they belonged to. While the boundaries between localities worked very well at maintaining a stable system based on opportunity hoarding, the urban–rural boundary, as suggested by Wang Fei-ling, did not. Discrimination between urban and rural residents from the same localities was not accepted, and when cadres mobilised other cadres, the urban–rural categorisation was also frequently in play.

The many boundaries between localities seemed to provide a stable infrastructure for claims making of both hard to control local cadres and citizens who all saw advantages in being in a special situation defined by their respective localities. When claims resulted in violence or close-to-disastrous social engineering, these problems were contained within a single locality, since boundaries between localities were regarded as 'natural'. Both rule and claims making were powered by difference.

Notes

1 This article builds on extensive fieldwork on Chengdu's urban–rural boundary, including more than 200 interviews and archival work. For a full list of interviews, see JW Zeuthen, 'Ruling through differentiation in China: Chengdu's urban–rural integration policy', unpublished PhD dissertation, Roskilde University, 2010.

2 Quotes are from two of the most path-breaking contributions to the field: Li Zhang, *Strangers in the City: Reconfigurations of Space, Power, and Social Networks within China's Floating Population*, Stanford, CA: Stanford University Press, 2001, p 1; and DJ Solinger, *Contesting Citizenship in Urban China: Peasant Migrants, the State, and the Logic of the Market*, Berkeley, CA: University of California Press, 1999, p 1. Bregnbæk in this issue discusses *suzhi*. See also A Anagnost, 'The corporeal politics of quality (Suzhi)', *Public Culture*, 16(2), 2004, pp 189–208; and C-P Pow, 'Securing the "civilised" enclaves: gated communities and the moral geographies of exclusion in (post-)socialist Shanghai', *Urban Studies*, 44, 2007, pp 1539–1558 use this concept to argue how the urban middle class constructs itself as the opposite of rural–urban migrants. R Murphy, 'Turning peasants into modern Chinese citizens: discourse, demographic transition and primary education', *China Quarterly*, 177(1), 2004, pp 1–20; and Pun Ngai, *Made in China: Women Factory Workers in a Global Workplace*, Hong Kong: Hong Kong University Press, 2005 shows how similar discourses contribute to the disciplining of rural subjects. On *hukou*, see A Chan & P Alexander, 'Does China have an apartheid pass system?', *Journal of Ethnic and Migration Studies*, 30(4), 2004, pp 609–629; KW Chan &W Buckingham, 'Is China abolishing the Hukou system?', *China Quarterly*, 195, 2008, pp 582–606; and Wang Fei-Ling,

Organizing through Division and Exclusion: China's Hukou System, Stanford, CA: Stanford University Press, 2005.

3 See, especially, Wang, *Organizing through Division and Exclusion*; and Pun, *Made in China*.

4 See S Thøgersen, 'Return of the Chinese peasant: farmers and their intellectual advocates', *Issues and Studies*, 39 (4), 2003, pp 230–239 for an overview of the open debate. On mobilisation, see Yu Jianrong, 'Maintaining a baseline of social stability' (translation of a speech to the Beijing Lawyers Association), *China Digital Times*, 17 February 2010, at http://chinadigitaltimes.net/2010/03/yu-jianrong-maintaining-a-baseline-of-social-stability-part-i/, accessed 10 February 2012.

5 Districts (urban) and counties (rural) are the administrative level just below the city prefecture. They are divided into street committees or townships that are again divided into communities of villages and sub-villages.

6 KJ O'Brien & Li Lianjiang, *Rightful Resistance in Rural China*, Cambridge: Cambridge University Press, 2006. On fragmented authoritarianism, see K Lieberthal & M Oksenberg, *Policy Making in China: Leaders, Structures, and Processes*, Princeton, NJ: Princeton University Press, 1988.

7 C Tilly, *Durable Inequality*, Berkeley, CA: University of California Press, 1998.

8 M Selden, *The Yenan Way in Revolutionary China*, Cambridge, MA: Harvard University Press, 1971.

9 Aihwa Ong, 'The Chinese axis: zoning technologies and variegated sovereignty', *Journal of East Asian Studies*, 4(1), 2004, pp 69–96. Historically, see GW Skinner, 'Presidential address: the structure of Chinese history', *Journal of Asian Studies*, 44(2), 1985, pp 271–292; and RB Wong, *China Transformed: Historical Change and the Limits of European Experience*, Ithaca, NY: Cornell University Press, 1997, pp 179–206

10 Cai Yongshun, 'Power structure and regime resilience: contentious politics in China', *British Journal of Political Science*, 38(3), 2008, pp 411–432; Wang, *Organizing through Division and Exclusion*; and O'Brien & Li, *Rightful Resistance in Rural China*. For a perspective on a well intended centre, see also Wang Shaoguang, 'Changing models of China's policy agenda setting', *Modern China*, 34(56), 2008, pp 56–87

11 G Smith, 'Political machinations in a rural county', *China Journal*, (62), 2009, pp 29–59. On the concept of social engineering, see JC Scott, *Seeing like a State: How Certain Schemes to Improve the Human Condition have Failed*, New Haven, CT: Yale University Press, 1998.

12 Wang, *Organizing through Division and Exclusion*.

13 For a review, see Chan & Buckingham, 'Is China abolishing the Hukou system?'. An example from the academic debate is Zhu Yu, 'China's floating population and their settlement intention in the cities: beyond the Hukou reform', *Habitat International*, 31(1), 2007, pp 65–76.

14 You-tien Hsing, *The Great Urban Transformation: Politics of Land and Property in China*, New York: Oxford University Press, 2010; and Zeuthen, 'Ruling through differentiation in China', p 119.

15 For details on documents collected and interviews on the city prefecture's policy, see Zeuthen, 'Ruling through differentiation in China', pp 106–122.

16 Hsing, *The Great Urban Transformation*; and P Ho, *Institutions in Transition: Land Ownership, Property Rights, and Social Conflict in China*, Oxford: Oxford University Press, 2005.

17 JW Zeuthen & MB Griffiths, 'The end of urban–rural differentiation in China? Hukou and resettlement in Chengdu's urban–rural integration', in B Alpermann (ed), *Politics and Markets in Rural China*, London: Routledge, 2011.

18 Interview, November 2007.

19 For details of documents collected and interviews on cases discussed in this sub-section, see Zeuthen, 'Ruling through differentiation in China', pp 169–178.

20 *Ibid*, pp 207–210.

21 *Ibid*, pp 155–163.

22 The data on urban residents are explored more fully in Zeuthen & Griffiths, 'The end of urban–rural differentiation in China?'.

23 Parts of the material on rural–urban migrants are also discussed in *ibid*.

24 For data on the case before resettlement, see A Mertha, *China's Water Warriors: Citizen Action and Policy Change*, Ithaca, NY: Cornell University Press, 2008. For further details on immigration to Chengdu, see Zeuthen, 'Ruling through differentiation in China', pp 147–148, 206–207.

25 Anagnost, 'The corporeal politics of quality (Suzhi)'.

Notes on contributor

Jesper Zeuthen has recently defended his PhD dissertation on Chengdu's urban-rural integration policy at Roskilde University, Denmark and teaches China Studies at the University of Copenhagen.

'Winning Hearts and Minds': emotional wars and the construction of difference

NANDINI SUNDAR

ABSTRACT *Exploring an ongoing civil war between Maoist guerrillas and the Indian government, this article looks at how emotions are mobilised, conscripted and engendered by both sides. The focus is, however, on the state's performance of emotion, including outrage, hurt and fear-inducing domination, as part of its battle for legitimacy. Intrinsic to this is the privileging of certain kinds of emotions—fear, anger, grief—and the emotions of certain kinds of people over others. Subject populations are distinguished from citizens by the differential public acknowledgement of their emotional claims.*

On 6 April 2010 76 personnel of the paramilitary organisation the Central Reserve Police Force (CRPF) were killed in an ambush by Maoist guerrillas in the Dantewada district of Chhattisgarh, central India. The ambush was part of a series of 'encounters' in an escalating war between Maoists and the government. While the Maoists had been active in the area since the early 1980s, the war intensified in 2005 after a state-sponsored vigilante movement called Salwa Judum burnt and looted several hundred villages (644 by official count) in Dantewada and forcibly evacuated their residents into camps. Many hundreds were killed and raped by the security forces and vigilantes. But it was not until 2009—following litigation in the Supreme Court against this vigilantism;[1] the arrest of a doctor and human rights activist, Binayak Sen, on charges of acting as a courier for the Maoists, which became a *cause célèbre*;[2] the transformation of a local operation confined to a single state into a nationwide 'Operation Green Hunt'; and the involvement of celebrity author Arundhati Roy in the issue[3]—that it began to receive national media attention.

The Tadmetla ambush, or '*chyatar kand*' (76 incident) as it became widely known,[4] was followed by sharp outrage on the part of the government, amplified by an equally indignant media. The 'Dantewada martyrs' became symbolic not just of the 'butchery' and 'savagery' of the Maoists, but of a political community—'India'—under siege, a message reinforced by the

Nandini Sundar is in the Department of Sociology, Delhi School of Economics, Delhi University.

IDENTITY, INEQUITY AND INEQUALITY IN INDIA AND CHINA

ubiquitous TV images of flag-draped coffins, last seen in the Kargil war against Pakistan. Headlines like 'The outraged nation', 'Government outraged over Maoist massacre—BJP wants fight to the finish (*Hindustan Times*) and 'War between India and the Maoists' (*Times Now* television channel), struck a note of infuriated anger, while others emphasised the pathos and sacrifice of the slain men: 'Country bids farewell to Dantewada martyrs' (*NDTV*), 'Amid heart-rending scenes 42 bodies reach Lucknow' (*The Hindu*), 'Brave and helpless' (*Outlook* magazine).

Government anger was directed not just at the Maoists but at their alleged 'sympathisers in civil society', whose verbal and written criticism of the government for violations of the Constitution and of fundamental rights was morally equated with the Maoist act of killing in retaliation for those policies.[5] Within minutes, then, given the government's role as the primary definer of news,[6] whether the alleged sympathisers had adequately condemned and expiated the attack became as critical to the framing of the news as the attack itself.

The largely one-sided government and media outrage—the targeted killings or rapes of ordinary *adivasis* (indigenous tribespeople) rarely, if ever, invite direct calls upon the Home Minister to condemn each such incident—easily call to mind Herman and Chomsky's distinction between 'worthy and unworthy victims' as part of what they call the media 'propaganda model'.[7] While news coverage of the worthy is replete with detail, evokes indignation and shock, and invites a follow-up, unworthy victims get limited news space, are referred to in generic terms, and there is little attempt to fix responsibility or trace culpability to the top echelons of the establishment.[8]

Critics of the government's counter-insurgency programme responded to this event in a clinical tone, pointing out that the CRPF personnel were on a combing operation when ambushed. Some argued that even mourning was not called for, since these were combatant deaths in war. This is in contrast to people in conflict areas, who make a distinction between moral indignation and mourning. When family members who have taken to arms die in a genuine encounter, their families feel sad, but accept it as part of life. But when it is a clear-cut case of an extra-judicial killing, there is widespread anger, and local citizens' committees to protest against such killings are common in conflict areas across India. A leading human rights organisation issued a statement the same day:

> People's Union for Democratic Rights believes that the death of 70 jawans in Dantewada on early hours of April 6th, 2010, is an unfortunate fallout of the government's willful policy of pursuing 'Operation Greenhunt'...Since war remains the preferred option of the Indian government they have no one else but themselves to blame if and when combatants die. We wish to remind them that security forces were returning from three day long operations when the ambush took place. As a civil rights organization we neither condemn the killing of security force combatants nor that of the Maoists combatants, or for that matter any other combatants, when it occurs. We can only lament the folly of the Indian government which lacks the courage and imagination to pursue a non militaristic approach which is pushing us towards a bloody and dirty war.[9]

IDENTITY, INEQUITY AND INEQUALITY IN INDIA AND CHINA

Sumanta Banerjee, a well known scholar and a former Naxalite, was even more critical of the 'bourgeoise-liberal response', pointing out that such killings were inevitable during civil war:

> The national media may shed tears for the death of the 75-odd CRPF soldiers in Chhattisgarh. But then, these soldiers, by being cannon-fodders of the Indian state, however tragic it might be, suffered the fate that—I'm sorry to say—they deserved. Should the bourgeois-liberals and human rights activists shed tears for the young dedicated Nazi soldiers (who massacred the Jews), and were killed in reprisal by the Soviet Red Army? Surely, there should be a limit to the tolerance that bourgeois-liberalism allows![10]

The Maoists themselves celebrated the event as a showcase of the dedication and bravery of their comrades. The photos of the eight Maoist martyrs who died in the ambush were published in the January–June 2010 issue of the Hindi organ, *Prabhat*, while a 15-foot high red cement memorial commemorating their sacrifice in the historic 'deliberate ambush' dominates the open plain in the village of Morpalli, neighbouring Tadmetla. A Maoist press release of 8 April 2010 noted: 'The heroic PLGA guerrillas led by the CPI (Maoist) have created history by wiping out an entire Company of the central paramilitary force in Dantewada district of Chhattisgarh'. Ironically, after describing the security forces as 'mercenaries' and 'uniformed *goondas* [thugs]', and describing the widespread torture, gang rapes and massacres the security forces had carried out in the course of their operations, the CPI (Maoist) goes on to say:

> The CC, CPI (Maoist) while offering its heart-felt condolences to the bereaved families of the dead jawans, appeals to the state and central paramilitary personnel to realize they are being used as cannon-fodder in this war waged by the exploiting ruling class in the interests of a tiny parasitic elite against the poor and oppressed people of our country led by CPI (Maoist)...We appeal to all peace-loving, democratic-minded organizations and individuals in India to *understand the context in which the Maoists are compelled to annihilate* the so-called security forces who are creating a virtual reign of terror in adivasi areas armed with mortars, LMGs and grenades. *When dacoits try to loot your house you have to fight back. And that is what the masses led by the Maoists are doing in all these areas.*[11]

While 'Tadmetla' became a signifier of the state's resolve to revenge itself, the Maoists evoked an alternative geography of loss and memorialisation:

> *Dantewada strikes back...*
> *For Gompad, Gachanpalli, Singanamadgu, Gattampadu, Gollagudem,*
> *For Gumiyapal, Palodi, Dokpad, Palachelima, Kachalaram...*
> *Hungry, starving, undernourished, emaciated,*
> *Suffering countless injustices and humiliations*
> *Dantewada strikes back*
> *To defend its right to live.*[12]

Indeed, a year later, in March 2011, 'Tadmetla' itself was overlain with another kind of significance after security forces attacked that village and the

135

neighbouring villages of Morpalli, Timapuram and Pulanpad, burning some 300 homes and granaries, and raping and killing villagers.[13] All these villages had been attacked in 2007 as well, leading to successive pauperisation, as families which had just about put their homes together after the first round of attack found them burnt again. In 2011, however, for the first time there was almost contemporaneous press coverage, and the Supreme Court ordered an enquiry.[14]

The 2010 ambush—and the reactions to it from different quarters—raise several questions: how are emotions mobilised, conscripted and engendered during the course of civil war? In what language do states and rebels portray emotion, especially outrage? How do certain kinds of emotions, like the fear and anger of the powerful, enter into discourses of national security, while others, like the desperation of hunger or the desire for dignity among the poor, are seen as irrelevant? Even when it comes to something common like grief at the death of combatants in war, how are the emotions of certain people (relatives of soldiers) privileged over others (relatives of insurgents)?

While the differential distribution of emotional rewards and punishments is intrinsic to stratification,[15] this article shows how emotional stratification works in times of war, as one of the more effective, if intangible, weapons deployed by the state, primarily through the media. As Butler argues, 'frames of war are part of what makes the materiality of war...media representations have already become modes of military conduct'.[16] War itself is about the production of righteousness and grieving, on the one hand, and non-recognition and deniability, on the other:

> We might think of war as dividing populations into those who are grievable and those who are not. An ungrievable life is one that cannot be mourned because it has never lived, that is, it has never counted as a life at all...The differential distribution of public grieving is a political issue of enormous significance.[17]

Referring to what she calls the 'precarity' of life, Butler points to the unequal distribution of the means to reduce vulnerability as both cause and effect of an inequality in perception or regard:

> This differential distribution of precarity is at once a material and a perceptual issue, since those whose lives are not 'regarded' as potentially grievable, and hence valuable, are made to bear the burden of starvation, underemployment, legal disenfranchisement, and differential exposure to violence and death. It would be difficult, if not impossible, to decide whether the 'regard'—or the failure of 'regard'—leads to the 'material reality' or whether the material reality leads to the failure of regard, since it would seem that both happen at once and that such perceptual categories are essential to the crafting of material reality.[18]

Conversely, resistance to economic and political inequality must necessarily involve asserting emotional equality, of insisting on a recognition of humanity and the capacity to suffer, as well as the right to be angry about this, of changing the terms of the 'feeling rules' imposed by the dominant.[19] Flam writes: 'We must map out emotions which uphold social structures and

IDENTITY, INEQUITY AND INEQUALITY IN INDIA AND CHINA

relations of dominance to then show how social movements work to counter them'.[20] Social movements are also essentially emotional movements—where the successful mobilisation of righteous anger or a sense of injustice, or the maintenance of solidarity through humour, songs (which evoke emotions) and other rituals of resistance are as critical to the existence of these movements as the structural reasons which drive people to participate in them.[21]

While this article does discuss some of the ways in which the Maoists mobilise anger to counter the state, as in the poem, *Dantewada strikes back*, cited above, the focus is on the state's deployment of emotion as part of a counter-insurgency strategy. Contrary to Collins, who argues that, since the state is not a social movement, in situations when an insurgent movement is pitted against the state, 'we have only one movement in the attention space',[22] this article argues that the state also vies for emotional attention in the public sphere. While rituals of rule have long been studied by political anthropologists and historians, through coronation ceremonies, public parades and a variety of other spheres, here I look at how even bureaucracies—which are classically meant to be impersonal organisations driven by rational–legal rules—deploy emotion as part of their repertoire. In times of civil war the emotions performed by the state range from the inculcation of fear to a calculated display of indifference to the exhibition of injured feelings, as if it was citizens and not the state who were violating the social contract, and as if the social contract consisted of the state's right to impunity.

Emotional silencing

Emotions—whether of happiness or feelings of loss and deprivation—are not *sui generis* but are located in particular institutional structures. Emotional resources in one institutional domain—such as familial love—can have positive effects in other domains like the workplace, or lead to a cascading sense of worthlessness across domains.[23] Even as emotions are differently experienced, expressed and narrativised by different cultures, the inequality in their attribution or expression is widely recognised as a signal of material inequality.[24]

As with the selective public acknowledgement of grief, anger is differentially sanctioned in state and public discourse: 'Since it normally constitutes the prerogative of the powerful, social movements have to re-appropriate the right to feel and display this particular emotion by their members'.[25] In India the claim to 'hurt sentiments' is used to justify mob vigilantism by the Hindu right, ranging from the destruction of the Babri Masjid in 1992 to justify a wrong allegedly committed 500 years ago to genocidal attacks on Muslims following the burning of a train in Godhra, Gujarat in 2002. However, *adivasis* whose villages have been burnt, or Kashmiris who suffer routine and daily humiliation by the army are castigated if they resort to counter-violence, and are expected to forever turn the other cheek.

In fact, in contrast even to Kashmiris, and to almost every other section of the Indian population which is allowed emotional citizenship, *adivasis* are not expected to have emotions at all, other than the simple pleasures of the carousing savage. When doing fieldwork in Dantewada in the early 1990s, two things I was frequently told were, first, not to go to *adivasi* villages in the evening because they would all be drunk and, second, that *adivasis* showed no emotion when people died. Rather than seeing the frequent deaths caused by malaria or easily treated diseases as egregious state failures, they were dismissed as an everyday part of life which *adivasis* took in their stride. In actual fact, all the deaths that I encountered in the field—whether through 'normal illnesses' or extra-judicial killings—were deeply mourned. People took considerable risks to come back when the security forces had finished attacking their villages and cremate the bodies of those killed.

In part this denial of emotion is because the relation between *adivasis* and the post-1947 state in India continues on largely colonial premises, where, as Mbembe writes, the dominant prototype of the native is that of an animal, and one of the primary attributes of *commandement* which characterises colonial rule (as well as rule in the postcolony) is the 'lack of distinction between ruling and civilizing'.[26] In the twinning of misery and abjection, such that the poor are blamed for the poverty in which they live, 'the physical suffering of indigenous peoples can be associated with their moral and intellectual degradation', providing 'both a justification for European intervention and as the necessary iteration of a fundamental difference between colonizer and colonized'.[27] Flogging was justified by colonial authorities on the grounds that natives understood no other language: 'it is no crime but a kindness to make them work ... The measures adopted are severe, but the native cannot be satisfactorily handled by coaxing; he must be governed by force'.[28]

A picture of the brute and animal—and emotionless—*adivasi* is reflected in a 'benign' tourism website (withdrawn after protest) which tells us: 'when drinking from a stream they (AbujhMaria) do not take up water in their hands but put their mouth down to it like cattle'.[29] From such dehumanisation to actual state violence, from acts of omission to acts of commission, is a continuous process. When some women Maoists were killed in West Bengal in 2010, they were suspended upside down with their hands trussed to poles like hunting trophies and carried out by paramilitary forces.[30] The emotional excuse in counter-insurgency is thus implicitly framed as: we kill them (*adivasis*) not because we do not feel anything about them, but because they are incapable of feeling.

This seeming silence, this affective invisibility is, however, itself an emotional quality—the silence of the passive sufferer driven to fatality, or 'the seething silence of coerced compliance'.[31] The problem is how to read this silence—as quiet off-stage resistance or resignation or both, depending on the context. As Scheper-Hughes argues, the violence of massive and everyday inequality and frequent illness and death must necessarily have an impact on how people feel and how they express emotion:

> If Paulo Freire erred in his unidimensional view of Nordestino peasants as mere objects of the rich and powerful so that their knowledge and experience of themselves as self-reflexive humans was all but destroyed, Fratz Fanon erred in his belief that the victims of colonialist oppression could remain strong throughout their torment and emerge altogether unscathed from cultural and economic enslavement, with their subjectivity and culture intact.[32]

IDENTITY, INEQUITY AND INEQUALITY IN INDIA AND CHINA

If the quest for human dignity is the intangible that can propel some people to risk their lives in seemingly hopeless rebellions,[33] keeping this spark alive is critical to any insurgent movement. The state, on the other hand, must count on extinguishing this aspiration—and on fear, resignation and the desire for survival being the more predominant emotion among civilian sympathisers. One of the basic claims of counter-insurgency doctrine is that people will support whichever side is winning or whichever side has control over their area, irrespective of their actual sympathies,[34] thus justifying the use of force to gain control regardless of its costs in terms of human emotions, suffering or even legitimacy. Thus the ups and downs of civilian (sympathiser) 'morale' is as much the battleground in insurgency and counter-insurgency as is soldier morale.

Emotional conscription during conflict

In a democracy, however, the state's dilemma is acute. On the one hand, it must rally behind its personnel and cheer them on in their fight against fellow citizens, resisting any attempt to depict them as cannon-fodder in a war to gain resources for industry. As one general said on a television show in response to this charge, the Tadmetla CRPF men who were ambushed were 'doing their duty'. On the other hand, the state must simultaneously claim to represent everybody (both the CRPF and the *adivasis* who are alienated and therefore joining the Maoists). The best way this can be done is to emotionally privilege the deaths of the CRPF and the trauma caused to their families, while denying the very existence of deaths on the other side, or of killings by the security forces. It is this 'emotional work' or 'emotion management' to mobilise or wear down the public to its side, that is the focus of this article.[35]

As states engaged in counter-insurgency have long recognised, 'media management' is essential to this task of emotional conscription. This is an especially powerful tool when the media are autonomous and not state-owned. The gold medal for cheerleading in the Indian print media goes to the *Indian Express* newspaper, which publishes detailed interviews with the families of security personnel killed by Maoists or militants on its front page, but rarely provides the same space to families of victims killed by the security forces. For instance, when doubts were raised about the extra-judicial killing of a Maoist leader, Kishenji, in West Bengal at a time when peace talks were being discussed, the *Express* carried a front page anchor quoting the widow of a policeman who died in a Maoist attack: 'My husband's body too was riddled with bullets'. There appeared to be no qualms about seeming to publicly justify revenge as a motive for counter-insurgency.

When governments are forced by human rights activists or courts to recognise the killing of ordinary villagers, they enter the public emotional ambit only in terms of compensation, without the immediacy of any emotional trauma attached to it. Even compensation is portrayed as a favour to the people, causing the villagers to worry that taking compensation will absolve the state of any criminal responsibility. In January 2012, against the backdrop of the Supreme Court-mandated enquiry, I discussed comparative culpability for the Tadmetla ambush, when CRPF men were killed, versus the burning of homes and killing of villagers with some men from the CRPF. One said dismissively: 'but they have got compensation for their losses' (the villagers got a measly Rs25 000 each for houses burnt but nothing for murder or rape). I pointed out that in that case, the families of the CRPF personnel had also been compensated, and that too in the several hundred thousands, to be told: 'no amount of compensation can suffice for the loss of a loved one'.

Like the government, guerrilla leaders must keep their cadre going by managing the emotions attached to combat deaths. Unlike the government, however, guerrilla leaders must minimise any hint of emotional distress to themselves and dwell on the sacrifice, bravery and fortitude of their cadres. And even as the Maoists downplay the tragedy of the CRPF deaths as inevitable and describe the soldiers as mercenaries, they must yet condole with their families because they too lay claim to an alternative government which represents everybody. Their press release performing this simultaneous act of condemnation and condolence asserts the moral stand of a state invoking the sad necessity of punishing the errant citizen that is often found in judicial death sentences.

However, this article is about more than just stratification along an emotional landscape of mourning and memorialisation, with some deaths achieving iconic status and others crumbling ungrieved. In fact, there are really parallel spaces of commemoration and grieving. The Maoists ensure that all their dead are commemorated and they are grieved locally. However, the state's grieving for its own has greater visibility, and purchase in determining what constitutes 'security policy'. The manner in which 'security' is defined, and the politics of fear it founds itself on, is essentially constructed on a process of obliteration. Questions of food insecurity, the insecurity created by military combing operations, the fear of being killed in random shootings while collecting fuelwood or cultivating one's fields, are downplayed in favour of other kinds of risk and insecurity, most notably the state's fear of losing control, and the fear of politicians and industrialists that they will no longer be able freely to exploit the land and resources of the poor. As Huysmans notes, 'security' functions as a thick signifier, forcing us to address its politics, and the way in which it defines order:

> The understanding of security in international relations involves a specific mediation of death and life which implies a mixture of two interdependent forms of security—ontological security, which concerns the mediation of chaos and order, and daily security, which concerns the mediation of friends and enemies.[36]

He goes on to ask:

> Since the signifier 'security' does not describe social relations but changes them into security relations, the question is no longer if the security story gives a true or false picture of social relations. The question becomes: How does a security story order social relations? What are the implications of politicizing an issue as a security problem?[37]

While the real problem for villagers is saturation paramilitary presence (in 2011 there were some 100 000 paramilitary forces active in the states of central India as compared with 10–15 000 armed Maoists), these areas are always referred to as 'Maoist infested', evoking the imagery of vermin and disease, and enabling a genocidal eradication drive in which non-combatant villagers become mere collateral damage.

In an obvious attempt to put some visual flesh on this written description, and to create revulsion towards the enemy, the Indian government has put out full page advertisements in the national print media with graphic images of bloody corpses, headlined: 'Maoists are nothing but cold blooded murderers'; this is replicated across the country with posters put up at roadside tea stalls with photos of local Maoists with prices on their heads (never mind that in many cases the Maoists concerned look so young and sweet that these might have the opposite effect). At the annual state exhibition during the Dussehra festival in Jagdalpur, in conflict-ridden Chhattisgarh, where the state displays its wares and development pro-grammes,[38] the government created large posters with comic characters and situations showing how the Maoists impeded development.

Yet when one of the most senior Maoist leaders, a member of the central committee, Mallojula Koteswara Rao, popularly known as Kishenji, was killed by the security forces in West Bengal in November 2011, thousands of people gathered at his funeral, including Members of the Legislative Assembly (MLAs):

> Since morning people started pouring in from places as far as Nizamabad, Adilabad and Visakapatnam. A serpentine queue could be seen at Kishenji's house at Brahmana Veedhi [street], where his body was kept.[39]

It is not clear whether even the government fully believes its own propaganda.

The unequal distribution of sanctioned fear

One of the fears which the government has actively promoted is the fear of a rural guerrilla take-over of the country. In 2005, at the height of the Salwa Judum campaign, when entire swathes of villages were being burnt, the Maoists distributed compact discs (CDs) containing footage of the burning villages to the houses of a number of MLAs. Nobody was concerned with the horrifying images these videos contained; instead the legislative assembly in Chhattisgarh chose to focus on the terrible fact that the Maoists were 'close enough to the state capital to distribute CDs to MLAs'. Sometimes, these fears sound ridiculous even to government supporters, as when GK Pillai, a former home secretary, tried to create hysteria at the prospect of a Maoist takeover by 2050! But frequent lectures by security experts, depicting a 'red corridor' from Pashupati (Nepal) to Tirupathi (South India), bolsters this imagery of an expanding communist swathe, the 'gravest security threat' to India that the prime minister is so fond of repeating. On the other hand, media coverage is a double-edged sword, and ensuring silence on the issue is often better for the state, as there is no room then for emotional reaction of either kind. Media coverage of Maoist action may create disgust but also a belief in the Maoists' powers. For instance, when over 300 prisoners broke out of the jail at Dantewada in 2007 and walked out, there was definite admiration.

Once, when I asked the top administrator of Chhattisgarh, an otherwise genial man, why the administration did not reopen schools in the interior villages from where they had been shifted after Salwa Judum started, he said, in all seriousness: 'but if we teach them chemistry in the villages, they will only learn to make bombs'. Even as the state has passed a Right to Education Act, on the ground counter-insurgency is driven by the fear of teaching children in their villages, and leaving them exposed to the insurgent ways of their parents. Huge hostels have been built by the roadside, next to paramilitary camps, to keep these children captive. Parents, on the other hand, are worried about sending their small children to these far-off schools, and many children themselves cry and want to come home. Familial bonds battle with the state in this particular emotional war.

The CRPF accuse human rights activists of being in league with the Maoists because they are unafraid to visit the villages. 'Why do they run away when they see us but talk to you?'. When combing operations started in 2009, people rushed to get their photos taken and have identity cards made, driven by the fear of going into the forest and being accosted by the CPRF, although how much use these would be if shots rang out and they were caught in the crossfire is a moot question. A CPRF commander in one of the remote outposts of Dantewada said he had come to an understanding with the local Maoists. He would patrol two kilometres in each direction, and the Maoists would patrol in the forests. Each in their own place; each happy.

When media organisations carry out surveys on popular support for the Maoists, they get a large number of 'don't knows', although the vast majority favour non-military approaches.[40] There is fear of openly voicing support for a banned organisation; fear of free speech. At the same time, villagers' attitudes towards the Maoists are also tinged with fear—fear of being branded an informer and fear of the exemplary and brutal punishments that are known to be publicly imposed. If a villager leaves the village for any length of time to visit relatives or work elsewhere, he or she must inform the party. And even as people are instinctively drawn to Maoist condemnations of the state, given the extent to which the state goes to prove the Maoists right by its policies, and attracted by the personalities of individual leaders, they are worried that a Maoist presence in their village will invite further state repression. Fear vies with familiarity and desire to produce 'don't know'; silence.

Between 2005 and 2007 I travelled to Salwa Judum camps in Chhattisgarh, where people had been forcibly brought, and to refugee outposts in neighbouring Andhra Pradesh where people had fled on their own from Chhattisgarh. All the people in the camps—speaking under the watchful eye of the camp leaders—said that they were there to escape the Maoists. The people in Andhra Pradesh said they had come to search for land. They were scared of describing what had happened to them. There were only whispers in the back lane if no-one was looking, scattered fragments that were swept up

IDENTITY, INEQUITY AND INEQUALITY IN INDIA AND CHINA

by human rights organisations to bring out the truth: that this was strategic hamletting by the state.[41] It was only in 2007 that the silence began to break, when villagers handed in scraps of paper to a local communist leader, Manish Kunjam, at a rally held just outside the state. These were later collated and submitted to the court:

> Two years ago, the headmen (*mukhia*) of our village and neighbouring villages who had joined the Salwa Judum came and threatened us that if we did not leave our villages and join the Salwa Judum camps in Geedam, then the police, SPOs, Naga forces and Salwa Judum would jointly kill us. Therefore, all of us out of fear, left our homes and came to the Salwa Judum camp established in the mandi of Geedam...We are scared that if we return to our village, the police, SPOs, CPRF and other paramilitary forces and members of the Salwa Judum will attack and kill us, or they will forcibly capture us and take us to one of the Salwa Judum camps or they will catch us, falsely accuse us of being Naxalites, and send us to jail. (Testimony, N village)

> The frightened villagers of Gangaloor, Cherpal and Bijapur, seeing the Salwa Judum, have fled into forests. Why is this happening in our country, why is this happening in Chhattisgarh. Why has the Chhattisgarh administration been running this? Has our Chief Minister been elected only for this? (Testimony, K village)

> In our village, there have been murders, physical assaults, arson and other inhuman atrocities due to which our people have been living in fear and terror. In the interior villages, transport has come to a complete stop and life has become incomplete. There is an acute shortage of essential items for us. People are starving of hunger or praying for their lives. All these reasons have resulted in the migration of at least 350 families to Andhra Pradesh in order to survive. There is nobody to understand us. Also, four villagers have been killed, one girl was murdered and another girl made to faint. (Testimony, L village)[42]

Anthropologists have written of the overriding sense of fear and suspicion that civil war creates,[43] but as Galeano writes, fear pervades capitalism more generally:

> Democracy is afraid of remembering and language is afraid of speaking.
> Civilians fear the military, the military fears a shortage of weapons, weapons fear a shortage of wars
> It is the time of fear.
> Women's fear of violent men and men's fear of fearless women.[44]

It is only the Maoists who have no fear.

Can a state be an outraged community?

In a recent issue of the journal *Samaj* on 'outraged communities', Amelie Blom and Nicolas Jaoul argue that much political action in India is driven by emotion—and particularly a sense of outrage that underlies collective action:

143

'Instigating, staging and managing this "righteous anger" is a crucial dimension in mobilizing "outraged communities"'.[45] However, the question I pose here is whether the state can be considered an 'outraged community'. Indeed, outrage might be said to be central to performances of stateness. Dictionaries define outrage as an act of violence or brutality; a violation of established norms; an extremely strong reaction of anger, shock, indignation, resentment; and as an emotion engendered by injury or insult.[46] While state violence is normalised as expressions of sovereignty, affronts to this monopoly over violence become punishable acts, thus coding outrage into the everyday act of ruling.

Even bureaucratic work depends on the creation of certain emotional attributes among the staff. Armies, for example, must enable their soldiers to kill.[47] As organisational sociologists have shown, while bureaucracies are defined as impersonal and rational modes of organisation, in fact, much bureaucratic activity is in practice mediated by the personalities and emotions of those who populate it, and certain bureaucracies must make emotional management a primary task.[48] Outrage is thus also an emotion that is inculcated in the bureaucracy.

In a civil war context this outrage is amplified through appeal to certain sections of the public. Here the 'imagined community' invoked by the state addresses the nation at large, but practically mobilises specific communities that help the state to display outrage and to manage surveillance. Apart from the government's own reports, blogs like http://naxalwatch.blogspot.com/ and others run by right-wing supporters and 'security experts' mobilise in defence of the government and against the Maoists. The government also summons and showcases outrage by the families of those killed by the Maoists, helping them to organise rallies and demonstrations demanding strong state action, thus creating its own 'public' to oppose the 'public' which supports the Maoists.

But outrage is not the only emotion that the state displays. In responding to the Maoists, the state has oscillated between being outraged, 'resolved' (it will do whatever it takes to wipe out the Maoists) and also vulnerable and helpless. In response to a letter from EAS Sarma, a retired civil servant who was one of the petitioners in the Supreme Court against Salwa Judum, asking for basic data on what compensation and rehabilitation the state had provided in the wake of Supreme Court directives, the Chief Secretary of Chhattisgarh responded:

> May I request you to pause for a while and put yourself in the position of these officers faced by your questions... Kindly reflect on the utility of haranguing these officers with questionnaire like the one you have sent. In Dantewada and Bijapur we have two Collectors whose commitment to the socio-economic development of the scheduled tribes is certainly not less than that of any of your generation or mine (for that matter) in the administrative services. I hope it is not too much to ask that you spend a little time to see for yourself the struggle they go through in implementing various development schemes in the shadow of unabated Naxalite violence and in the face of grave and continuous personal risk to their lives. Today when we have all these schemes, we are stopped on the

tracks by a violent movement spearheaded by runaway fugitives from other states who found not just that our pristine forests are convenient hideaways but also that the tribal communities here are easy to subjugate and convert in to their obedient foot soldiers. I do hope that your exertions would help the cause of development of Bastar and its people. And that, some day we would be able to work together to find solutions to the many problems facing our tribal areas instead of wasting our lives fighting in the dark jungles and in dreary law courts.[49]

The Indian state, as this letter illustrates and Shalini Randeria argues, is a 'cunning state'. While her argument is made in the context of globalisation, it highlights the way in which states deploy weakness to evade responsibilities to their citizens:

'Cunning' is a weapon of weak states, or, more precisely, of the stronger among subordinate states in the international system. It does not describe a characteristic of state structure or capacities but the changing nature of the relationship of national elites (very often in concert with international institutions) to citizens. The notion of a cunning state is thus a useful way to delineate a range of tactics deployed at various sites of negotiation where a shift in responsibilities and sovereignties occurs.[50]

The government constantly cites Maoist control as a reason why it cannot implement development programmes in certain regions. After the kidnapping of a district administrator in 2011, directives were issued to all senior state functionaries not to travel in Maoist areas without a security escort. However, while this affects those who want to work, staying away often suits local functionaries, whose failure to work precipitated the development crises in the first place. School teachers and health workers get their salary, without having to teach or look after the medical needs of the people. Village headmen get 'elected' because no-one has voted for them, but the ritual of voting is carefully maintained by the state. They carry out public works which exist entirely on paper. The cunning of the state in terms of its policy and self-presentation is deeply intertwined with the cunning of its functionaries, who enact a seeming helplessness in performing their functions, to extract advantage for themselves.

The war for hearts and minds

The phrase 'winning hearts and minds' (WHAM) brings out clearly the degree to which counter-insurgency is perceived as a war over public emotions; even though the warm and friendly connotations of the term are belied by the actual practice of counter-insurgency. The term was first pioneered by General Richard Templer in Malaya, arguing that it was not enough simply to intern villagers to isolate them from insurgents, but that grouping must involve improving the economic and living conditions of villagers, so that they have a reason to support the government rather than the insurgents. However, as Shafer and others have pointed out, in practice

IDENTITY, INEQUITY AND INEQUALITY IN INDIA AND CHINA

counter-insurgency follows a 'cost–benefit approach', which involves making the costs, including starvation, torture and other brutal forms of pacification, far higher than any benefit the public gains from supporting the guerrillas. In the Malayan case, which is seen as the prime example of successful WHAM, Francis Loh Kok Wah notes that, while the Chinese villagers were 'pacified', 'this is very different from saying that their hearts and minds had been won. At most a small group of elites came to identify with the British cause.'[51] In Dantewada, since starvation and force have been the major instruments of policy,[52] it is hard for the local forces to learn any other strategy. Thus orders from above to make friends with the locals by distributing clothes and other small gifts are carried out in battle mode. Villagers laugh as they describe how CRPF men carry a *saree* in one hand and a large stick in the other, to beat women into accepting their gifts. Some villagers said they threw their *sarees* away when out of sight.

Unlike propaganda, which involves the dissemination of 'information' that is designed to persuade, counter-insurgency erects an entire ladder of feeling among citizens, whose rungs clash against each other. Much research remains to be done on how effective propaganda is at creating patriotism, indignation and pride, when directed at one's own citizens. Coming down to smaller units, what happens when members of families fight each other? In 2011 at least three of the special police officers who burnt the villages of Tadmetla, Timapuram and Morpalli were local youths who had 'turned bad'. Even as the Maoists put pressure on villagers in their areas not to send their children into the police or army, the government targets precisely these areas for recruitment, creating divided loyalties. Even as people hate the government for what it has done to them, they are desperate for some justice from this very government. And even as they support the Maoists in their boycott of the state, they want to be able to access the benefits which the state provides.

Berlant uses the phrase 'slow death' to describe 'the physical wearing out of a population and the deterioration of people in that population that is very nearly a defining condition of their experience and historical existence'. While she uses it in the context of capitalist structural subordination and governmentality, it is especially the case where capital is imposed through force and in the face of insurgency.[53] Slow death here means not just physical wearing out but also emotional atrophy. If the state wins the emotional war against the Maoists, it will be through resignation or weariness rather than active support. On the other hand, because even under the worst conditions people continue to hope, life continues to flicker—slowly. Slow life battling against slow death, a symptom of the emotional schizophrenia that civil war creates.

Notes

1 *Nandini Sundar & ors v State of Chhattisgarh*, WP (Civil) 250 of 2007; and *Kartam Joga and ors v State of Chhattisgarh and Union of India*, WP (Cr) 119 of 2007.
2 See www.freebinayaksen.org; and www.binayaksen.net.
3 A Roy, 'Walking with the comrades', *Outlook*, 29 March 2010, at http://www.outlookindia.com/article.aspx?264738, accessed 12 November 2011.

IDENTITY, INEQUITY AND INEQUALITY IN INDIA AND CHINA

4 The actual site of the ambush was in the fields between Mukram and Tadmetla villages, and much closer to Mukram than to Tadmetla. For some reason it has come to be known as the Tadmetla ambush.

5 For example, after a Maoist attack in which four men of the Central Industrial Security Force were killed, the Home Ministry put out a statement asking 'What is the message that the CPI (Maoist) intends to convey? These are questions that we would like to put not only to the CPI (Maoist) but also to those who speak on their behalf and chastise the government . . . We think that it is time for all right-thinking citizens who believe in democracy and development to condemn the acts of violence perpetrated by the CPI (Maoist).' 'Chidambaram slams Maoist sympathizers', *Times Now*, 26 October 2009, at http://articles.timesofindia.indiatimes.com/2009-10-26/india/28067149_1_maoist-sympathisers-cisf-jawans-chhattisgarh, accessed 12 November 2011.

6 S Hall, C Critcher, T Jefferson, J Clarke, B Roberts, *Policing the Crises: Mugging, the State and Law and Order*, London: Macmillan, 1978; HJ Gans, *Deciding What's News*, Evanston, IL: Northwestern University Press, 2004.

7 ES Herman & N Chomsky, *Manufacturing Consent: The Political Economy of Mass Media*, New York: Pantheon Books, 2002, pp 37–86.

8 An enquiry was immediately ordered into the Tadmetla attack, headed by a former director general of the Border Security Force, EN Rammohan. He found several lapses in the leadership and functioning of the CRPF, including their failure to adhere to standard operating procedures. However, the commander responsible for this debacle, DIG Nalin Prabhat, while initially transferred, was given a gallantry medal a year later in 2011. Further, the government itself takes no responsibility for orchestrating this mindless war on its own people.

9 PUDR, 'Death of Jawans in Chhattisgarh—PUDR Statement', 6 April 2010, at http://sanhati.com/articles/2259/, accessed 9 November 2010.

10 S Banerjee, 'The other side of transactions in a violent system: the Maoist way of suppressing the paramilitary forces', at http://sanhati.com/articles/2259/, accessed 9 November 2010.

11 Communist Party of India (Maoist), 'On Dantewada guerrilla attack', press statement dated 8 April 2010, *People's March*, March–April 2010, p 42, emphasis in the original.

12 Front cover of *People's March*, March–April 2010.

13 Three women were raped, three men were killed, and three old people died of starvation after their houses were burnt.

14 *Nandini Sundar & ors*, Supreme Court order of 5 July 2011.

15 JH Turner, 'The stratification of emotions: some preliminary generalisations', *Sociological Inquiry*, 80(2), 2010, pp 168–199.

16 J Butler, *Frames of War: When is Life Grievable?*, London: Verso, 2009, pp 28–29.

17 *Ibid*, p 38.

18 *Ibid*, pp 24–25.

19 AR Hochschild, *The Managed Heart: Commercialisation of Human Feeling*, Berkeley, CA: University of California Press, 1983; and H Flam, 'Emotions' map: a research agenda', in H Flam & D King (eds), *Emotions and Social Movements*, Abingdon: Routledge, 2005, pp 19–40.

20 Flam, 'Emotions' map', p 19.

21 *Ibid*; J Goodwin, JM Jasper & F Polletta (eds), *Passionate Politics: Emotions and Social Movements*, Chicago, IL: University of Chicago Press, 2001; and R Aminzade & D McAdam, 'Emotions and contentious politics', *Mobilization*, Special Issue on 'Emotions and Contentious Politics', 7(2), 2002, pp 107–109.

22 R Collins, 'Social movements and the focus of emotional attention', in Goodwin *et al*, *Passionate Politics*, p 41.

23 Turner, 'The stratification of emotions'. But equally, Turner argues, emotional distress in one field can lead people to compensate in other fields. The famous British stiff upper lip imposed emotional costs on the elite; on the other hand, since displaying emotion was seen as a mark of lower class vulgarity, the careful concealment of emotion was valorised in status terms. Thus emotions are a complicated case of stratification.

24 See, for instance, among a huge range of anthropological/sociological literature, JL Briggs, *Never in Anger: Portrait of an Eskimo Family*, Cambridge, MA: Harvard University Press, 1970; R Sennet & J Cobb, *The Hidden Injuries of Class*, New York: Vintage Books, 1972; and M Trawick, *Notes on Love in a Tamil Family*, Berkeley, CA: University of California Press, 1990.

25 Flam, 'Emotions' map', p 20.

26 A Mbembe, *On the Postcolony*, Berkeley, CA: University of California Press, 2001, p 31.

27 D Spurr, *The Rhetoric of Empire*, Durham, NC: Duke University Press, 1993, p 78.

28 Glave, cited in S Lindqvist, *Exterminate All the Brutes*, New York: New Press, 1996, p 21.

29 www.bastar.nic.in.

30 While state mourning for the CRPF personnel killed in Tadmetla was instrumental in perpetuating the war, the state is often equally callous to its own when no political advantage is involved. In another

incident of necro-management, the bodies of three security personnel who were killed by Maoists were removed in a municipal garbage truck. When there was public protest, the administration claimed that no other vehicle had been available and the truck had been properly scrubbed.

31 N Scheper-Hughes, *Death Without Weeping: The Violence of Everyday Life in Brazil*, Berkeley, CA: University of California Press, 1992, p 533.

32 *Ibid*, p 533.

33 E Wood, *Insurgent Collective Action and Civil War in El Salvador*, Cambridge: Cambridge University Press, 2003.

34 S Kalyvas, *The Logic of Violence in Civil War*, Cambridge: Cambridge University Press, 2006, p 132.

35 See Hochschild, *The Managed Heart*, for this phrase.

36 J Huysmans, 'Security! What do you mean? From concept to thick signifier', *European Journal of International Relations*, 4(2), 1998, p 229.

37 *Ibid*, p 232.

38 N Sundar, *Subalterns and Sovereigns: An Anthropological History of Bastar*, Delhi: Oxford University Press, 2007.

39 *Hindustan Times*, 27 November 2011.

40 An August 2010 survey by an academic agency and two media houses (*The Week*– CNN–IBN– CSDS) across the 'red belt' claimed that 49 per cent support the government, and 60 per cent have faith in the democratic process, although 76 per cent want the political system to be reformed. But, remarkably, in the printed *Week* version of the survey, responding to questions about who the Naxalites are and what they stand for, on average 50 per cent of people had 'no opinion'. S Palshikar & Y Yadav, 'The Week–CNN–IBN–CSDS poll inside India's war zone', *The Week*, 20 August 2010, pp 20– 43.

41 PUCL, PUDR *et al*, *When the State Makes War against its Own People*, Delhi: PUDR, 2006; and Independent Citizens' Initiative, *War in the Heart of India*, Delhi, 2006.

42 All testimonies reproduced from *Kartam Joga and ors*, Vols 1, 2.

43 L Green, 'Fear as a way of life', *Cultural Anthropology*, 9(2), 1994, pp 227–256; and J Pettigrew, 'Living between the Maoists and the army in rural Nepal', in M Hutt (ed), *Himalayan 'People's War': Nepal's Maoist Rebellion*, London: Hurst and Company, 2004, pp 261–284.

44 E Galeano, *Upside Down: A Primer for the Looking Glass World*, New York: Metropolitan Books, 2000, p 79.

45 A Blom & N Jaoul, 'Introduction: the moral and affectual dimension of collective action in South Asia', *South Asia Multidisciplinary Academic Journal*, Special Issue on '"Outraged Communities": Comparative Perspectives on the Politicization of Emotions in South Asia', 2, 2008, para 27, at http://samaj.revues.org/document1912.html.

46 http://www.merriam-webster.com/dictionary/outrage; and http://oxforddictionaries.com/definition/outrage, accessed 7 January 2012.

47 C Browning, *Ordinary Men: Reserve Police Battalion 101 and the Final Solution in Poland*, New York: HarperCollins, 1992.

48 M Albrow, *Do Organizations have Feelings?*, London: Routledge, 1997.

49 J Oommen to EAS Sarma, 6 October 2010, DO No . . . 373/CS/2010.

50 S Randeria, 'The state of globalisation: legal plurality, overlapping sovereignties and ambiguous alliances between civil society and the cunning state in India', *Theory, Culture & Society*, 24(1), 2007, p 4.

51 F Loh, *Beyond the Tin Mines*, Singapore: Oxford University Press, 1988, p 161; M Shafer, 'The unlearned lessons of counterinsurgency', *Political Science Quarterly*, 103(1), 1998, pp 57–80; R Stubbs, *Hearts and Minds in Guerrilla Warfare: The Malayan Emergency 1948–1960*, Singapore: Marshall Cavendish, 2004, pp 169–172.

52 The government has imposed restrictions on the movement of rice across state boundaries on the grounds that this will give rice to the Maoists; fair-price shops selling cheap rice have been shut down in Maoist areas and people's grain stocks have been burnt.

53 L Berlant, 'Slow death (sovereignty, obesity, lateral agency)', *Critical Inquiry*, 33(4), Summer 2007, p 754.

Notes on contributor

Nandini Sundar is Professor of Sociology at Delhi University, and currently working on inequality, civil war and counterinsurgency.

Religion, Secularism and National Development in India and China

PETER VAN DER VEER

ABSTRACT *This article addresses the question of the relationship between religion and national development in India and China. It argues that instead of looking at secularisation as a necessary process in national development, one should focus on secularism as a powerful project of intellectuals and the state in these societies. In the post-colonial period, anti-consumerism in China took the form of Maoist secular utopianism, while in India it took the form of Gandhian religious utopianism. The article argues that religious elements can be found in both Indian and Chinese secularisms.*

In the imperial interactions between metropolis and colony, religion has always been central to explanations of why the metropolis had already developed and why some other societies had to be colonised to become developed.[1] The traditions of the colonised had to be acknowledged and interpreted first as 'religions' (such as Hinduism or Confucianism) and, second, as inferior religions. The pre-modern Christian view had been that the traditions of the peoples (heathens) outside Europe expressed falsehood and that those who were misled by them should be converted to the Truth of Christ. However, in the early Enlightenment and with European expansion the idea emerged that religion was natural and universal, but had many forms.[2] In the nineteenth century that idea could be fitted into evolutionary schemes in which Christianity was shown to be the most developed, civilised, scientifically correct and morally superior of existing religions. Universalism was thus connected to evolutionary history. This period also saw the birth of the notion of world religions with their own sacred texts: Buddhism, Hinduism, Confucianism, Islam, while Christianity and Judaism kept a special place in the analysis.[3] These world religions were supposed to carry a universal morality, in contrast to forms of animism or other localised magical beliefs. A sociological twist to this understanding of the moral nature of religion was the notion that we find with Max Weber, namely that certain religions or aspects of religion were conducive to development and others impediments to development.[4] This notion was followed by an entire branch of comparative sociology, in which the success of European modernisation

Peter van der Veer is in the Max Planck Institute for the Study of Religious and Ethnic Diversity.

was compared to the various failures in the rest of the world, in which invariably the nature of religious systems was found to be essential to these failures. The alternative to Weberian sociology was Marxist sociology but here again religion was seen as an impediment to progress, since it acted as a smokescreen that the capitalist classes used to hide their domination of the working class.

The nineteenth century imperial formations of Britain, Holland and France largely understood their domination of large parts of Asia as a proof of their civilisational superiority. They constituted the developed part of the world, while the colonised parts were underdeveloped. To be able to develop, one had to give religion a proper location in society, namely as a moral ingredient of the modern nation.[5] Since the colonised were not able to do so, there continued to be a need for empire that could provide the conditions under which the colonised could grow up and enjoy religion without misusing it to hinder the development of the political and economic system.[6]

The argument about the relation between religious traditions and modern development did not fundamentally change after decolonisation. In the USA, the new hegemonic power in the decolonised world, it was, for instance, continued in the 1950s project to study the 'new nations' at the University of Chicago. This project made a sharp distinction between the 'primordial sentiments' of religion and 'modern citizenship'.[7] It shared a moderate optimism about the ability of modern world leaders, such as Nehru and Sukarno, to create modern societies without the total revolution that had occurred in China. The optimism about the transition to modernity of the decolonised world, however, was replaced by a new 'realism' in the 1990s. The political scientist Samuel Huntington is probably the best example of this realism concerning the possibilities of replacing primordial sentiments with modern notions of citizenship. In his influential book, *The Clash of Civilizations*, he suggests that one should accept that the world is divided into civilisations that are characterised by their religious essences.[8]

The newly emergent pessimism about the possibilities of getting rid of religion in the 1990s puts an end to the modernisation paradigm and its corollary, the secularisation thesis. With all the attention to secularisation as an inevitable historical process, there has not been enough attention to secularism as historical project. Secularism as an ideological critique of religion and as a prerequisite of modern development is part of a number of social movements. It is important to examine not only the role of intellectuals in furthering this understanding of history, but also their relation to sources of power: state apparatuses and social movements. Secularism is a forceful ideology when carried by political movements that capture both the imagination and the means to mobilise social energies. It is important to attend to the utopian and indeed religious elements in secularist projects in order to understand why many of these movements seem to tap into traditional and modern sources of witchcraft, millenarianism and charisma. Much of this remains outside the framework of discussions of secularisation, but the cases of India and China show us how essential it is for understanding the dynamics of religion and the secular.

Secularism in China

Nationalists in the colonised world tended to accept the imperial idea that religion was a major explanation of the decline of the political and economic power of their societies. Religion and development were intricately linked. From this assumption, however, very different courses of action could be taken. The cases of India and China are almost at opposite points in the spectrum of possible responses to the problem religion poses to development.

Secularism as an ideology and as a practice in China is in the first place an anti-clericalism. Anti-clericalism has deep roots in Chinese history but at the end of the nineteenth century it gained the attention both of the popular media and of intellectuals who were grappling with modern, Western ideas. Intellectuals like Liang Ch'i-ch'ao (1873–1929), Chang Ping-lin (1869–1936) and Ch'en Yin-k'o (1890–1969) separated Buddhism and Taoism from their clerical roots and made them into national moralities that could serve the modernisation of China. Buddhist leaders such as Taixu (1890–1947) and Taoist modernists like Chen Yingning (1890–1969) made great efforts to bring their religions under the rubric of secular nationalism. The popular press was also not opposed to religion as such, but to Buddhist and Taoist clerics, who were described not only as ignorant buffoons but also as criminals, drunkards, gluttons and, foremost, sexually debauched. Temples and monasteries were described in the emergent press in the Late Qing period as dungeons for sexual debauchery, places of great pornographic potentiality. Clerics were portrayed in stories as visiting houses of pleasure. The main theme here is in fact that monastic celibacy and techniques of self-improvement are a disguise for a lawless, unbridled sexuality.[9] This theme of sexual scandal is certainly crucial in the emergence of the popular press in the nineteenth century everywhere, but the Chinese focus on clerics particularly recalls the pornography that was printed in the Netherlands and distributed in revolutionary circles in France in the decades before the French revolution. Here we see a genealogy of *laicité* in the underbelly of the Enlightenment that connects religion with sexuality in ways that are never made explicit, but which are, in my view, also behind the social energy in anti-Islamic gestures today in France.[10]

Clerics in China were also seen as dangerously violent, since their ascetic disciplines and martial arts that inflicted violence on their own bodies could be turned against others for criminal or rebellious purposes. This theme obviously gained prominence because of the failed Boxer rebellion in the late nineteenth century. Clerics were able to organise secret societies that threatened the state monopoly of violence. They combined fighting techniques with magic, which made the believers think they were invincible and thus extremely dangerous. The failure of the Boxer rebellion, however, showed Chinese intellectuals that there was no future in using magical means to defeat the imperial powers. Again, the themes of delusion and disguise come up here, with the notion that the illiterate masses were being led into meaningless and ultimately fruitless violence by cunning clerics.

As well as being a form of anti-clericalism, Chinese secularism was a form of scientism and rationalism. From a nineteenth century enlightened and evolutionary perspective it pitched scientific rationality against magical superstition. Secularism was thus a battle against the misconceptions of natural processes that kept the illiterate masses in the dark and in the clutches of feudal rulers and clerics. The term for superstition (迷信 *mixin*) comes from Japanese, as do many other terms that are employed in the discourse of modernity, including indeed the term 'religion' (宗教 *zongjiao*) itself. In using these neologisms Chinese secularism made a distinction between religion, which contributes to the morality of the state, and superstition, which is detrimental to modern progress. These views were shared by intellectuals of all persuasions, including the nationalists and the communists, but also by many reformist religious thinkers. This was both a discursive and an institutional shift as an aspect of the transition from the ancient regime of the Qing empire to the modern Republic. The traditional system of three teachings (*sanjiao*)—Confucian, Buddhist and Taoist—in which Confucian state ritual defined the framework for the other two was transformed in the Republic by the notion that there were five acceptable world religions: Buddhism, Taoism, Catholicism, Protestantism and Islam. Confucianism was kept outside of this arrangement, because it was considered to be both national instead of global and in essence secular rather than religious. Confucian intellectuals did try to turn it into a secular civil religion, but this met with little success outside the nationalist elite. Those religions that are officially still recognised today are organised along the models of Christianity in nation-wide associations that are ultimately controlled by the state. What remains outside this is what is often called popular religion (民间信仰 *minjian xinyang*), namely all those cults that are in fact closely connected to Buddhist and Taoist ideas and practices but are not part of these associations. Moreover, many of the Buddhist and Taoist local cults are hard to transform into nation-wide associations. Taoism in particular had been deeply intertwined with local cults. The opposition between officially approved religion and local forms of superstition gave the authorities great space for controlling and repressing all kinds of religious expressions.

Anti-clericalism and scientism together were deeply connected to Western, enlightened ideas about progress, in which magic had to be replaced by scientific rationality and by moral religion as the basis of national identity. Major currents of Western thought, like social Darwinism, neo-Kantianism and Marxism were absorbed in China. Not only did prescriptive thought about society come to stand in the light of rationality, but descriptive social sciences, such as sociology and anthropology, also lost their ability to describe the effects of these ideologies on society, since they could not distance themselves from them. Intellectuals played an important role in the secularist projects of nationalising and rationalising religion and, crucially, they were part and parcel of large-scale state interventions to produce a modern, national identity. While Buddhism and Taoism were to some extent sources for the creation of national religion, Confucianism was itself being considered as already both national and rational. The attempts to transform

Confucian traditions into a civil, national religion were extremely interesting as a form of social engineering, but ultimately failed, largely because Confucian teachings could encompass Taoist and Buddhist teachings but not the social energy that local Taoist and Buddhist cults could mobilise.

I do not want to detail the sordid history of the state persecution of clerics and destruction of temples both before and during communist rule. I only want to draw attention to the fact that, under communism, the anti-superstition and anti-clerical campaigns were combined with anti-feudalism campaigns. The 1950s saw the brutal elimination of millenarian movements like Yiguandao (一贯道), as well as the destruction of feudalism and thus the redistribution of temple land and temple property—secularisation in its original sense.[11] Mao, as a good Marxist, predicted the decline of religion as part of the creation of a socialist China in the following words: 'The gods were erected by peasants. When the right time comes, the peasants themselves will throw away these gods with their own hands.'[12] But, as a matter of fact, Mao and the Party did everything to destroy the gods, while the peasants did everything to rescue them.

One of the great puzzles of China today is not that it proves the secularisation thesis wrong, but that, despite a century of secularism, religion has not been destroyed. In fact we see everywhere in China a more open engagement with the gods. This raises a number of issues. First of all, if the secular and the religious are produced simultaneously, what has happened to the religious under secularist attack? What is the nature of Chinese religion today? Has it been hiding but is now coming out of the closet, and what does that mean? Second, how can we explain the fact that secularism has not been able to fulfil its world-historical task? Third, what may be the future of secularism in China under the current conditions of religious expansion?

First, then, what is the nature of Chinese religion and secularity today? On the one hand, we find a general acceptance in China of the idea that religion is not important to the Chinese, that the Chinese have always been rational and secular, and with modernisation even more so. This view is not only prevalent among intellectuals, it is also more generally held. On the other hand, there is a widespread interest in religious practices, in visiting shrines, especially during tourist trips, in religious forms of healing. Both in cities and in the countryside communities are rebuilding their temples and have started awkward negotiations with the authorities to perform their ceremonies again. Religious activity seems to be embedded in a fully secular life, in which job insecurities, health and the desire for success and profit create a demand for divine support. With the decline of the iron rice bowl of the state this demand has only increased. The same intellectuals who deny the importance of religion pray for their families' welfare wherever they can. However, the chain of memory, to use Hervieu-Leger's term, seems to have been broken and needs to be patched up.[13] Often common people who engage in religious activities are not very knowledgeable about them but in China this is quite extreme. This is enhanced by the fact that the clergy has been largely exterminated or so strongly brought under control of the Communist Party that it has lost its liturgical bearings. This situation in itself provides a lot of space for new religious movements in which lay people play an important role, but also cobble them together from various elements, like the many *qigong* movements.

Second, how do we explain the failure of a century of systematic destruction of Chinese religious life? One answer lies in the millenarian nature of Maoism itself. The Party absorbed quite a lot of the social energy that is available in religious movements. Yiguandao was a huge movement, with millions of followers, at the moment of the Communist take-over, but it was destroyed quickly after the killing and torturing of its leadership without inciting huge rebellions. One of the reasons for this was that the Communists, like the Yiguandao, also promised paradise on earth and seemed to have a better go at it. Mass mobilisation (群众运动 *qunzhong yundong*) for the transformation of self and society has a central place both in Chinese religion and in Maoism. Studying and especially reciting Mao's writings again recalls religious chanting. The finding and expelling of class enemies and traitors follows quite precisely the trappings of Chinese witchcraft beliefs and exorcism, even in the giving of black hoods as symbols of evil to the accused.[14] The practice of public confession likewise continues religious practice.

Third, what is the future of secularism in China? As I have already indicated, secularity is well established in China in daily life as well as in people's self-understanding. Secularism as repression of religion is also widely tolerated if a movement like the Falun Gong appears to threaten the social and political order. It is much less tolerated when local authorities try to intervene with local manifestations of popular religion. In fact, in many cases the authorities are pleased with religious activities that draw in outside money.[15] Secularism is also certainly still the frame in which clerics have to operate. The Buddhist and Taoist associations are still largely controlled by the state.

Secularism in India

Secularism in India has a number of elements in common with Chinese secularism, but the nature of the caste system and of inter-ethnic and inter-communal relations alters the meaning of these elements decidedly. In Hinduism Brahmans are the most important clerics but anti-clericalism has deep roots in Brahmanical thought itself. Priests who perform a religious service to the community and are paid for it in gifts are looked down upon by Brahmans who devote themselves to studying the Vedas. This strand of anti-clericalism fuelled many of the reforms of the large temples in South India, in which powerful middle-class laymen demand that ignorant priests be re-educated to learn Sanskrit and ritual performances.[16] More generally the Brahman caste as a whole came under attack in the nineteenth and twentieth centuries with the rise of explicitly secularist movements, especially in South and West India. Jyotirao Phule (1827–90) began a movement in Maharashtra against the alleged exploitation of low castes by Brahmans.[17] EV Ramaswamy Naicker (1879–1973), also known as Periyar, founded a social respect movement in Tamil Nadu that became the basis of an anti-Brahman Tamil nationalism. He connected his anti-clericalism with a theatrical atheism that was expressed in publicly burning sacred books, such as the Sanskrit *Ramayana*. The sources of this anti-clericalism, which evolved in the case of Periyar into atheism, were two-fold: Christian missionaries had for a long time vilified Brahman priests and their rapacity and ignorance in their project to convert tribal people and low castes away from Hinduism.[18] This rhetoric was taken over by the anti-Brahman movements and was combined with racial and linguistic theories, developed by among others Max Muller, which distinguished the Aryan invaders from the indigenous low castes. Brahmans were then shown to be really different from, say, the Dravidians and were portrayed as exploiting the indigenous peoples. We can already see that Indian anti-clericalism was decidedly different from Chinese anti-clericalism because of the connection between caste and religion. It was the Brahman caste that came under attack and Brahman priests were taken to be the symbols of that caste. On the other hand, both in China and in India the main issue was the introduction of modern egalitarianism in a hierarchical society and thus the connection between feudalism and religion.

We also find scientism and rationalism in India as an element of secularism as we did in the Chinese case. However, already in the nineteenth century Indian intellectuals were not emphasising the opposition between science and religion, but instead emphasising the scientific nature of indigenous traditions. Secularist attacks on traditional religion were rare, although attempts to purify religion from so-called superstition and to show its scientific foundations were taken up by reformers in a number of proto-nationalist and nationalist movements. Rational religion, as a major current in these reform movements, offered a home to intellectuals who wanted to reflect on developments in science from Hindu traditions. A good example was JC Bose (1853–1937), a renowned physicist and plant physiologist, whose work on electrical waves and on plant consciousness was animated by attempts to understand the unity of nature from the perspective of the Hindu philosophical school of Advaita Vedanta, in which Bengali intellectuals had been trained.[19] The social network formed by such scientists and by Hindu reformers, like Swami Vivekananda, shows how the development of scientific and religious thought was interwoven. Philosophers like Henri Bergson and Aurobindo embraced Bose's vitalistic science eagerly. While Chinese intellectuals also found rationality and science in some religious traditions, especially in the field of medicine, there was a much stronger sense than in India that progress could only be made by separating science from magic and by destroying magic.

Secularism in India emerged in the context of a secular colonial state that was professedly neutral towards religious divisions in society. The British in India were deeply concerned with projecting an image of transcendent neutrality. They were at least partially successful in doing this, since Indians today often see *dharma-nirapeksata*, the Hindi term indicating the neutrality of the state, as a distinctive character of Indian civilisation rather than a colonial invention. Sometimes, for example by Gandhi, this neutrality was more positively interpreted as *dharmasamabhava*, the equal flourishing of religion under the state's neutrality. After the Mutiny of 1857 the British were afraid to be seen interfering with the religious activities and sensibilities of their Indian subjects. This implies that the state had to hide its modernising and secularising interventions in society under a cloak of neutrality, because it derived its legitimacy not from India but from a democratic process in Britain. This neutrality, however, was interpreted by Indian nationalists as a form of divide-and-rule, especially in the area of Hindu–Muslim relations. The state was thus condemned as pseudo-secular, an argument that was later revived by Hindu nationalists against the post-colonial government. The postcolonial state derived its legitimacy from democratic elections in India and was thus even less able than its predecessor, the colonial state, to disguise its interventions in society and religion, such as the Temple Entry Acts and the abolition of untouchability, as neutral.

Since the colonial state is secular in the sense of being neutral towards religion, this provides a wide scope for connecting religion with anticolonial nationalism. Anticolonial nationalism in India draws deeply from religious sources, both ideologically and organisationally. In earlier work I have made a distinction between a moderate, pluralist vision of the Indian nation and a radical vision that wants to promote a singular religion as the core of national identity. The pluralist vision is the ideological foundation of India as a secular state, as distinguished from the radical vision of Muslims separatists, which was the foundation of Pakistan as a 'homeland for Muslims' and the radical vision of Hindu nationalists who are fighting for a Hindu India. The moderate vision has always been part of the secular ideology of the Congress Party, which has ruled India for the larger part of post-independence history.[20]

Congress found itself confronted with two major problems. First of all, Hindu–Muslim antagonism was a major threat to the creation of an Indian nation. This problem became more and more crucial in the struggle for independence and secularism was conceived as the answer to it. Second, Indian society was marked by one of the most pervasive systems of inequality in the world, one that was religiously sanctioned by Hindu traditions. Again, secularism was conceived as an answer to this. While state interventions were recognised as crucial to the transformation of Indian society into a modern nation, Congress leaders agreed that large-scale violence should be avoided. A major argument in developing Indian secularism was made by Gandhi when he made a plea for non-violence and tolerance. However, except for a brief period, Gandhi was not officially a member of the Congress leadership, but a moral exemplar outside party politics. Gandhi's moral example could be an element in producing secular tolerance, but such an example is not enough for the daily business of regulating social life. After independence the modern state could not refrain from intervening in society.[21]

Critics of Congress's secularism today, such as TN Madan and Ashis Nandy, have understood the rise of communalism in India as a backlash against the long-term campaign of an interventionist state to impose secularism on a fundamentally religious society.[22] While their emphasis on state power is correct, their criticism of Nehru's secularism seems fundamentally mistaken. Nehru's position was that the state should not attempt to make India a mono-cultural society in which the minorities would feel alienated. Pragmatically Congress adopted the role of neutral arbiter of religious difference, just as colonial administrators had done. Separate civil codes for Hindus and Muslims that had developed in the colonial period were continued in secular India. Potential sources of violent conflict, such as the disputed site of Babar's Mosque in Ayodhya, had to be controlled and managed, rather than fundamentally solved. In fact it is this policy to which a Hindu nationalist party like the BJP today objects. It does not claim that an anti-religious secularism has dominated Indian society, but that it has been a pseudo-secularism, which has given religious minorities special benefits in order to get their votes. Thus it does not argue that secularists have launched an attack on the religious traditions of Indian society, but that they have left minority traditions intact for electoral reasons. The BJP claims to be secular, but it has launched campaigns to destroy mosques built on Hindu sites and has rebuilt Hindu temples, claiming that the only traditions that have to be dealt with by the secular state are those of the minorities. Nehru's cautious but sometimes ambivalent policies towards multiculturalism, and the ways they came to be challenged in the 1970s and 1990s, show the importance of the state.[23]

The limitations of a secular Congress that tries to avoid violence in its interventions in society are clear from the failure to get rid of untouchability and caste hierarchies. Ambedkar, one of the great Untouchable leaders of Congress and architect of India's secular constitution, came to the conclusion that the secular, liberal state could not solve the problems of untouchability, which were deeply embedded in codes of honour and respect. While early in his career he demonstrated his stance against Hinduism by burning Hindu law books in public, at the end of his life he decided to convert to Buddhism in order to escape from the Hindu caste system.[24] In a very original manner he came to grips with the dualism of redistribution (class) and recognition (caste). His conversion shows that religious conversion can sometimes address these issues better than conversion to secular ideologies like socialism or liberalism.

Conclusion

While the Great Transformation is deeply connected with the rise of European empires, the rise of a new consumer culture has been crucial to the development of US hegemony in the world. According to Woodrow Wilson, in 1916 the USA's 'democracy of business' had to lead in 'the struggle for the peaceful conquest of the world'. Wilson argued that 'the great barrier in this world is not the barrier of principles, but the barrier of taste'; he connected statesmanship and salesmanship in his advice to his countrymen to 'go out and sell goods' and 'convert the world to the principles of America'. This indeed has been successful. The USA has become the Market Empire, as Victoria de Grazia has called it in her recent book on the way American consumer culture has conquered Europe.[25] This conquest became really successful in the aftermath of World War II. The Atlantic alliance between Western Europe and the USA was accompanied by the enormous popularity of American music and products. The older cultural resistances against it, especially in France, continued but they came to look more and more like a lost battle.

After decolonisation, both India and China tried to develop into modern industrial societies without becoming part of the capitalist world under US hegemony. Indeed, until the late 1980s India and China were remarkably resistant to American consumer culture, a resistance that basically took two forms. In China it took the form of Maoist secular utopianism, while in India it took the form of Gandhian religious utopianism. Foundational to both forms was an anti-imperialist nationalism.

Basic to the anticolonial imaginary in India is the opposition between Eastern spirituality and Western materialism. This opposition is part of an exceptionalism on both sides of the equation. It explains the exceptional material success of Western modernity and the material defeat of the colonised societies in the East, as well as the philosophical shallowness of that success in the face of the exceptional richness of Eastern traditions. Gandhi is the best example of this line of thought.

As we have seen, the response to imperialism in China was quite different. Chinese nationalism embraces material progress and scientific materialism. In China, both in the republican period and in the communist regime that followed it, science was the sign under which the nation and modernity were conceived. At the same time one notices the emergence of a new urban consumer culture, for example in Shanghai in the 1920s and 1930s. Nevertheless, after the victory of the Communists, consumer culture, especially in Shanghai, was no longer a sign of modernity but a sign of capitalist decadence and therefore violently repressed until 1980.

What we see in China from 1950 to 1990 is a long period of invoking the revolutionary spirit of the people against feudalism, against individualism, against the capitalist enemy, most clearly the USA. This invocation was necessary for a number of ill-fated campaigns, such as the Great Leap Forward and the Cultural Revolution. This was the period of socialist frugality and uniform appearance in Mao costumes, as well as the patriarchal repression of sexual liberty. A city like Shanghai, with its pre-war cosmopolitanism, a 'city of dreadful delight' (to cite William James on London), was seen as un-Chinese and had to be repressed until the death of Mao and the rise of Deng Xiaoping (a former leader of Shanghai). It is interesting to see that Chinese people often see the Mao period as one without religion and consumption but full of enchantment and collective illusion. Clearly, Mao became the ultimate leader, with something resembling a heavenly mandate, but one who focused on mobilising the peasants and celebrating the peasant. The bourgeoisie and the landlords were targeted as counter-revolutionaries. Peasants were the pure source of revolutionary spirit and during the Great Cultural Revolution urban people had to be re-educated by going to the countryside and learning from the peasants. It is this period of repression that is crucial for our understanding of the rise of consumption and the emergence of an urban middle class in China following the declaration of 'socialism with Chinese characteristics' by Deng Xiaoping in 1978.

What happens in China can perhaps be best understood as a socialist transition comparable with what happened in Eastern Europe after the collapse of communism. The anxiety about the rise of class differences, loss of solidarity and of the state's 'iron rice bowl' have mixed with the joy of consumerism in the cities. The disillusion with Maoist collective effervescence has promoted a world of great opportunism ('grasping one's fate'—*bawo zijide mingyun* 把握自己的命运), of magical belief in 'good luck' (*yuanfen* 缘分) and of cynicism. This is perhaps clearest in the generation that participated in the idealism of the Tiananmen student revolt and is now totally devoted to making money.

In contrast to the Chinese case, where we find a form of extreme secularism that is at the same time an enchanted materialism, in India we find a spiritual rejection of materialism in Gandhi's contribution to the struggle for independence. Gandhi was as charismatic as Mao in mobilising the masses for his vision. He was deeply aware of the connection between materialism and anti-imperialism in British intellectual circles when he started writing about India's struggle for independence in his book *Hind Swaraj* in 1910. He himself saw that struggle as primarily a spiritual one. The sources of that spiritual perspective were multiple: Hindu tradition, Tolstoy's understanding of Christian spirituality, Ruskin's thoughts about industry, and Nordau's views on civilisation. His anti-consumerism came from Bania frugality and asceticism, which came to be linked with Ruskin's critique of industrial products. Furthermore, he was strongly influenced by RK Dutt's argument that Britain had de-industrialised and underdeveloped India. These thoughts came together in Gandhi's decision to discard English dress and wear only homespun cloth (*khadi*), ultimately going as far as wearing merely a loincloth, signifying asceticism as well as solidarity with the toiling poor. This was a radical rejection of both European production and consumption as deeply embedded in imperialism. The Gandhian dress came to be as symbolic for political service to the nation as the Maoist peasant dress in China, with both signify a resistance to urbanity and consumerism.

Gandhi's 'experiments with truth' were attempts to strive for moral truth through disciplines of the body, such as fasting, celibacy, frugality. All this implied a strong anti-consumerism, an economic autarchy and a celebration of simple rural life. Gandhi wanted economic progress for India and saw the materialism of imperial power as one of the causes of India's decline. Gandhian philosophy deeply influenced even Nehru's secular modernism, which was strongly geared towards creating economic self-sufficiency and led the state away from violent modernisation of the type seen in Mao's Great Leap Forward, but it also left society's deeply ingrained hierarchies intact. Nevertheless, it is striking how much both India and China sought to secure their national independence in anti-consumerism, with an emphasis on heavy industry rather than on creating a consumer market.

A major element in economic policy in both India and China between 1950 and 1980 involved great restrictions on foreign trade and foreign investments, with a strong emphasis on self-reliance. This placed great obstacles to the development of a consumer market which could be legitimised by Maoist and Gandhian ideologies. However, since the 1980s both India and China have been opening up their economies to the world market. This has had wide-ranging effects on these societies, including rising income levels for the middle classes and a change in consumption patterns. What does the consumer revolution after the 1980s mean for India and China, politically and socially? First of all, we may see the new confidence and assertion of the middle class. In India this has been clearest in the connection between the middle class and an aggressive religious nationalism. In China this is much less clear because of political repression, but perhaps the violently suppressed Falun Gong, with its messianic nationalism, shows some of the tensions inherent in the rise of the middle class. Second, we see a kind of youth revolution, signified in the middle class by the new professions taken by young people and the different lifestyles enabled by the higher salaries they acquire. Parents often complain about the selfishness of these new generations, but are also bewildered by the new money and conspicuous consumption of these youngsters. Third, we may see new gender relations. This is quite clear in some parts of the Far East, such as Taiwan, where young professional women prefer not to marry men who seem old-fashioned and patriarchal. This trend is visible to some extent in China, but hardly so in India. Nevertheless, also in India one finds the 'modern woman' with new demands for career possibilities and gender equality.

Obviously these developments are not part of a global process of westernisation or Americanisation, but are part of a global modernity that is experienced in significantly different ways in China and India. Sometimes we may suggest that forms of conspicuous consumption seem to have survived the onslaught of Gandhian and Maoist anti-consumerism even at the height of their influence. In India it is marriage, with its dowry system, that seems not to have been controlled by a spirit of anti-consumerism. Deeply embedded in hierarchical thinking, it has spurred competitive spending and indebtedness in a nation devoted to a savings glut. In China it is the creation of *guanxi* relations, practised via banquets, that seems to have escaped the Maoist onslaught. The extent to which men in particular are involved in dining out in large groups and today also go to karaoke bars is remarkable and explains the existence of an elaborate restaurant culture.[26]

Where does this huge economic change leave secularism and religion in India and China today? The secularisms found in India and China are emancipatory projects and by their very nature they are violent. The transition to modernity is obviously violent; it does violence to traditional arrangements and therefore the relation of secularism to violence is crucial. The secular mobilisation of social energies in China is incredibly violent, discursively and practically. The Chinese secular utopia is strikingly millenarian and magical and thus reintroduces the traditional elements that it wants to eradicate but in another configuration. The mobilisation of social energies in India is also violent, but it is not secularism that produces anti-religious violence, but rather secularism that tries to stem the violence between religious communities. The secular utopia, as is clearest in Gandhi's campaigns, is thus one of the peaceful coexistence of equal religions within a neutral state. Non-violence was therefore the centre of Gandhi's attempts to create a secular India. It is not only the emancipation from the colonial oppressor that has to be non-violent, the emancipation from inequality and communal opposition must equally be non-violent.

Second, the Chinese and Indian cases show us that secularism is not simply anti-religious in these societies, although there are anti-religious elements in it, but that it simultaneously attempts to transform religions into moral sources of citizenship and national belonging. The masses have to be re-educated to realise their emancipatory potential and religions can be used as state apparatuses to perform this re-education. In the regime of secularism religions are nationalised and modernised. While religion is an important element in the production of these imaginaries, it can never be entirely contained by the secularist frame. It may produce linkages outside the nation-state as world religions do; it may produce alternative visions of the moral state and thus become dangerous for secularist control, as in millenarian movements that have emerged in China since the demise of Maoism. Precisely because secularism is a project and not a process, it is bound to be incomplete and to produce contradictions that it itself cannot explain.

Notes

1 P van der Veer, *Imperial Encounters*, Princeton, NJ: Princeton University Press, 2001.
2 C Taylor, *Sources of the Self*, Cambridge, MA: Harvard University Press, 1989.
3 T Masuzawa, *The Invention of World Religions*, Chicago, IL: University of Chicago Press, 2005.
4 M Weber, *Gesammelte Aufsätze zur Religionssoziologie*, Vol 1, Tübingen: Mohr, 1986.
5 For a particularly clear argument for the need for a 'modern religion' in socioeconomic development and the positive role envisioned for the colonial government, one can refer to the famous Dutch Islamic scholar Christiaan Snouck Hurgronje, who was the governmental advisor for 'Islamic Affairs' in Dutch Indonesia. Hurgronje, *Nederland and the Islam*, Leiden: Brill, 1915.
6 One can find this argument also in John Stuart Mill's ideas about the colonised as children who needed to be educated before they could have self-rule. See U Singh Mehta, *Liberalism and Empire*, Chicago, IL: University of Chicago Press, 1999.
7 C Geertz, *Old Societies and New States: The Quest for Modernity in Asia and Africa*, New York: Free Press, 1963.
8 S Huntington, *The Clash of Civilizations*, New York: Simon & Schuster, 1996.
9 V Goossaert, 'L'anti-clericalisme en Chine', *Extreme-Orient/Extreme-Occident*, 24, 2002.
10 J Scott, *The Politics of the Veil*, Princeton, NJ: Princeton University Press, 2007.
11 D Ownby, 'Imperial fantasies: the Chinese communists and peasant rebellions', *Comparative Studies in Society and History*, 43, 2001, pp 65–91.
12 Cited in T Dubois, *The Sacred Village: Social Change and Religious Life in Rural North China*, Honolulu, HI: University of Hawaii Press, 2005.
13 D Hervieu-Leger, *Religion as a Chain of Memory*, New Brunswick, NJ: Rutgers University Press, 2000.
14 JB ter Haar, 'China's inner demons: the political impact of the demonological paradigm', in WL Chong (ed), *China's Great Proletarian Revolution: Master Narratives and post-Mao Counternarratives*, London: Rowman & Littlefield, 2002, pp 27–46; and ter Haar, *Telling Stories: Witchcraft and Scapegoating in Chinese History*, Leiden: Brill, 2006.
15 K Dean, *Taoist Ritual and Popular Cults of Southeast China*, Princeton, NJ: Princeton University Press, 1993.

16 CJ Fuller, *Servants of the Goddess*, Cambridge: Cambridge University Press, 1994.
17 R O'Hanlon, *Caste, Conflict and Ideology: Mahatma Jotirao Phule and Low Caste Protest in Nineteenth-Century Western India*, Cambridge: Cambridge University Press, 2002.
18 NB Dirks, 'The conversion of caste: location, translation, and appropriation', in P van der Veer (ed), *Conversion to Modernities*, New York: Routledge, 1996, pp 115–137.
19 G Prakash, *Another Reason: Science and the Imagination of Modern India*, Princeton, NJ: Princeton University Press, 1999.
20 P van der Veer, *Religious Nationalism*, Berkeley, CA: University of California Press, 1994.
21 JC Heesterman, *The Inner Conflict of Tradition: Essays in Indian Ritual, Kinship, and Society*, Chicago, IL: University of Chicago Press, 1985.
22 TN Madan, *Modern Myths, Locked Minds: Secularism and Fundamentalism in India*, Delhi: Oxford University Press, 1997; and A Nandy, 'An anti-secularist manifesto', *India International Quarterly*, 22(1), 1995, pp 35–64.
23 P van der Veer, 'The ruined center: religion and mass politics in India', *Journal of International Affairs*, 50(1), 1996, pp 254–277.
24 G Viswanathan, *Outside the Fold*, Princeton, NJ: Princeton University Press, 1999.
25 V de Grazia, *Irresistible Empire: America's Advance through 20th Century Europe*, Cambridge, MA: Harvard University Press, 2005.
26 C Jaffrelot & P van der Veer (eds), *Patterns of Middle-Class Consumption in India and China*, Delhi: Sage, 2008.

Notes on contributor

Peter van der Veer is Director of the Max Planck Institute for the Study of Religious and Ethnic Diversity in Göttingen. He also holds professorships at Utrecht University, the University of Göttingen and the Tata Institute for Social Studies in Mumbai. He focuses on the study of religion and nationalism in India and elsewhere. He is currently working on comparative studies of India and China.

Between Party, Parents and Peers: the quandaries of two young Chinese Party members in Beijing

SUSANNE BREGNBAEK

ABSTRACT   *This article explores the lived contradictions entailed in being a young member of the Chinese Communist Party (CCP) today. The focus is on how political and existential issues intersect. It explores party membership as a strategy for personal mobility among Beijing elite university students by providing an ethnographic account of the quandaries of two young CCP members. Even though one student is of rural origin and the other has an urban elite background, in both cases party membership has been pursued as a strategy for opening paths to the future and tied to a quest for self-development rather than a matter of wishing to make sacrifices for the country. The article focuses on how the two students' efforts play out differently. At the same time it is argued that a sense of moral and existential ambiguity goes hand in hand with both of their party membership strategies, leading to an experience of division.*

What does it mean to be a communist in present day capitalist China? Chinese society is fraught with competing and contradictory influences, which have a hand in shaping the lives of Chinese urban youth. In this article I will focus on the experiences of Chinese university students who belong to the so-called post-1980s generation (*balinghou*) and who are members of the Chinese Communist Party (CCP). The picture that emerges is that what is at stake for young people in different circumstances is less a question of intellectually incompatible world-views than a matter of working out a viable balance between self and other, between public behaviour and private thoughts, as well as between political ideals and the messiness and contingencies of everyday life. This involves considerable tension and this tension is at once political and existential.

China has undergone tremendous societal transitions, having over a period of 20 years changed from being a poor agricultural society to being the world's second largest economy. Despite these massive transformations, which have also led to an increasing divide between the haves and the

Susanne Bregnbaek is a post-doctoral research fellow at the Department of Anthropology, University of Copenhagen.

have-nots, the CCP is still in power. About one-fifth of Chinese elite university students are members of the party and the students at Qinghua University and Beijing University, among whom I carried out 10 months of fieldwork in 2005 and 2007, clearly held mixed feelings about them. While some felt that being a member of the party was necessary in order to become highly respected and successful, others found party members to be either opportunistic, naive or both. These ambiguous views mirror Stig Thøgersen's framing of party members in rural China as 'parasites' or 'civilisers'.[1] But how do things look from the perspective of the young party members themselves? What is entailed in their party membership strategies? What is the relationship between loyalty to one's family and loyalty to the party? And what can the issue of becoming a member of the CCP tell us about the lived implications of social differences in China?

In this article I will explore the experiences and quandaries of two young men, Bai Gang and Zhou Lemin.[2] What can be learned through examining the experiences of two individuals? In the spirit of the Manchester School, these cases are not to be seen as 'apt illustrations' of ethnographic generalisations concerning types of socio-cultural practice or any abstract idea of 'value', 'political culture' or 'belief systems',[3] nor have they been chosen because they are typical.[4] Rather, they have been chosen because they entail some measure of conflict and crisis and thus they have the potential to throw into relief 'the social and political tensions that are at the heart of everyday life'. These two young men make an interesting comparison since they are both members of the CCP and thus provide a window to the Chinese state, not as a monolithic bureaucracy but as made up of individuals, who in different ways embody the state yet face different predicaments. Phrased in existential terms, the aim is to try to do justice to their *experiences* and to disclose the commonalities in our lives rather than any pursuit of abstract knowledge.[5]

From theories of governance to lived experience

Pointing out that social/political life in China is fraught with contradictions is not new. Let me briefly and somewhat opportunistically cover the literature with which I enter into conversation. Ann Anagnost's work has been influential, since she was the first to focus on the concept of population quality (*suzhi*),[6] which has played an influential role in studies of Chinese governance. The concept is an amorphous term, which has undergone various transformations. In a thought-provoking and widely cited article 'The corporeal politics of Suzhi', Anagnost has argued that, since the 1980s, the term is no longer merely used to denote the backwardness of the rural population but has become tied to a discourse of middle-class mobility. In this text she analyses the production of (human) value in contemporary China through a juxtaposition of the migrant and the urban middle-class child as 'ghostly doubles'. She argues that the cheap labour of migrant workers is a hidden prerequisite for China's economic take-off and the emergence of a booming Chinese middle-class and goes on to argue that

IDENTITY, INEQUITY AND INEQUALITY IN INDIA AND CHINA

value is abstracted from the labouring bodies of migrants and placed into the bodies of urban middle-class children.[7] While her approach powerfully displays structural differences, it tells us little about the lived experiences of either the migrant or the middle-class child and begs to be documented ethnographically.

It has been quite common, mainly in US literature, to characterise the Chinese reforms, or aspects of them, since the Period of Opening Up and Reform as neoliberal and thus comparable to the backlash against the welfare state in many Western countries since the late 1970s. The trope of neoliberalism does highlight some important aspects of Chinese governance, such as the retreat of the welfare state, the increasing role of the market and the intention to create responsible individuals. However, as Andrew Kipnis has argued, in a pivotal and also widely cited article, a strongly politically charged term such as neoliberalism has its disadvantages when applied to a Chinese context, where *suzhi* discourse is first and foremost 'authoritarian rather than liberal, government-driven rather than market dictated'.[8] Even though several anthropologists have in different ways argued that they do not intend to reify neoliberalism but on the contrary refer to a particular Chinese version of neoliberalism, 'neoliberalism as exception', 'neoliberalism with Chinese characteristics' or 'neoliberalism with a small n', the role of the market takes centre stage in these studies and the role of the state remains something of a black box. Significant for my purpose is the fact that these studies reveal little about how the state consists of individuals, who may contradict or disagree with the state with a capital S.[9]

The role of the state and the party, on the other hand, have been well described by Frank Pieke. In his book *The Good Communist*, Frank Pieke investigates how government officials are trained for placement in the Communist Party and this process is full of contradictions. He shows how, while the CCP has undergone radical transformation since the revolutionary years under Mao, it is still incumbent upon cadres, who are selected through a highly rigorous process, to be ideologically committed to the party. He instead calls this form of governance *neo-socialism*, since he deals with what comes after socialism but in the form of a 'condition of socialism'. In this way he argues against both a tendency to explore Chinese governance through the trope of neoliberalism and against the limitations entailed in the concept of post-socialism, which is dominated the study of the former Soviet bloc. According to Pieke, 'China's present administration is Mao Zedong's worst nightmare become real'.[10] Rather than being directly involved in the life and work of the masses, cadres have become a ruling elite who worship book learning and formal education. He also notes that 'the learning, discipline and privilege that cadre training provides is a key transformative experience in the construction of cadres' unique sense of personhood, a sense of self that straddles the boundaries between strong individuality, total submission to the party's will, elitist exclusivity and faceless anonymity'. In other words Pieke's work suggests that party membership entails managing contradictory social imperatives. Leaving aside unifying tropes such as 'neoliberalism', 'post-socialism' or 'neo-socialism', the focus in this article is on how the contradictions entailed in being a communist in capitalist China are experienced, embodied and dealt with. But first let me now turn to the question of Chinese youth.

The post-1980s generation and the experience of division

Several studies of the so-called generation of 'little emperors' or the 'post-1980s generation' (*baling hou*), representing the roughly 200 million Chinese born between 1989 and 1999, have focused on the values they are shaped by. Some studies have focused on assessing the extent to which they are individualist (read selfish, spoilt, materialist) or collectivist (read filial, self-sacrificial and responsible). While Martin King Whyte's great study concludes that Chinese youth are in fact more filial than one could have expected, more recent studies conclude that Chinese youth are becoming more individualistic. A recent body of literature argues that an individualisation, in Ulrik Bech's terms, is taking place in China, and thus speaks of an' individualisation' of Chinese society as such.[11]

Reflecting on the increasing pluralisation of Chinese society after 30 years of reform, Stanley Rosen concludes that Chinese youth are far from unified in their belief systems. He has explored the competing and often contradictory influences shaping Chinese youth today. Based on extensive surveys, Rosen concludes that Chinese youth are 'capable of exhibiting all of these tendencies [nationalism, internationalism, materialism and pragmatism] at different times, depending on the circumstances, or even at the same time'. In Rosen's account events such as the tenth anniversary of the NATO bombing of the Chinese embassy in Belgrade gave rise to nationalist tendencies. But if we shift the gaze from belief systems to individual experience or from worldviews (*Weltanschauung*) to life-world (*Lebenswelt*), how do different *individuals* who find themselves in different social circumstances experience the role of the party? To paraphrase Arthur Kleinman, what is at stake for them?

In a recently edited volume called *Deep China: The Moral Life of the Person*, Kleinman *et al* venture a deeper inquiry of the psychology of Chinese citizens. They argue that China's extraordinarily fast modernisation 'may have created a special cultural version of the divided self'.[12] The authors invoke a famous painting of an owl with one eye closed and the other open by the Chinese painter Huang Youngyu, which has been interpreted as a critical wink at the terrible times of the Cultural Revolution. The authors of *Deep China* argue that this image also speaks to our times. The image of division is telling of 'a deep structural tension in China's moral worlds and in the Chinese individual', who in different ways experiences a split between their actual social practice and an inner world of contemplation and thus struggle to keep one eye open and the other closed.[13]

When reading this account I was struck by the degree to which it speaks to the tensions that I found to be so pertinent among the Chinese university students in Beijing among whom I carried out fieldwork in 2005 and 2007. However, the issue of party membership is a theme which none of the authors

IDENTITY, INEQUITY AND INEQUALITY IN INDIA AND CHINA

of *Deep China* addresses. Let me now turn to the ethnography, starting with Bai Gang.

Bai Gang

Bai Gang, a law student at Qinghua University, clearly had a lot on his mind when we first met during spring 2005. He explained that his parents, who were farmers in rural Guanxi province, had worked hard tilling the fields and had sacrificed a lot in order to enable him, as the youngest son, to receive a university education. Bai Gang spoke very caringly about his parents and said that he respected them a lot as a good filial son ought to. Like other students from rural areas, Bai Gang and his parents lived in different worlds: 'My parents have never been to Beijing', he said.

> They don't know much about the world. Their lives are about working and saving money for their children. They work so hard that they even sacrifice their own health for money.

Whereas his parents were concerned with obtaining a basic sense of security, he had vivid dreams for his future and the thought of returning to his natal village to provide for his parents during their old age was very remote to Bai Gang. He shared with his urban counterparts a dream of making a career in Beijing, finding an apartment and possibly even travelling to foreign countries in the future.

In the case of rural students such as Bai Gang, who have entered high-ranking universities in the country's capital, the migrant and the middle-class child are in fact embodied in the same person, causing considerable tension. Students like Bai Gang sometimes take part in the same educational system, they live closely together in small dormitories and compete against each other, although on unequal terms. Anagnost's juxtaposition of the migrant and the middle-class child as 'ghostly doubles' is none the less a powerful image and good to bear in mind when seeking to understand what is at stake for rural students who attempt to cross the rural–urban divide.

Bai Gang found it unfair that students from Beijing can enter universities with lower degrees than is the case for students from other provinces.[14] On the one hand, non-Beijing residents, such as Bai Gang, may be respected for their higher grades, he felt, but at the same time they tend to be looked down upon, since they lack other kinds of social capital. Bai Gang put it this way when we met at a café off campus and he tasted his first cappuccino:

> Maybe the students from Beijing have a more open mind because they are accustomed to modern life. For example, the internet, eating in cafés, in modern restaurants, their ability in painting, dancing, music...But many students from the rural areas don't have access to this so there is a gap between the cities and the rural areas...Sometimes they look down upon us because they have grown up in the capital and feel that they have an advanced attitude. For

people from the rural areas this leads to a lack of confidence because we live in a modern city but we are from less developed areas.[15]

Bai Gang's perceived lack of confidence in relation to urban students, who are accustomed to 'modern life' in the form of consumption and distinction, can be likened to the difficulty of a migrant adjusting fully to the norms of the host society. Even though Bai Gang finds most students from Beijing to be 'friendly', he says he feels estranged from them. Although Bai Gang himself does not use the term *suzhi*, by mentioning diffuse aspects such as 'an open mind', being accustomed to 'modern life', consumption patterns and artistic abilities, his experiences reflect *suzhi* discourse.

Since the 1980s various attempts to reform the Chinese educational system have gone under the name of *suzhi jiaoyu*. This term, which is usually translated as 'education for quality', draws on American competence education. The idea is to reform the educational system in such a way that Chinese youth can become innovative, independent and self-actualised in the same way that American students are imagined to be.[16] In other words, according to *suzhi jiaoyu* logic, while there is a sense that Chinese students in general have not quite caught up with their American counterparts, students from rural China in particular are an ambiguous reminder of China's sense of distance from the first world.

For Bai Gang this feeling of inferiority had much to do with the question of achieving a residence permit (*hukou*). *Hukou* is the household registration system, which in effect means that there are different kinds of citizenship in China. Rural students have a temporary residence permit in Beijing while they are studying. But, unless they are able to find a job after graduation in which their employer can 'arrange a *hukou* for them', they must in principle return to their home provinces. If they stay, they become part of the so-called 'floating population', the millions of migrants living illegally as 'strangers in the city' without any legal rights.[17]

This brings me back to Arthur Kleinman's image of the owl. The state has been successful at creating prosperity, although with worsening social inequality, but it is also repressive and dangerous.[18] The party-state is as much a place of collusion and collaboration with ruthless pragmatic power as it is a place of aspiration for and achievement of a better life for many of its citizens. Thus Bai Gaing, like other students with a rural background, found himself betwixt and between in hoping to transcend his rural status.

One day Bai Gang told me that he was preparing to become a member of the Communist Party. We had just made our way through a crowd of street hagglers selling everything from watermelons to fake watches and minority craftwork, as well as past several beggars in old dilapidated Mao suits who clearly made Bai Gang speed up his pace. Having found refuge in a café called 'Sculpting in Time', he said:

> In fact, I might become a member of the Communist Party before my graduation. I don't think I will be so conscious of being a member of the party,

but I plan to become a member because it will be helpful in order to find a job in the future. Especially if you want to work within a government institution you have to, and this is sometimes written in job advertisements—they call for being a member of the Communist Party. I think this is a good thing for me because there is serious competition for jobs.

Coming from a poor rural background with no official connections, Bai Gang's commitment to join the party was, however, primarily a strategy to attempt to improve his chances in the labour market after graduation. The *suzhi jiaoyu* focus on personal development and on education as implying more than obtaining high test scores was something Bai Gang would try to overcome by becoming a member of the party. His primary concern was to be able to get a good job in an 'opportunity city' (Beijing, Shanghai, Guangzhou or Shenzhen) and to obtain urban citizenship.

Even though he had said that he would not be so 'conscious of becoming a party member', when I asked him more about what becoming a member of the party entailed, he responded using the language of the party in the form of a rhetoric of self-sacrifice:

> You should have selfless dedication and work for the country, work for the people. You must improve yourself constantly. As a member, you should strengthen your skills and be an example of an advanced mind. And in a group, you should strive to be the most advanced. If someone is in trouble, you should help him selflessly. I think this norm will be good for me to strive for, as it would really be good for any person, whether he is a member of the Communist Party or not. It would be good for every citizen to have this spirit.

By becoming a party member, he admittedly hoped to increase his chances of finding a well paid job and an urban Beijing residence permit (*hukou*). In this way, he also hoped to be able to reverse the generational contract, to be able to send remittances back to his parents.

However, Bai Gang said that his parents were ambiguous about their son's becoming a party member. Like many of the other villagers, they were frustrated with the corruption of local officials, who taxed their crops heavily. 'My parents miss Chairman Mao because Mao *cared* about the peasants of China, unlike the current party members, who are busy filling their own pockets', he said. He said that they had a picture of Chairman Mao in their living room and that they would burn incense for him along with the other ancestors. He said this with a compassionate smile, indicating that he found this practice to be out of tune with reality, although he shared their frustration in relation to the corruption of government officials and the widening disparity between China's booming urban coastal areas and the poverty of the countryside.

Let me turn to another student, Zhou Lemin, for whom party membership was also tied to his hopes of attaining social mobility but for whom the question of social mobility played out differently.

Keeping various paths open

Zhou Lemin suggested we could meet briefly by the sports track at Qinghua University, since he had a very tight schedule. It took me a while to recognise him in his green tracksuit. Normally he was dressed in a blue velvet suit and wore large-rimmed spectacles. In this way he stuck out from the usually more casual college-student look, but today he blended in with the crowd. Every semester hundreds of Qinghua students gather at the dusty running track in order to take part in the running event of the university. The slogan 'Study healthily for the motherland for the next fifty years' was visible on large red banners. Boys have to be able to run 3000 metres in 15 minutes, while for girls the requirement is 1500 metres. Most students dreaded this exercise, even though few found it difficult to complete.

Having stretched out his sore legs and put his glasses back on, Zhou Lemin told me:

> In fact I find this exercise annoying because it is too inflexible. I think the requirement to be fit and healthy is OK, but they should be more flexible in the planning of the event. Actually, I had to do some work for a company today, where I am working as an intern, but I had to cancel. My boss found this hard to understand. A running exercise? So it was a dilemma for me, but I *have* to show up, otherwise I will be punished. And as a member of the party, we have to do these things in an enthusiastic way. We have to be a model for others.

He went on to explain that, when a person is selected as a potential member of the party,[19] and the person also aspires to become one, he or she goes through a period in which his or her actions and character are observed. This is sometimes referred to as 'the engagement process'. During this period the person writes an application, which is an expression of his or her motivation for joining the party, and this has to do with convincing the other party members of the sacrifices he or she is willing to make for the country and the party. When a person is found to be suitable in terms of political thoughts and moral character, he or she may be selected for membership. This is popularly referred to as 'marriage'. In this way party membership is phrased as a way of growing up, through gaining recognition from significant others, who hold a position of authority. In other words, a person changes from being a child of the state to being recognised not only as a grown-up person, but as an exemplary person, a model for others to follow.

As a member, one is expected to serve as an example to others and to take part in meetings once a week or every two weeks, in which party members study the work of Zhou Enlai, Dengxiao Peng and Mao Zedong and discuss current affairs of the country and matters related to the university, including the attempt to reform the educational system.

However, in practice Zhou Lemin faced incompatible social imperatives that could hardly both be realised simultaneously. This can be seen as a concrete example of the contradictions of *suzhi jioayu*. The requirement to take part in a collective running exercise in which the body of the individual person is to be strong and healthy, representing the strength of the body politic, coincided with the requirement to improve his 'social skills' as an intern in a foreign company. Zhou Lemin emphasised that, working in this foreign environment, he was constantly learning a lot and felt that he was 'improving himself' and changing his personality. He learned to be assertive and confident and this, he emphasised, was what '*suzhi jiaoyu*' was all about. Here he is expected to live up to the requirement to be a flexible and autonomous person, ready to live up to the demands of a competitive market economy.

Some authors have argued that a new neoliberal Chinese subject based on self-governance has replaced a self that was more oriented towards family, state and the collective.[20] Kleinman also has argued that Chinese phenomena such as the increasing popularity of personal memories, internet-based chatrooms, television soap operas, a turn in popular religion to more spiritual quests, post-retirement education, and the development of volunteerism all reveal a preoccupation with the cultivation of subjectivity that is reminiscent of the German *Bildungsroman*.

The slogan of 'working healthily for the motherland for the next 50 years', which echoes Chinese martial arts exercises seems strangely outdated when compared with pursuing personal credentials and fulfilment as an intern in an international company or through the appreciation of music or art. In the same way, the party rhetoric of working selflessly for one's country seems a far cry from the forms of self-development, exploring one's sense of selfhood and enhancement of personal 'quality' that *suzhi jiaoyu* promotes. In this way I think the view of 'the triumph of neoliberalism' misses the way in which mutual imperatives coexist in the lives of Chinese citizens, whose sense of self has not merely been absolved by neoliberal governance.

Let me return to Zhou Lemin's reflections about growing up as it were 'under communism':

> In fact I am quite unique. What I mean is, I am neither from rural or urban China, and even though I have grown up during the Period of Opening Up and Reform, I have grown up under communism.

He went on to explain how he had grown up in an oil-field in a part of Shenyang with many state-owned oil companies. This area continued to function as a *dan wei*, a work unit which provided for the families of the workers, until 1998, when former prime minister Zhu Rongji came to power and partly privatised the state-owned companies. There was a rationing system whereby at four o'clock in the afternoon people would queue up for eggs, the following day for soap, at five o'clock people went to the water station, etc. Zhou Lemin has fond memories of his childhood as a time when 'everybody had what they needed'. He emphasised that this area was sparsely populated because of the poor quality of the soil, but people were quite prosperous because of the oil industry, and they continue to be granted state pensions. In addition to this his father had set up his own small business from which he had derived quite a lot of profit.

Zhou Lemin seemed to experience some sort of division from his childhood memories to present life, but being a *'bei nan dang'*,[21] a member of the party, and a masters student of international relations, with parents who were party members, wealthy and well connected, he felt confident about his future. He had already established himself in his own apartment in Beijing and said that he was aware that he was in a fortunate position, and that having good 'material conditions' (*tiaojian*) also made him an attractive marriage partner. His dream was to enter the foreign ministry and to work as a diplomat in foreign countries in the future.

Zhou Lemin did not pretend to be making sacrifices for his country. He said bluntly that this was merely rhetoric. He explained that the procedure for obtaining party membership was a masquerade. Having parents who were party members was something that was 'helpful' if one wanted to join the party, he said. 'There is more or less a standard way of writing these applications, all the stuff about making sacrifices for the country...'. Zhou Lemin was a member of the party for strategic reasons, as were other party members, he believed. 'That is just the way the system works, and if you want to join the foreign ministry, this is the road you have to take'.

Could this not invite charges of hypocrisy and corruption of the ideology by which it justifies itself? According to Stephen Feuchtwang, the CCP is a 'fossil, whose continuing life is an ever present reminder of other possibilities. Habits and recollections of collective organization and socialist ideals live on after the exhaustion of revolution. They cast a shadow over the commercialization of exchange and the privatization of formerly collective or state-controlled economic relations...The persistence of this fossil represents a permanent potential provocation.'[22] In the case of Zhou Lemin this fossil did not come across as a provocation, but as a contradiction in terms none the less.

Notice the contrast between the egalitarian, simple life that he associated with the communism he grew up with and the standing as a party member, which had become an element of his personal striving for elite status. He seemed to have moved with the changing tides, and as such they never came across as a source of conflict in his life. Rather, it seemed that he and his family had adapted to and derived advantage from the political and economic changes. Zhou Lemin was both a party member and an intern in a foreign company, and in this way he seemed to keep various paths open and to present himself as being very confident about his own future. Zhou Lemin's account made apparent how becoming a party member was a strategic choice, one which did not seem problematic to him. Even though he did not 'believe in communism', he found it wise to keep various paths open.

It is possible that there are many Zhou Lemins like him, in the sense that so far the party has been able to represent the interests of the Chinese elite to a substantial degree, as the work of Stanley Rosen suggests.[23] However, even though this mostly quantitative work has shown that the Chinese elite supports the party, I think the autobiographical sketch outlined in this article points to the ambiguities at stake in terms of how this is experienced. Even though there is no political alternative to the CCP, and even though becoming a party member is pursued as a strategic choice, Zhou Lemin's reflections also revealed a certain ironic distance from the empty ideals. Following Kleinman *et al* he seemed to experience a split between the role he felt obliged to play and his inner thoughts, or between his public and his private self. A sense of moral disillusion was noticeable in the kind of mild discomfort that appeared in his flickering eyes when talking about political issues. With a shrug of the shoulders he said that he felt that in the future the party might become irrelevant but for the time being one just had to put up with it. Even though Zhou Lemin was able to navigate in a terrain of conflicting imperatives and find paths towards the future, his thoughts were more nuanced than could be captured by labelling him either 'nationalistic', 'internationalist', 'materialistic' or 'pragmatic'.

A double-bind

When I met Bai Gang again during the second part of my fieldwork in 2007, he seemed more disillusioned than the cheerful boy I had met two years earlier. He seemed to be stuck in a dead-end. He had recently graduated and was looking for a job in Beijing but without any luck. He also explained that he found it difficult to envision a viable solution, since people with a BA degree earn only 1500 RMB a month and people with postgraduate degrees as little as 2000. This money makes it hard to settle permanently in Beijing, find a place to live, provide for a family and send remittances back to one's parents and siblings. Although Bai Gang knew he could probably easily get a job in another part of China, closer to home, he was unwilling to give up the idea of making a life for himself in Beijing.

He was deeply distressed by what he experienced as the increasing corruption in society in general and within the educational system. In particular he mentioned a friend of his, whose father had a friend who was a secretary to a high-ranking party official. This friend wanted to do a PhD but felt that he would not be able to live up to the requirements of the exam. Through his father's connections he was promised a position the following year. According to Bai Gang, this friend now spends a year on campus without doing anything and is going out to bars in the evenings and spending his time leisurely having fun (*wan*) with his girlfriend.

As for his commitment to the work of the party, Bai Gang said that, as a party member, he now also took part in the recruitment of new members among the university students. 'This procedure is equally corrupt', he said. 'What happens is that we recommend our friends. In principle, we are supposed to observe them, hold meetings and discuss their assets and flaws, but this is done superficially. It is all about "*guanxi*" [connections]'. By becoming a party member, Bai Gang in a sense 'became the party'—he became part of the structural logic of the party, whereby connections (*guanxi*) were far more important than values and virtues. While he assisted in recruiting new members, in his own case party membership had not provided a means for social mobility.

For Bai Gang becoming a party member was tied to a strategy of trying to transform his rural status to an urban one, thus making him a fully recognised citizen. In this way he could also grow up in a moral sense in relation to his parents and siblings and repay their sacrifices. His desire to come into his own, by working and living in the capital of the country, also had to do with a desire not to be looked down upon as a 'stranger' and a second-class citizen in his own country. However, becoming a party member did not seem to have paid off.

Bai Gang's attempts to transcend his social status put him in a double-bind.[24] On the one hand he felt emotionally attached to his parents and obliged to respect them and eventually take care of them during their old age. On the other, he found it hard to escape a sense of looking down on them as primitive peasants who knew little about what the world has to offer. And how could he justify wanting to stay in Beijing or another 'opportunity city', when he could easily get a job in a place closer to home? How could he fulfil his filial obligations if it meant abandoning his own dreams and confining himself to the same poverty that oppressed his parents? Having tasted a bit of urban life he wanted more; in his own words he would like to continue moving 'forwards' not 'backwards'.

Bai Gang's political disillusionment and existential dissatisfaction is far from unique. Young men like Bai Gang, who work hard and whose families have sacrificed so much for their education, yet who do not feel that their efforts bear fruit, have increased dramatically over the past decade, in which unemployment for Chinese college graduates has sky-rocketed.[25] There are currently about three million unemployed Chinese university graduates living in Beijing's suburbs, to some extent sharing the same fate as China's many migrant workers, who live in crowded apartments in Beijing's suburbs, getting by on low or no income. Bai Gang told me while shrugging his shoulders: 'Can you believe it? This is the life of a Qinghua graduate.' The Chinese sociologist Lian Si coined the term 'China's ant tribe' and the government fears that the ants may become restless and pose a threat to political stability.[26] Existentially young people such as Bai Gang feel betrayed. Were these years of studying hard and the sacrifices his parents have endured in order to provide for his higher education really in vain?

Conclusion

The quandaries tied to being a communist in capitalist China were experienced less as a product of intellectual contemplation than as a matter of trying to create viable paths to the future. Arguing against any abstract concepts that encapsulate the particular forms of Chinese state governance as well as attempts to characterise Chinese youth in terms of their values or belief systems, I have tried to provide an account of two young men who in different ways experienced certain moral quandaries in relation to being a member of the party. The stories of these two young men in their very different ways seem to attest to how the CCP is comprised of individuals whose life chances are so different that it is failing to work as an embodiment of the country as a whole. For Bai Gang this means that his parents feel abandoned by the state, as they are at the mercy of corrupt local cadres. But it also means that he has been able to get a higher education, something his parents were never able to do. However, Bai Gang seemed stuck and unable to move on.

To Zhou Lemin it means that he idealises his 'communist childhood', yet feels estranged from the political slogans that he readily admits to opportunistically using as gate-openers to an alluring and unpredictable future. For Zhou Lemin becoming a member of the party was in some ways at odds with his other plans to work as an intern in a foreign company but, knowing that the political content was merely jargon, he seemed able to have it both ways. Rather than being torn in two directions, for him it was a matter of staying afloat and seizing the opportunities at hand. A closer look at his life story and perspective, however, reveals that, although he was able to manage contradictory social experiences and eventually succeeded in going abroad for further studies, this did not mean that he was not highly reflective and experienced some degree of ambivalence between the role he felt obliged to perform—enthusiastically working for the nation or talking in slogans, while his thoughts were elsewhere, yet swallowing his pride.

By contrast Bai Gang struggled to reconcile his belief in the remnants of socialism, which had been part of his rural upbringing by parents who still worshipped Chairman Mao, with what he experienced to be the corrupt reality of the party. When I first met him he seemed to jump between repeating party slogans to expressing political critique. Gradually party membership came to denote mere opportunism and self-interest, rather than sacrifices based on a promise of future return. He felt disenchanted at seeing himself fall into the role of a corrupt party member, as he was in the structural position of selecting other candidates for party membership because of *guanxi*, rather than of motivation or dedication to the common good. He felt that peasants, like his parents, were paying the highest price for that kind of hypocrisy and moral corruption.

Whereas Bai Gang initially more or less consciously echoed party rhetoric, Zhou Lemin self-consciously dismissed it as jargon that one had to put up with but that had little direct bearing on reality. Being included as a party member, however, entailed certain ritual requirements, such as the expression of one's political convictions. However, this seemed to have little to do with inner beliefs than with a pragmatic attempt to open a path to the future. I think this split between the political rhetoric and actual social practice can be understood in term of Kleinman's notion of a sense of split subjectivity—as a matter of keeping one eye open and one eye closed.

For Bai Gang, who both embodies rural and urban China and experiences a deep split between his filial obligation to provide and care for his parents and his own desire to lead a cosmopolitan form of life in Beijing, the sense of division is all the more pertinent since he is failing in both senses. He guiltily turns a blind eye to his family obligations and presses on with new ways to find the key to a Beijing *hukou*, a girlfriend and a well paid and fulfilling job, neither caring for his parents, nor living out his own dreams but stuck in what has been termed 'China's ant tribe'.

While both young men opportunistically became members of the party in order to improve their chances in a competitive job market, seeing this as an example of the 'individualisation' of Chinese society misses the way in which social responsibilities remain highly important to them. Since Zhou Lemin's parents had good state pensions, he did not feel pressure in terms of having to provide for them in an economic sense, but he also emphasised that being close to them when they grew old was important to him. A sense of family obligation evidently weighs heavily on Bai Gang and as a result he feels torn between competing social imperatives that cannot easily be reconciled.

While these contradictions relate to a particular point in Chinese history, I do not see this sense of division as a *uniquely* Chinese phenomenon. Rather than speaking of a 'cultural version of the divided self', as is the case of the authors of *Deep China*, inspired by the work of Michael Jackson, I see this sense of being torn in several directions to be part of the human condition itself.[27] The two young men whose stories I have outlined in this article experienced varying forms and degrees of existential dilemma—between parents, party and peers. Because of China's radical transformations the contradictory nature of all our lives is perhaps even more readily visible. However, this is a difference in degree not in kind. Following Hannah Arendt, social life is full of contradictions and 'most of the time we do not know *what* we are doing what we are *acting*'.[28] In other words rather than painting a picture of near-schizophrenic individuals, I hope to have highlighted some of the quandaries faced by young party members in China today, arguing that the tensions they experience are less a result of intellectual contemplation (*vita contemplativa*) than of the existential dilemmas or double-binds between self and other, as well as between moral ideals and lived experience that emerge in the course of everyday life as it is chaotically lived (*vita activa*). Finally, since the dynamics of the social world are continuously in flux at different points in their biographies, people are likely to experience them differently.

Acknowledgements

Special thanks are due to Ayo Wahlberg and Ravinder Kaur for bringing together participants from the 'governing difference' workshop under the Asian Dynamics Conference (ADI) held in Copenhagen in 2010. I also wish to warmly thank my colleagues at the 'political bodies' research group at the Institute of Anthropology for fruitful comments, as well as my colleagues at the Nordic Institute of Asian Studies, University of Copenhagen for support.

Notes

1 S Thøgersen, 'Parasites or civilisers: the legitimacy of the Chinese Communist Party in rural areas', in KE Brødsgaard and Zheng Yongnian (eds) *Bringing the Party Back In: How China is Governed*, London etc: Eastern Universities Press, 2004, pp 192–216.

IDENTITY, INEQUITY AND INEQUALITY IN INDIA AND CHINA

2 In order to protect the anonymity of informants I have used pseudonyms.

3 MH Gluckman, *Analysis of a Social Situation in Modern Zululand*, Rhodes-Livingstone Papers No 28, Manchester: Manchester University Press, 1958.

4 For an analysis of the Manchester School, see *ibid*. For overviews of the Manchester School, see TMS Evans & Don Handelman, *The Manchester School: Practice and Ethnographic Praxis in Anthropology*, New York: Berghan Books, 2006; and B Kapferer & L Meinert (eds), special issue of *Social Analysis: The International Journal of Cultural and Social Practice*, 54(3), 2010.

5 M Jackson, *Existential Anthropology: Events, Exigencies and Effects*, New York: Berghan Books, 2005. Jackson, among other things, draws on Hannah Arendt's distinction between *vita activa* and *vita contempletiva*, or the difference between life as it is chaotically lived and the explanations we generate *post hoc* about the events that befall us. Arendt identified diminishing human agency and political freedom in terms of the paradox that, as human powers increase through technological and humanistic inquiry, we are less equipped to control the consequences of our actions. H Arendt, *The Human Condition*, Chicago, IL: University of Chicago Press, 1998.

6 According to Andrew Kipnis, while the term *suzhi* used to be associated with inborn characteristics and eugenics, it has increasingly become linked with social and moral characteristics that are the result of child-rearing and education. Since the 1970s the term has undergone a transformation. *Suzhi* (素质) is a compound of the characters *su* 素 and *zhi* 质. *Zhi* means 'nature, character, or matter', whereas *su* has many meanings, including 'unadorned, plain, white and essence'. *Suzhi* no longer connotes the natural in a nature/nurture dichotomy, but refers to individually embodied human qualities. A Kipnis, 'Suzhi: a keyword approach', *China Quarterly*, 186, 2006, pp 295–313. See also Kipnis, 'Neoliberalism reified: suzhi discourse and tropes of neoliberalism', *Journal of the Royal Anthropological Institute*, 13, 2007, pp 383–400.

7 A Anagnost, 'The corporeal politics of quality (Suzhi)', *Public Culture*, 16(2), 2004, pp 189–208.

8 Andrew Kipnis argues that, while a neoliberal approach masks hidden differences by 'blaming the victim', *suzhi* discourse rather reifies differences. He sees 'blame the victim' discourses as a critique of the neoliberal welfare policies articulated in the rhetoric of Ronald Reagan. This style of discourse works by denying that, for instance, 'welfare moms' are victims at all. It denies the relevance of structural factors to the explanation of their disadvantages and argues that, if welfare moms cannot get off welfare, they are just not trying hard enough. Kipnis, 'Neoliberalism reified'.

9 D Harvey, *A Brief History of Neoliberalism*, Oxford: Oxford University Press, 2005; G Sigley, 'Chinese governmentalities: government, governance and the socialist market economy', *Economy and Society*, 35(4), 2006, pp 487–508; and A Ong, *Neoliberalism as Exception: Mutations in Citizenship and Sovereignty*, Durham, NC: Duke University Press.

10 FN Pieke, *The Good Communist: Elite Training and State Building in Today's China*, Cambridge: Cambridge University Press, 2009.

11 Yunxiang Yan, *The Individualization of Chinese Society*, Oxford: Berg, 2009; and M Halskov Hansen & R Svarverud (eds), *iChina: The Rise of the Individual in Modern Chinese Society*, Copenhagen: NIAS Press, 2010.

12 A Kleinman, Y Yan, J Jun, S Lee, E Zhang, P Tianshu, W Fei & G Jinhua (eds), *Deep China: The Moral Life of the Person—What Anthropology and Psychiatry Tell us about China Today*, Berkeley, CA: University of California Press, 2011, p 23.

13 *Ibid*.

14 See Wang Fei-Ling, *Organizing through Division and Exclusion: China's Hukou System*, Stanford, CA: Stanford University Press, 2005 for a discussion of how the same test results give urban students access to better universities than is the case for students from China's rural areas.

15 See Lei Guang, 'Rural taste, urban fashions: the cultural politics of rural/urban difference in contemporary China', *Positions*, 11(3), 2003, pp 613–646 for a discussion of the close affinity between state practices and popular urban discourses creating a view of migrants as lacking in distinction and value.

16 TE Woronov, 'Chinese children, American education: globalizing child rearing in contemporary China', in J Cole & D Durham (eds), *Generations and Globalization: Youth, Age, and Family in the New World Economy*, Bloomington, IN: Indiana University Press, 2007, pp 29–52.

17 Li Zhang, *Strangers in the City: Reconfigurations of Space, Power, and Social Networks within China's Floating Population*, Stanford, CA: Stanford University Press, 2001. For a more detailed description of the concept of *hukou*, see Jesper Zeuthen's article in this issue.

18 Kleinman *et al*, *Deep China*, p 285.

19 About one-fifth of Chinese university students are members of the party (as opposed to three per cent of the general Chinese population), which gives an indication of its elitist character.

20 See Anagnost, 'The corporeal politics of quality (Suzhi)'; Ong, *Neoliberalism as Exception*; and L Rofel, *Desiring China: Experiments in Neoliberalism, Sexuality, and Public Culture*, Durham, NC: Duke University Press, 2007.

IDENTITY, INEQUITY AND INEQUALITY IN INDIA AND CHINA

21 The term invokes the idea that being from Beijng (*Bei* jing), being a man (*nan* shi) and being a member of the party (*dang* yuan), a person is in a position of social status or mobility. Shenyang is close to Beijing and being from there gives more or less the same entitlements as does being a person from the capital itself.

22 S Feuchtwang, 'Remnants of revolution in China', in CM Hann (ed), *Postsocialism: Ideals, Ideologies and Practices in Eurasia*, London: Routledge, 1992, pp 196–197.

23 Stanley Rosen has analysed issues of party recruitment from the perspective of those being recruited and found that China's youth cohort see party membership as an avenue to opportunities within a competitive job market. Rosen, 'The state of youth/youth and the state in early 21st century China: the triumph of the urban rich?', in P Hays Gries & S Rosen (eds), *State and Society in 21st Century China: Crisis, Contention and Legitimation*, London: Routledge, 2004, ch 8.

24 Gregory Bateson coined the term 'double-bind' to characterise the situation faced by a person who is receiving contradictory messages from another powerful person. The classic example is that of a child who is confronted with a parent who communicates withdrawal and coldness when the child approaches, but then reaches out towards the child with simulated love when he or she pulls back from the coldness. The child is then caught in a double-bind. No course of action can possibly prove satisfactory. Bateson felt that this kind of mixed communication may underlie the development of autism and schizophrenia. G Bateson, *Steps to an Ecology of Mind*, Chicago, IL: University of Chicago Press, 2000, pp 271–279. However, it is necessary for my purpose to clearly separate the notion of a double-bind from any clinical content of this sort. I see double-binds as conveying the experience of being torn in two directions and as tied to existential dilemmas that have no definite answer.

25 See also V Fong, *Only Hope: Coming of Age under China's One Child Policy*, Stanford, CA: Stanford University Press, 2004.

26 Si Lian, *The Ant Tribe: Between Hope and Reality*, Beijing: Beijing University Press, 2008.

27 Michael Jackson calls these dilemmas *aporias*, which literally means 'lacking a path (*a- poros*), a path that is impassable. However, whereas the classical Greek *aporia* was primarily a logical puzzle that was to be resolved through rational ingenuity, Jackson here refers to dilemmas between self and other, as well as between moral ideals and lived experience that define the human condition. M Jackson *Excursions*, Durham, NC: Duke University Press, 2007; and Jackson, *The Palm at the End of the Mind: Relatedness, Religiosity, and the Real*, Durham, NC: Duke University Press, 2009. Although both Kleinman *et al* and Michael Jackson are inspired by the phenomenology of William James and RD Laing, Jackson's work places less emphasis on the role of culture and rather makes universalist claims about the human condition.

28 On *vita activa* and the human condition, see Arendt, *The Human Condition*, pp 1–12.

Notes on contributor

Susanne Bregnbaek holds a PhD in anthropology and is conducting post-doctoral research at the University of Copenhagen. Her main research interests are (post)-socialism in Cuba and China, religion, Chinese higher education, generations, the state and existential anthropology.

Index

Page numbers in **bold** type refer to figures
Page numbers followed by 'n' refer to notes

activism 44–5, 88–9, 95, 104, 133–5, 139, 142
Adam, G. 69
Advaita Vedanta 155
aesthetics 6, 65, 70, 80, 108
Africa: sub-Saharan 26n
agency: human 70
agrarian economy 115
agrarian modernity 102–5, 113
agriculture 9, 21–3, 101–6, 109–15, 118–26,
    163; development 118
Ahmad, A. 65–7
Ali, Mansoor **77**, 78
Ambedkar, B.R. 157
American Heritage Dictionary 26n
Amin, A. 109
Anagnost, A. 164, 167
Anderson, B. 68
Anholt, S. 35
animism 149
aporias 178n
Appadurai, A. 65, 71
Arendt, H. 176, 177n
Arni, C.: and Pushpamala, N. 74–6
Arni, Clare 74–6, **74**, **75**
art 65; contemporary 65–83; fairs 67; global
    65–7, 80
Art Newspaper, The 69
asceticism 151, 159
Asia: imperialism 17–21
Asia Rising 2
Asia Society Museum (New York) 69
Asian Biotech (National Science Foundation)
    52
*Asia's Rising Science and Technology
    Strength* (NSE) 52
Assembly Elections 86, 102
atheism 155
Aurobindo, Sri (born Aurobindo Ghose) 155
authoritarianism 1–2, 165
authority 9, 12–16, 22–5, 60, 72, 170
autonomy 33, 45, 88, 113, 119, 139, 171

Babri Masjid (Babri Mosque) 137, 157

Bachchan, A. 45
Bai Gang 167–9, 173–6
Banerjee, S. 135
Bateson, G. 178n
Baudrillard, J. 47
Beaudry, C.: and Hicks, D. 70
Bech, U. 166
Beijing 124, 163–78
Bengal *see* West Bengal
Bergson, H. 155
Berlant, L. 146
Bhabha, Huma 79
Bharadwaj, A. 52
Bharatiya Janata Party (BJP) 34, 85–97, 101,
    134, 157
Bhatt, A. 89, 94
biobanking 56, 60
bioeconomy 52
bioethics 54, 57, 60–2
bioinformatics 54
biology 51, 59
biomedicine 51–3, 56–62
Bionet 53, 61; Expert Group 64n
biopolitics 111
Biopolitics in Asia (Gottweis) 52
Biopolitics in Asia (NSE) 52
Biopolitics in China (NSE) 52
bioscience 51
biotechnology 6, 51–64
Biswas, A. 107
Blom, A.: and Jaoul, N. 143–4
Bobbio, T. 6, 85–100
Bose, J.C. 155
Bourdieu, P. 72
Bourguignon, F.: and Morrison, C. 20
Boxer Rebellion (1899–1901) 151
Brand India 6, 31–6, **40**, 42–7
branding: as scientific knowledge hub **40**
Breckenridge, C. 70
Bregnbaek, S. 163–78
Breman, J. 24
British India 15, 18–21
Brookes, D. 17

INDEX

Brosius, C. 72
Buckingham, W.: and Chan, K. 120–2
Buddhism 149–54, 157
Bugatti Automobiles 42
Butler, J. 136

capital 11–15, 22–3, 34, 86, 114, 146, 174; global 31, 43; neoliberal 65–83; social 110, 167; working 107
capitalism 16–17, 22–4, 26n, 35, 143–6, 150, 158, 163–6; global 11–12, 101–3; imperial 5, 18; industrial 15, 102; networking 11
caste 80, 101, 114, 154, 157; lower 94, 155; upper 87, 91–4, 97–8, 105
Catholicism 152
Central Reserve Police Force (CRPF) 133–5, 139–43, 146
Chan, K.: and Buckingham, W. 120–2
Chang, P-L. 151
chauvinism 93–7
Chen, N.: and Ong, A. 52
Chen, Y. 151
Ch'en, Y-K. 151
Chengdu: ranked districts and counties **122**; urban–rural boundary 117–32
Chinese Communist Party (CCP) 7, 153–4, 163–5, 168–9, 172–4
Chiu, M. 69
Chomsky, N.: and Herman, E. 134
Christianity 149, 155, 159
Christie's 66
Ciotti, M. 6, 65–83
citizenship 7, 11, 137, 150, 161, 168
civil war 133–7, 143–6
Clark, G. 18–19
Clash of Civilizations, The (Huntington) 150
class 44, 80, 101, 105–7, 135, 150, 174; middle 24–5, 71–3, 85–97, 113–14, 159–60, 164–7; ruling 12–13; second 174; struggle 107; working 104, 128, 150
clericalism, anti- 152–5
coercion 3, 13, 59–61, 110
Cold War (1947–91) 17
collectivism 60, 166
Collins, R. 137
colonialism 39, 75–7, 138, 155–8, 161
colonisation 71, 150–1, 158
commercialisation 60–1
commodity 4–6, 42, 65, 68–71, 80
Commonwealth Federation 44
Commonwealth Games (CWG) (2010) 43–6
communalism 156
communication 91
communism 102, 141–3, 152–4, 158–9, 163, 166, 171–5
Communist Party, India (Marxist) (CPI (M)) 88, 104, 107, 114

community 35; imagined 35, 68–9, 144; outraged 143–5
conflict 7, 13–15, 32, 45, 141, 164
Confucianism 149, 152
Confucius 61–2, 152–3
Congress Party, India 21, 156
conscription 133, 136, 139
consumerism 4, 39, 47, 71–3, 90–1, 158–60, 168; anti- 149, 159–60; global 79
Cornia, G.: and Kiiski, S. 20
corruption 4, 45–6, 61, 175
cosmopolitanism 2, 158
crime 130, 151
crisis 164; financial 1, 66–7; industrial 90
cultural difference 5, 53
cultural economy 10
Cultural Revolution (China) 119, 128–9, 158, 166
culture 3–5, 10, 53–6, 60–5, 91–3, 103, 137; exclusion 93–7

Dance of Democracy (Ali) 78
Darwinism, social 152
Datt, G.: and Ravallion, M. 28n
Deaton, A.: and Dreze, J. 22
Declaration of Helsinki (1964) 55
decolonisation 25, 34, 150, 158
Deep China: The Moral Life of the Person (Kleinman) 166–7, 176
deindustrialisation 24
Deleuze, G. 4, 8n
democracy 22, 33–5, 38, 46, 75, 135, 156–7
Dengxiao, P. 170
Depression, Great 16
Derrida, J. 4
Desai, M. 88
development 86, 98, 107–11, 126, 144; agricultural 118; economic 13, 17, 87, 90–2, 96–7; global 17; human 4, 21; industrial 39, 104, 115; modern 150; national 21, 149–62; programmes 35, 128, 141, 145; social 65, 80
devolution 21–2
difference 1–8, 52–7, 62, 70, 81, 115–32, 159; construction 133–48; cultural 5, 53; governing 1–8, 101–16; religious 157; social 1, 72
discourse 1–4, 10, 137
discrimination 94
disease 56–7, 141
Dodd, P. 69
domination 101–16
double-bind term 178n
Dreze, J.: and Deaton, A. 22
Dutt, R.K. 159

East India Company 15

INDEX

Eclipse (3) (Kallat) 79
economy 3, 80, 111; agrarian 115; cultural 10; development 13, 17, 87, 90–2, 96–7; global 1; growth 1–4, 15–18, 21–5, 43–6, 52, 90–7, 101; market 9, 171; power 20, 151; reform 9, 124–5, 128
education 21–4, 106, 112, 120, 161, 165–75
egalitarianism 101–16, 155, 172
Embryo Protection Act (1990) 59
emotion 136–9, 143–6; public 145
Empire Strikes Back: Indian Art Today, The (Saatchi Gallery, 2010) 65–8, 73–6, 79–81
employment 17, 23
Enlightenment 149–51
Escobar, A. 3, 53
Ethical Principles for Medical Research Involving Human Subjects 55
ethics 6, 51–62
Ethics Commissions 59
ethnicity 22
Euro-modernity 62
Europe 12, 52–4, 58–62, 67–9, 158
European imperialism 24
evolution 149, 152
exclusion: culture 93–7; social 94
exploitation 59–61
extremism 85–7, 94–5

fairs: art 67
Falun Gong 154, 160
Federation of Indian Chambers of Commerce and Industry (FICCI) 46
Feuchtwang, S. 172
feudalism 103–9, 153–5, 158; anti- 153
financial crisis 1, 66–7
Financial Times 55
First World 2, 15
Flam, H. 136
foreign direct investment (FDI) 32–4, 47
foreign policy 32
foreign trade 160
France 150–1, 158
free market 9, 16–24, 35–8, 47
freedom 11, 108, 125; speech 4, 142

Galeano, E. 143
Gandhi, M. 76–7, 92–4, 149, 155–61; religious utopianism 149, 158
Gaurav Yatra (Procession for Pride) 86, 96
gender 22–3, 75–6, 80, 101
genomics 52–4, 57
Germany 18, 59
Gini coefficient 21–2
girls: evening safety 99n
global art 65–7, 80
global capital 31, 43
global capitalism 11–12, 101–3

global consumerism 79
global development 17
global economy 1
global mobility 62
global modernity 73, 160
global power 1–2, 38
globalisation 9–18, 23–5, 52–4, 65–6, 70–2, 90–4, 145
Good Communist, The (Pieke) 165
Gottweis, H. 52
governance 1–8, 44, 164–6; deficit 45–6; difference 1–8, 101–16; ethical 51, 61
Graeber, D. 72
Gram Panchayat 108–10
Gram Sabha 102
Gram Sansad 108, 112
Grazia, V. de 157–8
Great Leap Forward (1958–9) 120, 158–9
Gross Domestic Product (GDP) 18–20, **19**, **20**, 23, 91, 97–8
growth: economic 1–4, 15–18, 21–5, 43–6, 52, 90–7, 101
Guha, R. 110
Gujarat 85–100; Assembly Elections (2002) 86
Gupta, Subodh 77–9, **77**

Hall, S. 3
Hardt, M.: and Negri, A. 12
Hazare, A. 45–6
health 17, 21, 24, 60–1, 153, 167
hegemony 1, 10, 53, 97, 110–15, 157–8
Heller, A. 114
Herman, E.: and Chomsky, N. 134
Hervieu-Leger, D. 153
Hicks, D.: and Beaudry, C. 70
Hinduism 149, 154–7
Hindustan Times 134
Hindutva 85–100
Hoogvelt, A. 11, 24
Hsing, Y-T. 122–3
Hu, J. 130
Huang, Y. 166
hukou 117, 120–2, 125, 128–31, 169, 175–6
human development 4, 21
Human Development Report (1996) 16
human embryonic stem cell (HESC) research 51–4, 57–60
human rights 86, 95, 133–5, 139, 142–3
Huntington, S. 150
Huysmans, J. 140

imagery 31–6, 46–7, 74, 141; frame 6; machine 36–43
Imagining Biotech India (National Science Foundation) 52
immigration 13, 130

INDEX

imperial modernity 5, 9–29
imperial power 13, 24–5, 151
imperialism 5, 9–29, 120, 149–51, 158; anti-
  158–9; Asia 17–21; capitalism 5, 18;
  European 24; inequality 21–4; inequity
  15–17
Independence (India, 1947) 19, 21–3, 32, 45,
  65–7, 87, 156
India: Right place, Right time (campaign) 39
India: new 31–49
India Art Collective (IAC) 68
India Art Fair 67
India Brand Equity Foundation (IBEF) 34–5,
  42
India Now 38
India Rising 32
India Shining 34
India vs India 45
Indian Express 139
Indian Rebellion (1857) 156
Indianness 65–83
Indira Awas Yogna 109
individualisation 166, 176
individualism 60, 158, 166
industrial capitalism 15, 102
industrial crisis 90
industrial development 39, 104, 115
industrialisation 6–7, 32, 44, 91–2, 113–14,
  140; post- 91
industry 31, 90, 102, 118, 123, 159; local 125
inequality predicament 15–17, 25
insurgency 139, 145–6
Integrated Rural Development Project
  (IRDP) 109
International Monetary Fund (IMF) 17
internationalism 166, 173
intervention 138, 156–7
investment 46, 85–7, 90–1; foreign 85, 160;
  foreign direct (FDI) 32–4, 47
investor: India best country **37**
Islam 149–52

Jackson, M. 178n
James, W. 158
Jaoul, N.: and Blom, A. 143–4
Japan 15
Jin, C. 56
Judaism 149
Jumabhoy, Z. 73–4
justice 108, 146

Kallat, J. 75–9
Kantianism, neo- 152
Kapoor, A. 74
Kaur, R. 6, 31–49; and Wahlberg, A. 1–8
Khaire, M.: and Wadhwani, R. 71
Khilnani, S. 46

Khurshid, S. 46
Kiiski, S.: and Cornia, G. 20
Killat, Jitish 76–7, **76**, **78**, 79
Kipnis, A. 165, 177n
Kiran Nadar Museum of Art (KNMA, New
  Delhi) 82n
Kishenji (Rao) 139–41
Kleinman, A. 166–8, 171, 175; *et al* 166, 173
Korea: South 51
Kruta, J. 42
Kunjam, M. 143

labour 44–7, 72–5, 90–1, 104–12, 117; market
  85, 91, 169; power 72
land: reform 21, 103–4, 105–7, 110, 113
language 1–4, 85, 88–9, 110, 138, 143, 155
Latin America 26n
law 12, 145
Left Front government (West Bengal) 6, 101–
  7, 113–15
Li, L.: and O'Brien, K. 119
Li, Y. 123–4
Lian, S. 174
Liang, C. 151
liberalisation 21–2, 25, 73, 80, 90–1, 113
liberalism 33–5, 38, 97, 157, 165
Lin-Hill, J. 69
Local Committee (LC) 106
Ludden, D. 5, 9–29

McKinsey & Company 113
Madan, T.N. 156
Maha Gujarat *Andolan* (Movement for a
  great state of Gujarat, 1956–60) 87–9
Maha Gujarat Conference (Ahmedabad) 88
Maha Gujarat Janata Parishad (Maha
  Gujarat People's Association) 88–9
Mahatma Gandhi National Rural
  Employment Guarantee Act
  (MGNREGA, 2005) 110
Malaysia 34
Mao Zedong 153–4, 158–9, 165, 168–70, 175
Maoism 7, 133–5, 140–6, 149, 154, 159–61;
  secular utopianism 149, 158–61
Maoist attack 147n
marginalisation 5–6, 9, 89, 93, 110–15, 126
market 11, 33, 42, 65–83, 157, 171; consumer
  39, 160; economy 9, 171; free 9, 16–24, 35–
  8, 47; global 43, 69, 71; labour 85, 91, 169;
  logic 65, 71; neoliberal 2; transaction 13
Marx, K. 12, 150
Marxism 152–3
mass mobility 109, 154
materialism 158–9, 166, 173
Mathew, P. 81n
Mathur, Saloni 80
Mazarella, W. 48n

INDEX

Mbembe, A. 138
medicine 51, 54, 57, 120, 155; research 60–1
Members of the Legislative Assembly (MLAs) 141
memoranda of understanding (MOU) 86
middle class 24–5, 71–3, 85–97, 113–14, 159–60, 164–7
migration 2, 75, 76, 130, 167
military 136, 140, 143
millenarianism 150, 153–4, 160–1
Minimum Wages Act (1948) 105–6
Ministry of Health (China) 55–6
Ministry of Science and Technology (China) 55–6
Mitchell, W.J.T. 47
mobility 11–16, 45–7, 52–3, 117–28, 131–9, 159–61; global 62; mass 109, 154; personal 163; social 13, 23–4, 111, 169, 173
modern development 150
modernisation 85, 93–5, 149–53, 166
modernism 4, 46, 66–8, 71, 101–7; high- 125; secular 159
modernity 38–9, 90–4, 114–15, 150–2, 158–60; agrarian 102–5, 113; Euro- 62; global 73, 160; imperial 5, 9–29
Modi, N. 85–7, 92–8
morality 7, 55–9, 97, 134–8, 161, 174; national 151–2; universal 149
Morrison, C.: and Bourguignon, F. 20
Muller, M. 155
multiculturalism 2–3, 157

Nandy, A. 94, 156
Naoroji, D. 18
nation-branding 6, 31–5, 42
nation-building 5–6, 20, 31, 34–5, 51–2, 62
national development 21, 149–62
national religion 153
National Sample Survey (2004) 22
national territory 18–21
nationalisation 161
nationalism 11–21, 85, 94, 151–2, 155–60, 166, 173
nationalist rhetoric 85
Native Women of South India: Manners & Customs (2000–2004) **74, 75**
Naxalites 135, 143–4
Negri, A.: and Hardt, M. 12
Nehru, J. 32, 38, 87–8, 150, 157–9
neoliberalism 9–12, 17–18, 24–5, 31–5, 90–1, 165, 171; capital 65–83; market 2; reform 85–6, 97
Nepal 9, 23–4
Netherlands 150–1
networking 11
neutrality: state 155–6

New Delhi: Kiran Nadar Museum of Art (KNMA) 82n
New Genetics and Society (2009) 52
New Industrial Policy (NIP, 1991) 90
New York: Asia Society Museum 69
New York Times 17
non-governmental organisations (NGO) 17, 107–8
Nordau, M. 159
North Atlantic Treaty Organisation (NATO) 17, 158; Yugoslavia bombing (1999) 166
Nuremburg Code (1949) 60

O'Brien, K.: and Li, L. 119
Olympic Games: Beijing (2008) 43
Ong, A. 119; and Chen, N. 52
Operation Barga 106
Operation Green Hunt 133–4
Orientalist, The (Bhabha) 79

Pakistan 32, 73
Panchayat 102–8, 113–14
Panchayat Pradhan 108–9
Panchayati Raj 105, 108
Patel, C. 89
patronage 11, 42, 46
People's Liberation Guerrilla Army (PLGA) 135
People's Union for Democratic Rights (PUDR) 134
Periyar (Ramasamy) 154–5
personal mobility 163
Petryna, A. 56
Phillips de Pury 70
Phule, J. 154
Pieke, F. 165
Pillai, G.K. 141
Pitman, J. 79
pluralism 156
Polanyi, K. 24
policy 47; foreign 32
political power 151
political rhetoric 89–90, 94–5
popular religion 152
postcolonialism 11, 46, 69–73, 81–7, 138, 149, 156
postliberalisation 101
postmodernism 47
postsocialism 35, 165
poverty 2–4, 15–24, 26n, 29n, 46, 75–80, 91, 138, 174
power 9–16, 19, 43–5, 51–64, 110–12, 150; economic 20, 151; global 1–2, 38; imperial 13, 24–5, 151; labour 72; political 151; social 114–15; state 4, 22, 157
pragmatism 166, 173
Praja Socialist Party 88

INDEX

Pratt, M.L. 68
Pritchett, L. 17–18
privatisation 90–3, 113, 172
Progressive Artists' Group (Bombay, 1947) 67–8
propaganda 32, 87, 90–1, 95–6, 134, 141, 146
prosperity 31–2, 47, 119, 168
Protestantism 152
protests 31–2; violent 31–3
protonationalism 155
Public Notice (2) (Kallat) 76
Pushpamala, N. **74**, **75**; and Arni, C. 74–6

racism 3
Rajan, S. 55
Ramasamy, E.V. (Periyar) 154–5
Ramayana 155
Ranciere, J. 36
Randeria, S. 145
ranking 13–16, 21, 131; imperial 19, 25
Rao, M.K. (Kishenji) 139–41
rationalism 152, 155
Ravallion, M. 15; and Datt, G. 28n
Raza, S.H. 68
Reagan Revolution (1980) 16
realism 150
Red Army (Soviet) 135
Reddy, M.A. 23
reform 31–2, 43–7, 90–2, 121, 129, 152–5, 166–70; economic 9, 124–5, 128; land 21, 103–4, 105–7, 110, 113; neoliberal 85–6, 97
regionalism 85
relations: social 72, 140
religion 24, 58, 80, 95–8, 101, 149–62, 171; anti- 7, 161; difference 157; national 153; popular 152; violence 24, 75
Renaissance 65–83
Report on the World Social Situation (UNDP, 2005) 15–16, 24
Reubi, D. 55
Revolution Continues: New Chinese Art, The (2008–2009) 73
rhetoric 87, 107–8, 130, 169, 172, 175; nationalist 85; political 89–90, 94–5
Right of Children to Free and Compulsory Education Act (2009) 142
rights 122, 125, 168; human 86, 95, 133–5, 139, 142–3
Rosen, S. 166, 172, 178n
Roy, A. 133
Roy, T. 18, 25
Rudra, A. 106
Ruiyun Group 124
ruling class 12–13
rural–urban boundary 117–32
Ruskin, J. 159

Saatchi Gallery 74–6, 79–80
safety: girls in evening 99n
Saffronart 66, 69, 72
Salwa Judum 133, 141–4
Samyukta Maharashtra Samiti (United Maharashtra Committee) 88
Sangh Parivar 91
Sanghvi, V. 44
Santhosh, T.V. 70
Sarkar, S. 6, 101–16
Sarma, E.A.S. 144
Scheper-Hughes, N. 138
scientism 152, 155
Scott, J.C. 123–5
secular modernism 159
secularisation 7, 149; thesis 150, 153
secularism 7, 97–8, 149–62
security 103, 136, 139–41, 144
Sen, B. 133
separatism 2, 88, 156
Seth, S. 31
sexual violence 66, 80
sexuality 3, 151
Shafer, D.M. 145–6
Sheikh, M. 111, 112
Shining India campaign 101, 115n
Shinoda, T. 99n
Singh, M. 22
social capital 110, 167
social development 65, 80
social difference 1, 72
social exclusion 94
social mobility 13, 23–4, 111, 169, 173
social power 114–15
social relations 72, 140
socialism 157–9, 165, 175
society 53, 71; transitional 101–16
socioeconomics 54, 57, 60–2, 80, 110, 144
Sosrodihardjo, Kosno (President Sukarno) 150
Sotheby's 66; Institute of Art 69
South Africa 34
South Asia Multidisciplinary Academic Journal (Samaj) (2008) 143
South Korea 51
sovereignty 12, 31–3, 42
special economic zones (SEZ) 85
speech: freedom 4, 142
stability 103–5, 117, 120, 131, 174
state: neutrality 155–6; power 4, 22, 157
States Reorganisation Act (1956) 88
stem cell research 51–4, 57–60
struggle: class 107
sub-Saharan Africa: poverty 26n
subnationalism 85–100; chauvinism 93–7
Suk, H.W. 52, 56

INDEX

Sukarno (President of Indonesia) (born Kusno Sosrodihardjo) 150
Sumner, P. 70
Sundar, N. 7, 133–48
Sung, W-C. 52
supermarket **41**
superstition 152–5
Supreme Court 46, 133, 136, 139, 144
suzhi 177n

Tadmetla ambush 133, 135–6, 139, 140, 146, 147n
Taixu 151
Taoism 151–4
Tata Group 31
technology 39
Tehelka Magazine 68
Temple Entry Proclamation 156
Templer, R. (General) 145
territorialism 9–14, 21
territory 11, 15, 25, 85–9; national 18–21
Third World 2, 8n, 15, 32, 39, 80
Thøgersen, S. 164
Thompson, C. 52
Tiananmen Incident (1976) 130
Tiananmen Square Protests (1989) 159
Tilly, C. 119, 129
Tolstoy, L. 159
tourism 34–5, 45–7
trade 15, 18–20, 93; foreign 160; unionism 92
transitional society 101–16

U.F.O. (Gupta) 77, 79
Union of Soviet Socialist Republics (USSR) 17
Union Territory (India) 88
United Kingdom (UK) 17, 18, 18–19, 21, 59, 62, 67, 150, 159
United Nations Children's Fund (UNICEF) 108–10
United Nations Development Programme (UNDP) 10, 16
United Nations (UN) 15–17, 24
United States of America (USA) 10, 15–19, 51–5, 67–71, 150, 157–8, 165
Universal Declaration on Bioethics and Human Rights 55
universalism 149
Unveiled: New Art from the Middle East (2009) 73
Urban Land Ceiling Act (1976) 113
urban–rural boundary 117–32
utopianism 150; Gandhian religious 149, 158; Maoist secular 149, 158–61

Vazirani, M. 69
Veer, P. van der 7, 149–62

vegetarianism 99n
Vibrant Gujarat campaign 6
Vibrant Gujarat Global Investors Summit 92, 97; (2003) 86; (2011) 87
Victoria, Queen 18
violence 61, 89, 95, 104, 131, 144–5, 156–7; anti-religious 160–1; non- 77; protests 31–3; religious 24, 75; sexual 66, 80
Vishwanathan, S. 98
vita activa (active life) 176, 177n
vita contemplativa (contemplative life) 176, 177n
Vivekananda, S. 155

Wade, R. 16
Wadhwani, R.: and Khaire, M. 71
Wah, F.L.K. 146
Wahlberg, A. 6, 51–64; and Kaur, R. 1–8
Wang, F-L. 121, 131; and Yongshun, C. 119
war 7, 15, 43, 134, 145; civil 133–7, 143–6; Cold (1947–91) 17; emotion 133–48; Kargil 134
Warnock Committee 58–9
wealth 11–21, 24–5, 42, 80–1
Weber, M. 149–50
welfare 91–3, 111, 120–2, 153, 165
Wen, J. (Premier) 130
West Bengal 6, 47; Agribusiness Vision (2010) 113; Assembly Elections (2006) 102; Left Front government 6, 101–7, 113–15
West Bengal Industrial Development Corporation (WBIDC) 113
Whyte, M.K. 166
Wilson, R. 76
Wilson, W. 157
winning hearts and minds (WHAM) 145–6
Winther-Tamaki, B. 68
working capital 107
working class 104, 128, 150
World Bank (WB) 16, 17
World Economic Forum (Davos) 32, 36, 39
World Trade Organization (WTO) 93
World War: First (1914–18) 18; Second (1939–45) 17–18, 158

Yagnik, I. 89
Yongshun, C.: and Wang, F-L. 119
Yugoslavia bombing (1999) 166

Zeuthen, J. 6, 117–32
Zheng, Y. 21
Zhou, E. 170
Zhu, R. 171
Zonal Committee members of CPI (M) 106, 109
zoning 119–25, 130–1

www.routledge.com/9780415593854

Related titles from Routledge

Renewing International Labour Studies

Edited by Marcus Taylor

Through a combination of theoretical works and a series of case studies, the volume highlights the cutting edge of international labour studies. Its expands on three pivotal areas of study within the discipline: 1) the social construction of new labour forces across an expanding international division of labour; 2) the self-organising potential of workers, particularly within non-traditional sectors; and 3) the possibilities for transborder labour movements to help address the asymmetrical power relationships between globalised capital and localised labour.

In addressing these themes, the volume helps explain not only how the contemporary international division of labour is produced and reproduced, but also the strengths and limits to current attempts to overcome its unequal and divisive nature.

This book was published as a special issue of *Third World Quarterly*.

Marcus Taylor is an Assistant Professor in the department of Global Development Studies at Queen's University, Canada.

October 2010: 246 x 174: 216pp
Hb: 978-0-415-59385-4
£90 / $133

For more information and to order a copy visit
www.routledge.com/9780415593854

Available from all good bookshops

www.routledge.com/9780415503532

Related titles from Routledge

Movement, Power and Place in Central Asia and Beyond
Contested Trajectories
Edited by Madeleine Reeves

From the *ThirdWorlds* book series

This book explores the workings—and unintended consequences—of policies aimed at sedentarizing, collectivizing and resettling populations as a means to fix and territorialize space. The book also examines ethnographic studies attuned to the role of movement in sustaining social life, from Soviet-era trade networks to pilgrimage routes through which 'kazakhness' is articulated, to the contemporary moralization of migration abroad in search of work.

Rather than analysing 'flows' as abstract processes, the book enquires about effortful activity, material infrastructures, political relations and social habits through which people, ideas, knowledge, skills and material objects move or are prevented from moving. As such, it offers new insights into the complex intersections of movement, power and place in this important region over the last two centuries.

Madeleine Reeves is an RCUK Research Fellow in Conflict Cohesion and Change at the University of Manchester. She teaches in the Department of Social Anthropology and is a member of the ESRC Centre for Research on Socio-Cultural Change.

April 2012: 246 x 174: 216pp
Hb: 978-0-415-50353-2
£90 / $155

For more information and to order a copy visit
www.routledge.com/9780415503532

Available from all good bookshops

www.routledge.com/9780415680998

Related titles from Routledge

Youth in the Former Soviet South
Everyday Lives between Experimentation and Regulation
Edited by Stefan Kirmse
From the *ThirdWorlds* book series

This book offers the first comprehensive analysis of youth, in all its diversity, in Muslim Central Asia and the Caucasus. It brings together a range of academic perspectives, including media studies, Islamic studies, the sociology of youth, and social anthropology

This book maps out the complexity and variance of everyday lives under post-Soviet conditions. Youth is not a clear-cut, predictable life stage. Yet, across the region, young people's lives show forms of experimentation and regulation. Male and female youth explore new opportunities not only in the buzzing space of the city, but also in the more closely monitored neighbourhood of their family homes. In many ways, they stand at the cutting edge of globalization and post-Soviet change, and thus they offer innovative perspectives on these processes.

This book was published as a special issue of *Central Asian Survey*.

July 2011: 246 x 174: 184pp
Hb: 978-0-415-68099-8
£90 / $148

For more information and to order a copy visit
www.routledge.com/9780415680998

Available from all good bookshops